B	Bridge passage
C	Cadential passage
cd	Cadenza
e	Piano episode
F	First Subject
F1 F2 etc	Sections of the First Subject
I	Introductory passage
m	Main theme, motif, or main unit
NT	New tutti or ritornello
pb	Piano bridge
pi	Piano introductory passage
ps	Piano second subject
px	Piano climax
R	Relief passage
S	Second Subject
T	Transition passage

Passages combining elements of two subjects or groups are marked thus: F/T; B/S etc

MOZART'S CONCERTO FORM

A

Mozart's Concerto Form

The first movements
of the piano
concertos

Denis Forman

PRAEGER PUBLISHERS
New York · Washington

BOOKS THAT MATTER

Published in the United States of America in 1971
by Praeger Publishers, Inc., 111 Fourth Avenue,
New York, N.Y. 10003

Library of Congress Catalog Card Number: 77-165529

Printed in Great Britain

Acknowledgements

I acknowledge that in writing this book I am an amateur who has strayed into a professional reserve. I would not have been so bold had it not been for professional encouragement, and I could not have done it without professional help.

One person in particular thought the project worthwhile: the late Jill Vlasto, Music Tutor of Girton College, Cambridge and Librarian of the Rowe Music Library, Kings College, Cambridge, who gave this book its early impetus. I am grateful to Barbara Trofimczk, particularly for her dauntless enterprise in researching the concertos of J. C. Bach and his contemporaries, and also to Kate Reed for her help in the final stages. I acknowledge my debt to three earlier writers: Sir Donald Tovey and the Professors Girdlestone and Hutchings. Also to the late Emily Anderson for her edition of the *Letters*, to which all of us who write about Mozart must so often refer, for authentic and intimate evidence of Mozart's state of mind.

Little Garnetts
Essex March 1970

Contents

THEMATIC INDEX TO MOZART'S PIANO CONCERTOS

CONCERTO AND KÖCHEL NUMBER	TYPE	MAIN REFERENCES

The tempo of each first movement is *allegro*, but the word 'allegro' is sometimes qualified, and where this happens the qualification only is given in brackets. 467 is an exception: it has no marking at all.

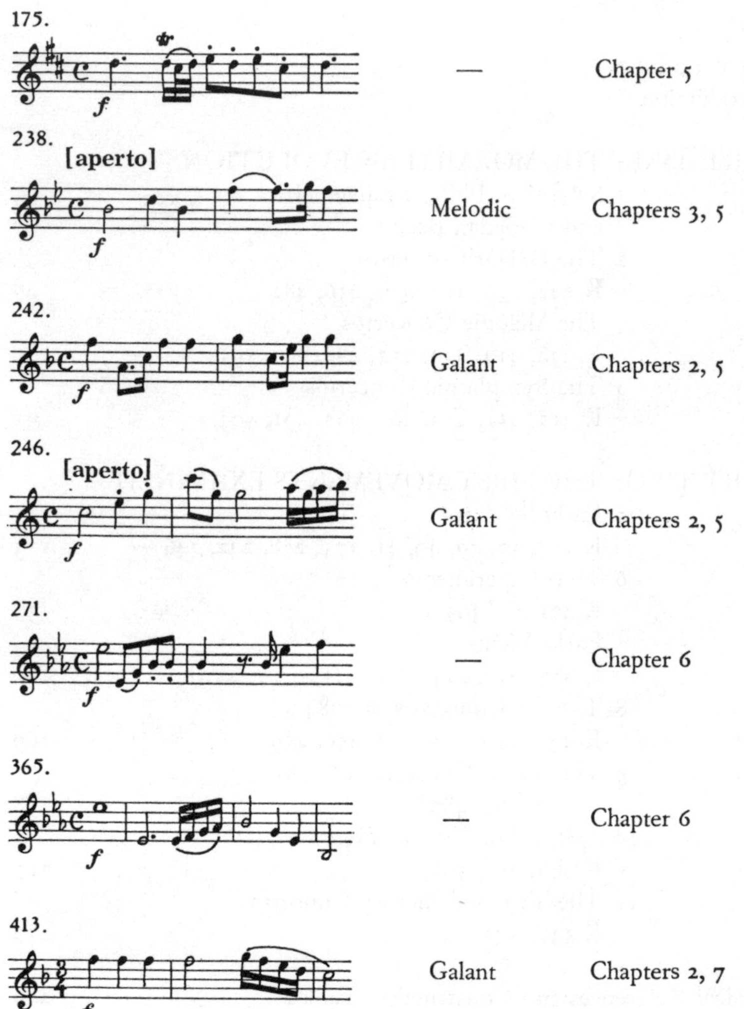

CONCERTO AND KÖCHEL NUMBER	TYPE	MAIN REFERENCES
175.	—	Chapter 5
238. [aperto]	Melodic	Chapters 3, 5
242.	Galant	Chapters 2, 5
246. [aperto]	Galant	Chapters 2, 5
271.	—	Chapter 6
365.	—	Chapter 6
413.	Galant	Chapters 2, 7

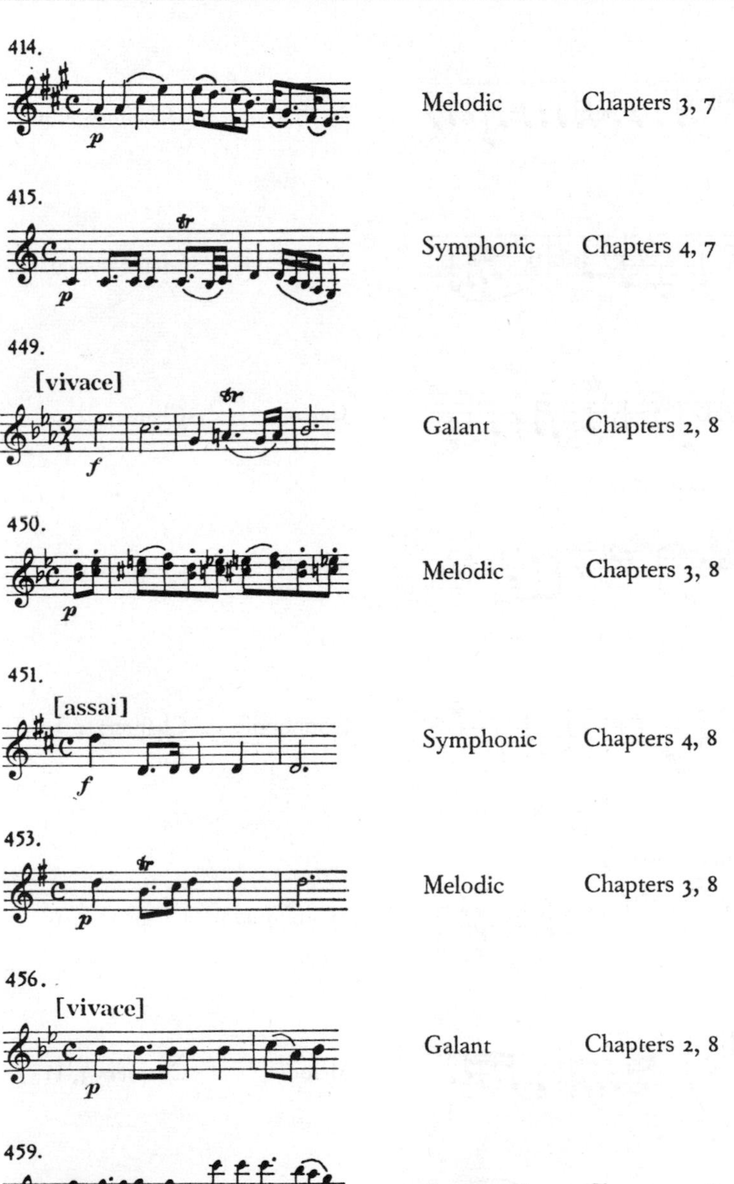

CONCERTO AND KÖCHEL NUMBER	TYPE	MAIN REFERENCES
414. *p*	Melodic	Chapters 3, 7
415. *tr* *p*	Symphonic	Chapters 4, 7
449. [vivace] *tr* *f*	Galant	Chapters 2, 8
450. *p*	Melodic	Chapters 3, 8
451. [assai] *f*	Symphonic	Chapters 4, 8
453. *tr* *p*	Melodic	Chapters 3, 8
456. [vivace] *p*	Galant	Chapters 2, 8
459. *p* 3	Symphonic	Chapters 4, 8

CONCERTO AND KÖCHEL NUMBER	TYPE	MAIN REFERENCES
466. 	Symphonic	Chapters 4, 9
467. 	Symphonic	Chapters 4, 9
482. 	Galant	Chapters 2, 9
488. 	Melodic	Chapters 3, 10
491. 	Symphonic	Chapters 4, 10
503. 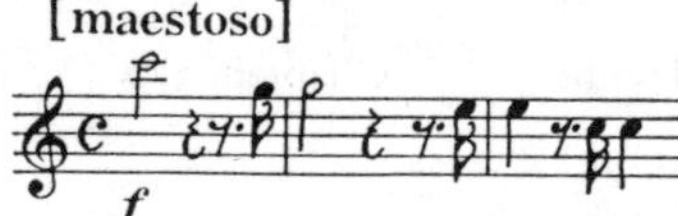	Symphonic	Chapters 4, 10
537. 	Melodic	Chapters 3, 11
595. 	Melodic	Chapters 3, 11

Introduction

The word 'Classical' is a convenient label for the period of music that lies between the Baroque and the Romantic. In one sense it is apt, for a classical taste and a classical sense of proportion pervade the spirit and the forms of the music. In another sense it is misleading, because it implies that the art of music had settled into golden proportions which offered a set of fixed disciplines to the creative talents of the day.

This was certainly not true of the musical scene in Mozart's lifetime. The composers of the later eighteenth century, with the Bach family, Haydn and Mozart himself in the van, vigorously developed and enlarged the musical forms within which they worked. It was one of those periods of rapid expansion in the practice of an art which usually earns a more dynamic title, for although it may be 'classical' in retrospect, at the time it was a period of revolution.

The reasons for the sudden advance were both social and mechanical. In the fifty years before Mozart's birth the centre of musical activity had begun to spread outwards from the Church into the courts, opera houses and concert halls of the capitals and main provincial cities of Europe. The high art of polyphony was passing out of vogue, and, because of the great demand for music which was more entertaining, composers wrote for their new public in the Galant style, less 'learned' than the old contrapuntal types of composition and more sophisticated than the traditional forms of the dance. Germany, France and England were rediscovering the riches of Italy in all the arts and her voice was heard in every centre of musical fashion. The orchestras of Mannheim and Paris were beginning to sound like the orchestra of Beethoven, and by the 1790s the harpsichord was outmatched by the more powerful hammer piano. And the forthcoming romantic and social revolutions of the nineteenth century were beginning to cast a scarcely discernible shadow during the later years of Mozart's life.

Mozart and his contemporaries did not consciously set out to be pioneers or experimentalists. Music was required to serve the needs of the court, the concert hall and the opera house, and as cooks provided food to satisfy one appetite, composers provided music to supply another. Their status might have been a little higher, but until the end of the eighteenth century they were still commonly in service or under patronage. Music was therefore mainly written to meet the requirements of the court calendar, and the greatest demand was for entertainment. Musical forms were available to suit all occasions. An aria, an overture, a symphony, all had an appropriate form which was in common use from Moscow to Naples. 'Free' music (partly, perhaps, because it would take longer to compose) was seldom heard, and extempore performance was then, as now, a separate art.

The evolution of the great classical forms such as sonata form and the sonata rondo came about through the art and inventiveness of composers like Christian Bach, Haydn and Mozart who worked fast and worked continuously to delight and surprise a small and discerning audience. They made a great leap forward in an astonishingly short time, and with an assurance unclouded by any academic or philosophical concern about the theory of what they did.

Mozart wrote his twenty-three original piano concertos within this tradition. At first, as we shall see, all three movements were written in forms that were handed down to him. As his experience grew, he found that the slow second movements could still be contained within the structure of the adagios and andantes of the day and that the fast third movements too (although he enlarged their range and scale) could be handled effectively within the rondo or variation form. The first movements, however, presented a problem.

The form he inherited from Christian Bach was a hybrid, still bearing traces of its origin as an aria. This prototype he strengthened, refined, enlarged and ultimately transformed into a symphonic concerto movement as different in scale and in breadth from the concerto of Christian Bach as a Beethoven piano sonata from one by Scarlatti.

In contrast to this evolution of the concerto first movement, the first movements of the symphonies from first to last could be contained within sonata form, with only an occasional departure. There was no need for Mozart to change it, for when the proportions were greater, as they were in the later symphonies, sonata form served his purpose just as well as in the miniature symphonic essays of his childhood. Again, unlike the early symphonies, many of which are run-of-the-mill works, at least half of the twenty-four piano concertos, from the lively K175 to the last sad K595, are masterpieces, and each first movement marks the completion of a stage in a journey of discovery which reached its destination in the D minor, the C minor and the big C major concertos.

The secret of Mozart's hard-wrought achievement, however, died with him. The piano concerto had never seriously engaged Haydn's interest, and Beethoven, although he absorbed many of Mozart's felicities, did not grasp, or did not want to use, the subtle architectural plan that he had perfected. Brahms brought yet another approach, and at the same time the structure of the first movement of the piano concerto began to crumble beneath the onslaught of the romantics and the virtuosos.

For over a century Mozart's concertos were largely neglected both by the composers and musical public. Within the last twenty years, however, their quality has been recognised again, and today they are played more often than ever before, usually with affection and skill. But not always (so far as the first movements are concerned) with understanding. The reason for this may lie in the history of musical criticism, for it can fairly be said that the form of the first movements of Mozart's piano concertos has never been described in terms that are wholly true and at the same time wholly comprehensive.

So far as the Mozart concertos are concerned modern musical analysis begins, perhaps, with Tovey's essay on the Classical Concerto, written in 1903 (*Essays in Musical Analysis*, *Volume III: Concertos*, Oxford University Press, 1937). This is characteristically penetrating and discursive. It bases its approach on a full analysis of the first movement of K503 (the big C major concerto), and it begins by brushing away some cobwebs.

Tovey challenges the standard theory of first movement concerto form which was to be found in the textbooks of the day. This 'standard theory' is perhaps best defined in Stewart Macpherson's book *Form in Music* (Joseph Williams, 1908) as follows:

> It was not until the time of Mozart that the concerto definitely assumed the form with which we are now familiar, viz. that of a work, usually of the dimensions of a sonata, for a solo instrument with orchestral accompaniment. The concertos of Mozart and his successors are mostly on the three-movement plan, and consist of an Allegro in sonata form, with a notable modification – the Double Exposition, the plan of which will be discerned by the following diagram:

Exposition I (Orchestra)	Exposition II (Solo and Accompaniment)
1st subject in Tonic	1st subject in Tonic
2nd subject in Tonic	2nd subject in Dominant or Relative Major, both subjects being presented with a good deal of florid ornamentation for the soloist.

> The development and recapitulation usually open with orchestral tuttis of some importance...

There is no doubt that Mozart's concertos will not fit the 'standard theory' and Tovey rejected it impatiently. He had, however, no real alternative to offer, and indeed implied that to seek for any general plan was to chase a chimera:

> ...there is no foreseeing what the solo will select from the ritornello. All that we can be sure of is that nothing will be without its function, and that everything will be unexpected and inevitable. I doubt whether three important concertos of Mozart (at least

> fifteen are important) could be found that agreed as closely in form as Beethoven's three greatest concertos.

This, as we shall see, is far too sweeping. Five more of Mozart's piano concertos appear amongst Tovey's notes (reprinted from the programmes of the Reid concerts) which make up the rest of the volume. Each concerto is described as if it were one of five different houses built, it is true, by the same architect, but with no structural plan in common. He does, however, define two main principles (and makes one lesser generalisation which we will meet later on).

First, he points out that the idea of a classical concerto derives from the alternating ritornello and solo of the aria and that however complex the opening orchestral section may be, it remains a true ritornello and not a symphonic exposition. Tovey's definition of ritornello and solo falters, however, in describing his second main principle.

This asserts that the great masters of sonata form adapted the ritornello and solo of the older form of concerto to make a 'sonata form concerto'. He describes the four main sections of the concertos as the opening ritornello, the solo exposition, the development and the recapitulation, and these labels were to stick. They imply the concept of a work in the standard sonata form with a separate ritornello in front. But beyond these general principles it is clear that Tovey feels Mozart's concertos to be widely variable.

Girdlestone's book *Mozart's Piano Concertos* was written in French in 1938 and published in English ten years later. It is a detailed and affectionate work. But it is an account of the concertos written by a lover who is content to describe no more than their outward charms. In his chapter on form he does, however, attempt to draw up some general principles. After a very few broad rules that apply to first movement form he enters a maze of alternatives, either this, or that. Even so, a strong subcurrent of footnotes lists the errant works that will conform to no kind of generalisation.

He, like Tovey, sees their structures in terms of sonata form, and he too accepts, with a kind of fatalism, that there is no pattern which can be generally applied. He adopts the terms of sonata form, First (or Tutti) Exposition, Second (or Solo) Exposition, Development and Recapitulation, but his eye is more attracted by the external decoration of the concertos than by their structural design, and he is happier with an anthropomorphic vision of the piano and the orchestra as two personalities sometimes locked in conflict, sometimes working together in amity, than in calculating the logic of the musical and dramatic construction. To give only one example, he will frequently report, each time with surprised admiration, how the piano will 'reject' the succession of themes from the orchestral Exposition and 'strike out' with its own ideas, how it will 'shake itself free' of the orchestra, then once more become 'subdued' by it and so on. All of this is no more than a description of the regular pattern of the first concerted section, which, as we shall see later, Mozart had inherited from Christian Bach. His acceptance of sonata form as the basis of the concertos is less by deliberation than by default. He does not feel that the problem is important.

Arthur Hutchings' book, however, *A Companion to Mozart's Piano Concertos* (Oxford, 1948) is more radical. Like Tovey he discredits the 'standard theory' but like him also says 'there is no such work as a "typical Mozart concerto"'. He does, however, define afresh the elements of the first movements in order to reach his own general formula.

He again lays emphasis upon the 'ritornello principle' and describes the first orchestral section as the Orchestral Prelude. Then he calls the first concerted section the Exposition, with its closing Ritornello; then a Development; then a Recapitulation ending again with a Final Ritornello.

This, as far as it goes, is a fair description of the major landmarks in the course of a movement. But in dealing with the thematic material he tends to use the approach of a quantity surveyor rather than an architect. Themes are given labels of identity, not of function; sections are assessed in terms of bulk rather than of shape. The ritornellos he sees as islands of orchestral music amidst concerted sections, not as the closing part of a continuous act in a drama. But apart from the 'ritornello principle' he still saw the first movement after the Prelude as the Exposition, the Development, and the Recapitulation of sonata form, in short, a three-section movement with a Prelude before and Ritornellos amid and aft.

The truth is that to base any analytical approach to Mozart's first movements on Sonata Form is a mistake. It seems that the 'standard theory' was written into the textbooks at a time when Beethoven's concertos were well known and Mozart's were not. Beethoven's C minor piano concerto fits the 'standard theory' precisely. His other piano concertos and the violin concerto can be construed in terms of it by making allowances for the irregularities demanded by a sonata form movement written for two voices instead of one. As Mozart's concertos became known, the commentators of the twentieth century rejected the 'standard theory', but their outlook was so dominated by sonata form, which had established itself over the previous hundred years as the almost universal plan for first movements, that they saw it even when it was not there. Tovey's main essay is headed indeed 'The Sonata Form Concerto' to distinguish it from the Baroque form which preceded it and the Virtuoso concerto which followed.

It was as if a group of scholars in some ancient forms of architecture were to stumble across the ruins of a related but different civilisation. Their natural tendency would be to describe the points of difference as deviations from the style they knew. Strange and unusual features would be defined in terms of what they should be, not in terms of what they were. Similarly we are apt to tell children that mammoths were an earlier, and irregular, form of elephant.

So the four sections of the Concerto movement came to be described in terms of the Sonata movement, although it is sometimes recognised that they fit in a little uneasily. Tovey makes a generalisation in a note written many years later that the fourth section is not a true recapitulation of the solo exposition, but rather a reprise which puts together, in a different order and at a different length, elements of both the first orchestral ritornello and the solo exposition. But he draws attention to it as a departure from standard practice by saying 'we can see very clearly one of Mozart's peculiar principles of concerto form; a principle far less easily traced in either Beethoven or Brahms. With Mozart the principle is definitely this: that the recapitulation recapitulates not so much the first solo as the opening tutti'. When we come to examine the concertos we shall see that this is not true, for the last section is a synthesis which has a logic of its own. The point here is that because Tovey *expected* a precise recapitulation of the first solo (or concerto) section he throws heavy emphasis on what strikes him as an irregularity.

Similarly Hutchings, who defines 'the principle of ritornello' so well, is not perhaps so happy in calling the First Ritornello an Orchestral Prelude and the first concerto section the Exposition. The First Ritornello is not outside the main drama; it is an organic part of it. The first concerto section is not an exposition, because it varies, enlarges and adds to the material given out in the first ritornello. Girdlestone muses in a puzzled manner over this point:

> ... the real development begins with the solo entry, and instead of dividing a concerto first movement into four parts as do the textbooks, it would be more sensible to keep a threefold division as for the sonata or the symphony: tutti exposition; *development* (including the solo exposition and the development in the textbook sense), and recapitulation.

He does not, however, follow his own advice, and perhaps this is just as well. Instead, he sticks to the usual terms. He displays further perplexity (caused by the subcurrent of comparison with sonata form) in phrases like 'the mock second subject' which he applies to a 'second subject' which appears in his First Exposition and not in the Second. Since in most concertos there are two 'second subjects', one from the orchestra and one from the piano, he expends considerable toil in deciding each time which is the 'true' and which is the 'mock' second subject.

The first step therefore for the student of Mozart's concerto form is to move away from the standpoint of sonata form as it came to be known and to step back to a much earlier point in time (perhaps 1730) when all of the classical forms were still in embryo.

The simple dance movement of a Baroque instrumental suite started in the tonic and led to a close in the dominant. (Or the tonic parallel, or occasionally the mediant. Whichever it might be, it served as the opposite polarisation to the home key, and from now on for the sake of brevity 'the dominant' should be read as meaning 'the polarised key' whichever one it may be.) The second part of the dance, then, began in the dominant and led back to the tonic. Sometimes the first strain of the dance was repeated in the home key before the final close. Thus the 'a b' of the simple dance form could become the 'a b a' of sonata form. Or it could be extended to form the 'a b a c a' of the rondo.

As the thematic material became more elaborate, the sonata principle inspired a thematic succession of subjects within 'a', a free-working central section for 'b', followed by a repeat of 'a'. The rules of tonality for the 'a' section dictated that the shift to the dominant came within a transition or link passage after the first group of themes, that it was followed by a second group and then some concluding material, all firmly in the dominant. The middle section 'b' remained free, so long as it observed the tonal rule of starting in the dominant and leading back to the tonic. In the repeat of 'a' the original themes were repeated in the same order, this time all of them in the tonic. This called for some adjustment in the link passage and a different register for the themes from that point to the end of the movement.

It is worth pausing for a moment to assess the function of this elaborate formula that stemmed from the sonata principle, and which came to be early sonata form.

The first section, 'a', or as it came to be called, the Exposition, was, as we have seen, made up of a succession of themes, the second group usually being in contrast to the first with some strong conclusive material at the end. This would have read as a complete statement in itself but for the switch to the dominant which left the statement incomplete and carried with it some sense of a question unanswered—the first half of an argument which awaits an affirmative reply. The middle section, 'b' (the Development), deferred this answer by introducing an imaginative excursion in which known material might be re-worked or new material introduced. There was usually an element of fantasy and sometimes of dramatic plot development. This last concept, first used by Scarlatti in the few pregnant bars within the microscale of his sonatas, was one of the new gifts of sonata form to music. It carried the imagination beyond the simple forms based on dances and heralded the possibilities of drama and conflict in instrumental music.

The middle section, having beguiled attention for some time, gave its cue for a return to the tonic and a repeat of the original material (unfelicitously labelled, by musicologists, 'the Recapitulation'). This time, the whole succession of themes remaining in the tonic, the 'a' section, reads as an affirmative, the answer or complement to its own first statement which had ended in the questioning dominant. In particular, the concluding material reinforced and hammered home the tonic key with an insistence that could be compared to the tonic pedal at the end of a fugue.

The form so far described (and so well known) was designed for a single instrument or for a group of instruments working as a team. When we come to music written for two voices, an aria or a concerto, it becomes clear at once that the importance of function transcends that of tonality or theme. To the listener it is more obvious and more important that a passage is performed by the soloist, or by the orchestra, or by both together, than that it is moving towards or away from the dominant. The aria form therefore had as its salient feature a set of rules which allowed for an alternation between the solo and the orchestra, a first ritornello, a first solo, a second ritornello and so on. Underlying this dramatic relationship between the single voice and the group there later came to be the same tonal principle as in the sonata, namely an 'a' section leading to the dominant, a free 'b' section returning to the tonic and a repeat of the 'a' section all in the tonic.

The thematic rules which developed from the sonata principle into sonata form did not, however, apply to aria form because the overriding functional importance of alternating ritornello and solo would not permit them to do so. Instead the orchestra has a first ritornello with its own succession of themes all in the tonic, then the solo begins, usually with the same material, but soon it develops a new thematic line of its own during which the switch to the dominant is made. The concluding material is given to the orchestra, now in the dominant, in a ritornello which ends the first section. After the free middle section which ends with a return to the tonic, an amalgam of all the material heard in the first and second parts is repeated, this time all in the tonic.

Thus the sonata principle of tonality underlies a part of the broad structure of the concerto, but the form built above this foundation is entirely different. An opera and a play both based on the same plot have a common origin, but the critic who for this reason expects both of them to conform to the same rules of construction is misguided. One will follow the dramatic traditions, the other those of opera. Yet this is not the approach that musicologists have brought to bear on Mozart's concerto form, and this may be why its true nature has been obscured.

This book is therefore an attempt to throw some light on this unique and ingenious musical structure which fell into disuse nearly two hundred years ago. It was one of Mozart's greatest and most personal achievements and the wonder is that a musical form that must be of interest to every pianist and every conductor who plays the concertos has never been subjected to the sort of thorough analysis that has been applied to the fugue, the sonata and the symphony.

The original motive behind this inquiry, however, was far from academic. It started involuntarily, out of sheer affection for the concertos. Familiarity bred an irresistible curiosity to find out how and why Mozart worked as he did. Previous writers on the concertos did not supply a full and satisfactory answer to all the questions. The only thing to do was to find out.

Accordingly, over many years scores and books were assembled, recordings collected (and in the case of K39 and 41, new recordings were made). Mozart himself was not so difficult; his contemporaries more so. The scores of all of Christian Bach's London concertos were copied out and subjected to comparative analysis. His brother Emmanuel, and other less famous men, were reconnoitred, not with any easy success. Finally the collected data began to settle into stable patterns, deductions could be made with increasing certainty and a line of historical succession became clear.

I hope this study will interest those practitioners in music who share a love for Mozart and a desire to understand how a great and resourceful composer achieves mastery over a musical form, how he starts where others left off; how he recognises problems, then solves them; how he draws upon stored experience; how he can make a negative experiment into a successful work; and finally how he can build on ancient foundations a fabric spacious enough to contain musical ideas which have grown ten times too big for the form with which they started.

I have presumed to mint a new vocabulary to describe the concerto form. The terms in common use are mainly applicable to and associated with sonata form and do not fit the construction of a concerto. The four main sections of the movement I have called the Statement (first exposition, opening ritornello, orchestral prelude); the First Concerto (second, piano and solo exposition); the Fantasy or the Development, whichever is the more appropriate (middle section); and the Concerto Reprise, or Reprise for short (Recapitulation).

Within each section the terms used are more conventional. A glossary is printed inside the back and front covers. Diagrams are used extensively to help those who see the shape of music more clearly in symbols than in words; they are, however, never more than accessories to the text.

And finally, for those who like to know where they are going before they set out, this study follows the evolution of Mozart's concerto form through four stages:

1 Aria. The North German School were familiar with Sebastian Bach's form of the Extended Aria. They adapted it, but not greatly, for the keyboard.

2 Galant. From North Germany Christian Bach took this form to London and after a variety of experiments settled on a version which Mozart used in his earlier concertos.

3 Melodic. Mozart continued to use the Galant form throughout his life: he also developed a variant in a series which I have called the Melodic Concertos.

4 Symphonic. He further devised a distinct and more complex form for a series of what I have called the Symphonic Concertos.

PART ONE

The Mozartean Evolution

I

Sebastian, Philip Emmanuel, and Christian Bach

There is no advantage in pursuing the piano concerto into the recesses of antiquity. The Baroque instrumental concertos of Handel and Bach are well known; the concertos of Sebastian Bach's sons and their contemporaries less so, and it is these works that provide the missing link between the age of polyphony and the classical period of Mozart. A convenient point at which to take up the story is therefore in 1750, the year of Sebastian Bach's death at the age of sixty-five and six years before the birth of Mozart.

At this time Carl Philip Emmanuel Bach, Sebastian's third son, was in his mid-thirties and held a high position amongst the circle of musicians at the court of Frederick the Great at Potsdam and Berlin. The monarch's interest in music is said to have centred mainly in his own performance on the flute, although he is also alleged to have been a composer. He did, at any rate, attract to his court many leading musicians, and perhaps the royal interest inspired as much fashionable interest in music then as it does in horses today.

Philip Emmanuel had been appointed court harpsichordist in 1740 and he both composed and performed many of the court keyboard concertos. The musical climate surrounding him was learned; in 1747 his father, Sebastian Bach, had sent to the king the Musical Offering, one of the most elaborate essays in counterpoint ever written and a compliment which would have been incomprehensible to a less musical monarch.

The demand, however, was now for a different kind of music, especially for the flute. Joseph Quantz, who tutored the king on the instrument and built the royal flutes, also composed over three hundred flute concertos. Wind concertos were not a particularly good medium for counterpoint, neither was the old Baroque form of concerto of Vivaldi and Sebastian Bach well suited for a display of virtuosity. This may have been one reason for the search for a new kind of concerto, or it may have been caused by no more than a general swing in musical taste. There is no doubt, however, that the composers at Potsdam, the leaders in the musical life of North Germany, were seeking a concerto form that would give a solo instrument a more individual role. They did not have to look far, for there already existed a vocal form that suited their needs.

This was the Aria. From the turn of the century the Aria had been the most common, indeed almost the universal, form of presenting an important solo for voice and instrumental accompaniment. The first and most stable pattern had been the *da capo* Aria, which was to provide the basis of much that was to come. Nearly all previous writers on the concertos have accepted the general statement that 'the concerto was based on the aria' but never, it seems, has the comparison been pressed home to show the remarkable similarity of the two original forms.

The *da capo* Aria opened with an orchestral ritornello which was headed by an important theme. Next came the first solo which usually began with some reference to the main theme but then moved into a vocal line of its own. This solo (and those to follow) were punctuated by side- or sub-ritornellos. To close the first section came the second ritornello. So far, except perhaps for some passing modulations in the first solo, this whole work had remained in the tonic.

The second solo provided a modulatory middle section and ended in the dominant or the tonic parallel. Then came the *da capo*, the first ritornello, first solo and second ritornello played again note for note as they had been on their first appearance.

The *da capo* Aria could therefore be construed in terms of the rondo principle as well as the sonata principle. If the ritornello is regarded as the rondo subject, it appears four times always in the tonic. The episodes are provided by the first solo, the second solo and the repeat of the first solo. The modulation in the second solo and the close in the dominant were acceptable practice at that time for episodes in strict rondo form. (The *da capo* Aria is summarised in Table 1.)

TABLE 1

The *da capo* Aria

The sections played by the orchestra are shown in capitals, the solo sections in lower case.

Section	*Description*	*Key*
FIRST RITORNELLO	Opening with the Main Theme	Tonic
First Solo	Usually opening with a reference to the Main Theme either by the solo or in the first short sub-ritornello. May modulate a little and return to tonic	Tonic
SECOND RITORNELLO	Often opening with the Main Theme; made up from elements of the First Ritornello; usually shorter	Tonic
Second Solo	The Middle Section. New Material: free and modulatory Ending in the dominant or tonic parallel	Modulatory Dominant
THIRD RITORNELLO	(*da capo*) The First Ritornello repeated	Tonic
Third Solo	The First Solo repeated	Tonic
FOURTH RITORNELLO	The Second Ritornello repeated	Tonic

TABLE 2

The Extended Aria: Quoniam from J. S. Bach's Mass in B minor

Section	*Bars*	*Description*	*Key*
FIRST RITORNELLO	1–13	Opens with the Main Theme (the horn tune) bars 1–4; continues in sequences	Tonic
First Solo	13–45	Opens with a new solo phrase; answered by a sub-ritornello of the Main Theme. Solo develops with its own melodic line, sequences and conclusion. Modulates firmly to the dominant (note well) and ends in that key	Tonic To Dominant
SECOND RITORNELLO	45–53	Opens with the Main Theme; is a shortened version of the First	Dominant
Second Solo	53–89	The Middle Section. New material; free; modulatory; orchestral support and sub-ritornellos	Modulatory Dominant
(THIRD RITORNELLO)		None. When omitted, the Fourth Solo will always start in the same way as the First Solo. This gives the necessary sense of reprise. The alternative is a Third Ritornello which opens with the Main Theme, then lets in a third solo which may be varied, and ends with a Fourth Ritornello. This is usually made up of the remainder of the First Ritornello	Tonic
Third Solo	90–116	Opens as the First Solo. Develops new sequences and a conclusion of a higher emotional pitch than in the First Solo	Tonic
FOURTH RITORNELLO	116–127	Reprise of the First Ritornello	Tonic

TABLE 3

The *da capo* Aria: the Extended Aria and the North German concerto compared

Section	da capo *Aria*	*Extended Aria*	*North German Concerto*
FIRST RITORNELLO	Main Theme Sequences Close	Main Theme Sequences Close	Main Theme Sequences Close
First Solo	Opening reference to Main Theme as described. Solo section sometimes modulates but always ends in the tonic	Same as *da capo* Solo section sometimes moves to the dominant and ends there	Same as *da capo* Solo section always moves to the dominant and ends there
SECOND RITORNELLO	A part of the First, in tonic	Same as *da capo* but can be in tonic or dominant	Same as *da capo* but always in dominant
Second Solo	Fresh material; free; modulating; end in dominant	Same as *da capo* but may start in the dominant	Same as *da capo* but starting in the dominant
THIRD RITORNELLO	Repeat of First: tonic	Sometimes omitted; if not, a reprise of part of the First. Tonic or tonic parallel	Nearly always present, a reprise of part of the First. Tonic.
Third Solo	Repeat of First: tonic	Variation or extension of First; may reprise some material; tonic	Same as Extended Aria, tends to a greater element of reprise. Tonic
FOURTH RITORNELLO	Repeat of Second: Tonic	Reprise of part of First (Tonic)	Same as Extended Aria

The Aria had already proved to be a thoroughly satisfactory form of music, and it was to remain in constant use for another half century. It happily combines an element of drama (not only in the words of the text but also in the contrast between the solo and the tutti) with an opportunity for an almost unlimited display of virtuosity. There were many varieties; for comic opera the *aria buffa*, for religious devotion the *aria da chiesa*, for one style of singing the *aria cantabile*, for another the *aria di bravura*. There were variations in form too, and one of these, the Extended Aria, was to be selected by the alert band of composers at King Frederick's court to become the form for instrumental and particularly for keyboard concertos.

The Extended Aria was used by Sebastian Bach in many of his works. (It is described in Table 2, using the Quoniam from the Mass in B minor as an example.) It was not merely an 'extension' of the *da capo* Aria. Indeed it could have the same number of solo and ritornello sections, and it was not necessarily any longer in 'extent'. There were, however, two important differences.

The first solo sometimes moved into the dominant and the following second ritornello would confirm the dominant tonality. The *da capo* Aria, on the other hand, had always closed its first solo in the tonic and the second ritornello had continued in this key. But now the Extended Aria could launch its middle section from the dominant and, after allowing the usual free progression, would end there (or in the tonic parallel, etc).

Secondly, the last part of the aria after the middle section was not a repeat of the first part. It could not be so if the first ritornello had moved into the dominant, because it must now stay in the tonic throughout. Not only that, the Extended Aria made its main advance (or extension) over the *da capo* form by introducing new material into the reprise of the first solo, thus heightening its emotional pitch in order to raise the solo part to an even greater supremacy than in the first solo section.

When the North German composers adopted the ground plan of the Extended Aria for their concertos they made an invariable rule of two of the features which had been optional in the vocal form. First, the early move into the dominant in the first solo became the regular practice, and second, the third ritornello was never absent from its place at the head of the last part of the work, which therefore always gained a definite sense of reprise at this point. The form was thus adopting some features of the developing Sonata Form and beginning to diverge from the Couperin-type of rondo.

It is not easy to explain why Sebastian Bach had not himself developed the aria form as a basis for his concertos. For some reason the composers of the older school did not see, or did not choose to exploit, the possibilities offered by substituting an instrument for the human voice in the aria. They wrote their concertos in the Baroque form established by Vivaldi, which could accommodate a concerto for a single mass of instruments, for two groups one stronger than the other, or for a solo, more often for the violin or a wind instrument rather than for the weaker voice of the clavier. Whatever the opposition of forces, however, the ground plan remained the same. The works were built on a main theme with sequences, relief passages and a modulatory middle section, but beyond that there was no fixed alternation of ritornello and solo, no formal observance of a key cycle and no attempt to cast a solo instrument in so human or so dramatic a role as in the 'aria' concerto.

The new form was, however, quickly and widely adopted by the composers at Potsdam and Berlin. Quantz, when writing his flute concertos for the monarch, preferred a slender and abbreviated version of the Extended Aria, free of all sub-ritornellos so that the light tone of the flute would not be outmatched. Philip Emmanuel and the keyboard composers, on the other hand, used the full version with a great deal of orchestral intervention so that they might exploit the dramatic contrast between the harpsichord and the orchestra. They adapted the traditional style of solo writing to suit the characteristics of the clavier, and of the ritornellos to conform with the more modern and vigorous orchestral practice of King Frederick's court.

Uldall in his essay on the *Clavier Concertos of the Berlin School*

(Breitkopf and Härtel, Leipzig, 1928) although he does not fully recognise their similarity to the Extended Aria, leaves no room for doubt that the North German form described in Table 3 became a settled and recognised standard from which variations were judged to be irregularities. He goes into the greatest detail in describing the practice of the different composers (Philip Emmanuel Bach, Quantz, Nickelman, Graun, Schaffrath, Schale and in Dresden, Hasse), in the way they managed their sub-ritornellos, the degree of reprise in the third solo and so forth, and lays down the standard length for each section and sub-section, which he measures exactly in numbers of bars (a measurement more arbitrary, incidentally, than the available evidence will support). There were, of course, variations, the most common being the addition of a fourth solo and a fifth ritornello. Philip Emmanuel himself tired of the extended aria pattern in later life and after 1762 went on to fresh experiments. Nevertheless it is clear that within the two middle decades of the century the extended aria was appropriated and practised by the North Germans as the common form for the clavier concerto.

A comparison between the three forms, the *da capo* Aria, the Extended Aria and the North German concerto form is shown in Table 3. Most of Philip Emmanuel's concertos of 1740–59 will serve as examples of the North German form; those that are best known are, perhaps, the concertos in G minor (1740), D minor (1748), F major (1755), and the two concertos in E flat and A major (1753/4) attributed to Christian.

Since the Extended Aria was the point of origin of the classical concerto, before tracing its development through successive innovations at the hands of Christian Bach and Mozart it is worth pausing to review the functional characteristics of the founder member of the family. Some of these are so strongly marked as to strike the ear at once.

First the ritornellos with their insistent re-entries seem to stand like a succession of sturdy pillars supporting the more delicate tracery of the solo sections. Each time the solid tone of the ritornello breaks in with its affirmation of the known material the listener gains a sense of reassurance, of returning home after an excursion into foreign places.

Second, the Middle Section (the second solo) is of a nature quite apart from the rest of the work. The progress of the music halts; the solo is allowed to follow its own fancy, to visit foreign keys and develop new ideas. It is a short imaginative essay embedded in the centre of a narrative.

Third, there is a special relationship between the two protagonists. They do not play together as in a duet, nor is one subordinate to the other. Instead they take the stage turn and turn about; the orchestra does accompany the clavier, it is true, but only to supply a light background, and when it does so it assumes a different character. Soon it will butt in with a ritornello and become itself again. The solo makes use of the Main Theme and other snatches of orchestral material; the orchestra borrows nothing from the solo. In the solo sections the performer is given every chance to display virtuosity and, because he is contending single-handed with a powerful instrumental chorus, his stature is raised to heroic proportions.

A second or third hearing will disclose a definite shape within sections. The First Ritornello opens (and often closes) with the Main Theme which is the dominant musical idea of the movement. Sequences flow from it, and pound along in the steady four-square rhythm of the day until they slacken off into a quieter passage, a relief both in tone (it is scored more lightly) and in pace. These Relief passages generally occur about half-way through the ritornello, which then gathers impetus once again in another string of sequences and ends with two or three Cadential figures, often the most tuneful of the orchestral themes. One of the Cadentials (usually the penultimate) often provides a second Relief Subject, and the last Cadential is often related to the Main Theme.

The first solo, as we have seen, opens with a reference to the Main Theme either by the orchestra, or, more usually, the solo. A sub-ritornello seals off the known material, and then the solo sails out on its own course, often passing through two distinctly lyrical passages, one during its early sequences bridging the gap towards the dominant, the second when it has settled into the new key.

TABLE 4

North German form: detail of sections

Orchestral material is shown in capitals; solo in lower case.
Variable material is shown in brackets.

Section	*Detail*	*Key*
FIRST RITORNELLO	MAIN THEME SEQUENCES RELIEF PASSAGES (SEQUENCES) CADENTIALS	Tonic Tonic
First Solo	Main Theme/SUB RITORNELLO Solo/SUB RITORNELLOS Solo (Cadentials)	Tonic Tonic To Dominant Dominant
SECOND RITORNELLO	(SEQUENCES) (CADENTIALS)	Dominant Dominant
Second Solo	Main Theme developed followed by a free fantasia *or* new material in the form of a fantasia	Modulatory Dominant
THIRD RITORNELLO	(MAIN THEME) (SEQUENCES)	Tonic Tonic
Third Solo	May follow the course of the First Solo either more or less; usually opens in the same way	Tonic Tonic
FOURTH RITORNELLO	(SEQUENCES) (RELIEF PASSAGES) (SEQUENCES) (CADENTIALS)	Tonic Tonic Tonic

The solo may end with some concertante treatment of the Cadential material from the First Ritornello. The Second Ritornello recalls some part of the First. Then follows the Middle Section. In the concertos of Philip Emmanuel this usually starts with a definite development of the Main Theme. It is always, however, modulatory, and in its later stages the Middle Section settles back into the dominant or the tonic parallel with a sense of reaching a destination.

The Third Ritornello, in the tonic, or more rarely the tonic parallel, recalls given material once again; next comes the third solo with a variable element of reprise from the first; and finally the Fourth Ritornello. Often the Third and Fourth Ritornello are together no more than the First, split open to let the third solo take its place between the two halves. The character of the seven sections is outlined in Table 4.

The North German form spread fast. During the 1750s Wagenseil, Joseph Haydn and Vanhal in Vienna, and the Stamitz family in Mannheim were writing concertos in this style. But the composer who was to take it furthest was, to study it at source.

Christian Bach was the eighteenth child of Sebastian, and the third by his second wife Anna Magdalena. He was fifteen years of age in 1750 when his father died, and he went at once to study under his half-brother, Philip Emmanuel. We do not know what sort of relationship developed between the two, separated as they were by a gap of twenty-one years, but four years later, at the age of nineteen (1754) Christian left Berlin for Italy, where he studied under Padre Martini at Bologna. In 1760 he took the post of organist at Milan Cathedral. In 1762 he left Italy for the court of George III in London and after a sustained and agreeable spell of popular (but not financial) success, he died there at the age of forty-seven (1782).

The change of scene from Northern Germany to the Po Valley at the age of nineteen (accompanied by a change from the Protestant to the Catholic faith) naturally had a considerable effect upon him both as an individual and as a composer, and it is likely that of his two common nicknames, one, 'The London

Bach', took account of geography alone, whereas the other, 'The Italian Bach', may have related to the quality of his music.

Philip Emmanuel's style of composition, which Christian had left behind him in Germany, makes a serious appeal to the solid, humane, but not unenterprising German spirit. His major works have a vigorous attack and a great depth of feeling, but within a limited range. In his writings on music Philip Emmanuel states his preference for 'feeling' over virtuosity. He favoured the minor key, and his allegro movements are characterised by a faintly anguished striving, conveying even at the climax of a work, whether in the major or minor, a negative sense of fatalism. He echoed the feeling of some of the music in the Passions of his father; he never reflected the confidence and jubilation of, for instance, the *Gloria*, the *Cum Sanctu Spiritu* or the *Resurrexit* of the B minor Mass.

The concertos were no exception. Their themes are mathematical in the true Pythagorean sense in that they depend greatly upon the simple harmonic relationships. Although figuration and scales might be used to fill the gaps, the outlines of the themes favour the basic arithmetical ratios of the octave's two to one, the fifth, the sixth and the third. The Main Themes have wide intervals, a jagged outline, and are often stated in unison. It is the music of a string and keyboard player and in no sense music for the human voice. He was, however, a marvellously inventive and successful composer and is surely due for a fashionable revival such as has already been enjoyed by Vivaldi and Telemann.

Christian arrived in Italy at a time when Padre Martini was still the supreme scholar of the old world of contrapuntal music. Outside the confines of the academies, however, the opera was sweeping into the full favour of musical fashion. And in Italy, as elsewhere, the human voice had never cared much for mathematics. The songs which had for centuries resounded throughout the Italian countryside had always run easily from note to note, perhaps only settling in the diatonic mode when a marriage with man-made instruments made it necessary. Christian Bach must have heard much music which through its grace and beauty made an immediate appeal to the senses. Such qualities had never flourished in the colder musical climate of the Protestant North. Evidently he found the new music to his liking, for he, and later Mozart, did more than any of their contemporaries to introduce into instrumental music the felicities of the Italian vocal style and of the Italian opera.

There are a number of clavier concertos attributed to Christian Bach in the period before he left Berlin. Their authenticity has, however, been questioned, for at least the two best-known (in E flat and A major) have a maturity, a seriousness of purpose and a style of composition which could seem to mark them out as the work of Philip Emmanuel. Christian lived with his brother and worked as his pupil and amanuensis, and so such a confusion could easily have arisen. Whether it was he, however, or his brother who wrote these early concertos is a question of little importance, for they were in the North German style and composed by a different Bach from the Italianate young man who arrived in London in 1762. The first London set of concertos were published within a year of his arrival in London and may even have been written before he left Milan.

In England he became one of the earliest champions of the forte-piano. Perhaps partly because of this, his solo parts were written with a firmer outline and at the same time in a more Italianate and lyrical style. Both of these qualities were to influence Mozart. More important, however, Mozart was to inherit the changes that Christian was making to the older North German form.

Christian Bach opened the First Ritornello with one of two kinds of First Subject, both of them new, and neither so striking as the Main Theme of the North Germans. One type was a quiet lyrical First Subject, often over a pedal bass (which was to be the forerunner of Mozart's Melodic first subject). Because of its gentle song-like nature it was unsuitable for sub-ritornellos and for development in the free sections. Hence it came to stand at the head of each section only. It could not easily be knitted into the texture anywhere else.

The second type of opening subject was more typically Galant; four-square, with dotted rhythms, often no more than a hunt up and down the tonic chord with the effect simply of a call for attention. This was more useful as material for side-ritornellos and for development, but it was short and staccato and its power as a unifying force was limited. Both types of Christian's First Subject were far removed from the stringent and dominating Main Themes of Philip Emmanuel.

Christian led straight from the First Subject into a sonata-type Bridge, faster in tempo and often over a rubbing bass. This ended by hovering on the dominant but did not truly enter it, thereby preserving one traditional characteristic of the ritornello—a lengthy assertion of the tonic key.

This swerve towards the dominant tonality served as a point of entry for the second or 'Relief' subject, for this was still far away from the character of a true 'sonata' Second Subject or group. The Relief subjects that lay amongst the billowing sequences of the North German ritornellos had been more a contrast in volume, rhythm and tone than in melody. The solid string chorus would fade down and, for a few bars, two or three solo instruments would play with some fragment plucked out from the rolling sequences that had gone before.

Christian's Relief subjects were not altogether unlike these passages, but with more individuality and sometimes with a definite tune. After the Relief subject he ran straight on to a string of Cadentials, often more numerous and always less geometrical in their shape than those of the North Germans. They were seldom related to the first subject.

In this way Christian diminished the importance of the Main Theme and broke up the continuous sequential run of the aria ritornello into short sections, each in dramatic contrast to the next.

He modernised the thematic material by importing Italianate and Galant First Subjects which ran directly into a Bridge of the kind that he and others were already developing in sonata form. The difference was, however, that in sonata form the transition passage had the real function of moving into the dominant key, while in the concerto the transition did no more than make a feint at the dominant.

It was a valuable innovation, however, in that both the slow Italianate and the jerky Galant First Subjects were static and needed the complementary hustle and drive of the Bridge passage to give the music an impetus and to furnish a noisy introduction to the soft Relief subject.

The North German First Ritornello is compared with Christian's in Table 5. The pattern quoted is used in the First Ritornello of thirteen out of his eighteen London piano concertos. Two of the five exceptional works were experiments in Sonata Form, and labelled *concerto o sinfonia* (Opus 1 Nos. 4 and 6): one was a genuine departure (Opus 13 No. 1) and two varied the scheme only by dipping into the dominant for the Second Subject (Opus 13 Nos. 5 and 6).

TABLE 5

The changing First Ritornello: the practice of Philip Emmanuel and Christian Bach compared

C. P. E. Bach	*J. C. Bach*	*Symbol*
MAIN THEME	FIRST SUBJECT	F
SEQUENCES	BRIDGE	B
RELIEF SUBJECT	RELIEF SUBJECT	R
(SEQUENCES)	FIRST CADENTIAL	C1
FIRST CADENTIAL	SECOND CADENTIAL	C2
SECOND CADENTIAL	THIRD CADENTIAL	C3

The pattern of the first solo remained fluid in Christian's hands. He introduced, however, three new characteristics, and, as we shall see later, one new principle. First, the piano's own new material was more lyrical. Second, when the solo moved into the dominant he usually introduced a new kind of piano passage with some of the nature of a sonata Second Subject. (Occasionally this was followed by the Relief subject from the Ritornello as well.) Third, he tended to introduce more material from the Ritornello into the first solo.

The sequence of events in the first solo was nearly always as follows. After the First Subject, now always given by the piano, the old Bridge would provide the side-ritornello, and then there might be some concertante treatment of the familiar Bridge material before the piano struck out on its own. The solo no longer dived into a new stream of material but began by developing a piano bridge passage from some fragment of the old Bridge before moving into the dominant for the second group. After the second group there was usually a more extended concertante treatment of the Cadential figures.

More important, however, than these modifications, which seem to be a change of emphasis rather than of form, Christian developed at the end of the solo a new section which can best be described as a 'piano climax'. In the four Opus 1 works two of the solos run straight into the second Ritornello in the old fashion. The other two, however, have a few bars of virtuoso writing before the closing trill. These show the idea of a piano climax in embryo. Three of the Opus 7 set, however, develop this passage at considerable length, and all of the Opus 13 concertos have a sustained climax, those of Numbers 2 and 4 being of twenty bars and more in length.

We must pause to look both forward and back to appreciate the importance of this new idea. Nothing was more sharply in contrast to the old perpetuum mobile of the Baroque and the North German schools than the idea of the soloist taking the lead in what can only be compared to an operatic climax in the middle of an instrumental work. It is true that there had been a tradition of an occasional cadenza at this point. But a cadenza broke the rhythm of the work; the soloist played his scales and arpeggios in free time whilst the orchestra waited like a stopped clock. The piano climax is based on the opposite principle. It is designed so that the piano can generate pace and tension with varied rhythms, but always with increasing vigour and urgency until, with the speed of a runner breasting the tape, it arrives at the final trill.

In Mozart's hands the piano climaxes were to become an important structural feature of the movement. It was Christian

Bach, however, who first saw the logic of appropriating an Italian operatic convention and of popping it in, duly recast for the piano, at this point. For the piano climax is a theatrical device to 'make a curtain' with a storming virtuoso exit for the star performer, just as the testing virtuoso writing at the end of an aria is designed to give the singer his or her moment of supremacy. The piano ends its climax with all the panache of a prima donna, and in the thump of the tutti there are overtones of applause.

Thus the Ritornello gains a sense of finality. When the steady beat of the First Solo ended with a cadenza or merely a trill, the following ritornello sounded like the beginning of a fresh section. After the piano climax, however, it swings into the role of closing ritornello to round off the first solo. (The first solo section is summarised in Table 6.)

TABLE 6

C. P. E. Bach and J. C. Bach: first solo sections compared

Capitals for orchestra alone; lower case for piano and piano and orchestra. (Brackets round optional material. Many sub-ritornellos in the concerted sections not shown.)

C. P. E. Bach	*J. C. Bach*	*Symbol*
(main theme)	first subject	f
SUB-RITORNELLO	BRIDGE	B
solo (into dominant)	piano bridge into dominant	pb
more solo & concertante	piano second subject	ps
	(relief subject)	(r)
(cadentials)	cadentials	c^s
(cadenza)	piano climax	px
	leading to	
SECOND RITORNELLO	CLOSING RITORNELLO	

The Fantasies of Christian Bach's concertos have generally less relationship to the rest of the work than those of Philip Emmanuel. They range more widely both in their material (though occasionally 'given' material is still developed) and in tonality. They usually touch on the traditional relative minor or major key but not with so strong a sense of reaching a destination, nor do they dwell there for any length of time. They are free in every sense, and they are among the most arresting and persuasive sections of the movement.

The Reprise opens with the First Subject in the orchestra, just as the Main Theme entered in the North German concertos. As soon as the Bridge follows it, however, we know the First Subject is in a new context. It is the first unit in a Reprise of the First Concerto and the First Ritornello knitted together; it is no longer a separate ritornello in its own right. The Reprise is often shortened, in particular the piano's subject is dropped in most of the concertos, and only very seldom is any new material introduced. Again, after the piano climax the final ritornello has the effect of a short final burst of applause for the soloist. Then sometimes there is a cadenza, and finally the later Cadentials as a tutti to end the section.

If we cast a retrospective eye over the whole movement we will see that Christian Bach had removed the main prop of the North German concerto, for his First Subjects lacked the power and unifying force of the old Main Themes. In the concertos of Philip Emmanuel the Main Theme enters five times to signal the start of a new section and also, through its use in the last Cadential, it could also mark its close. Add to this some development in the Fantasy and the striking character of the theme itself, and it can be seen why all else in the movement was, by comparison, subsidiary. Christian, however, by opening with a mild lyrical or Galant subject and by bringing to life the component parts of the First Ritornello created unity through a new kind of logic. This was the logic of succession; the listener could follow a sequence of events, each one distinct and immediately recognisable. The concerto was turning its back on the old rondo principle and appropriating more of the elements of the sonata.

The complete cycle, with the piano's interpolations thrown in, occurred three times, in the Statement, the First Concerto and the Reprise. The Fantasy, as ever, stood outside the rest of the work. Thus the concerto fell into four parts, three of them alike in that they all began with the First Subject, all ran on to the same Bridge material, sometimes all had the same Relief subject, and all ended with some or all of the Cadentials. Although appearing to do very little, Christian Bach had in fact done a great deal, for by a mysterious alchemy he had transformed the seven sections or three main parts of the old North German form into the four-part Galant form which was to serve the piano concerto for nearly two decades and provide Mozart with a firm basis for the next advance.

He had, in fact, given a new logic to the join between the first solo and the Second Ritornello so that the latter read now as the complement or the conclusion to the former. Thus he made a single unit (the First Concerto) out of what had been two. Similarly the Third and Fourth Ritornellos became the beginning and end of a general reprise of the whole work (the Reprise). The transformation into the four-part shape is shown in Table 7.

This metamorphosis may well have sprung quite incidentally from the experiments of performer/composer working at the keyboard. From what we know of Christian Bach's methods and nature it is not likely that he would sit down to devise a new theory for concerto form. However that may be, his innovations not only set the concerto on a new road, but also served to confuse the critics some one hundred and fifty years later. Christian has often been credited with adapting the 'Baroque concerto' to 'sonata form'.

So far as the overall structure of the movement was concerned he did, of course, nothing of the sort. Only the emphasis was shifted, so that similar sentences construed into different paragraphs. Apart from this, he did bring to the opening ritornello the same logic of thematic succession that he and others were also beginning to apply to the sonata. He did not, however, alter the tonality of the opening section nor did he change the structure of the first solo except through the happy invention of the piano climax, which had, of course, nothing to do with sonata form at all. Perhaps his real achievement was that he had moved the concerto out of the first half of the eighteenth century and into the second.

Table 7

The Transformation from North German to Galant

C. P. E. Bach		*J. C. Bach*	
FIRST RITORNELLO	MAIN THEME SEQUENCES RELIEF SUBJECT SEQUENCES CADENTIALS	FIRST SUBJECT BRIDGE RELIEF SUBJECT — CADENTIALS	STATEMENT
First solo SECOND RITORNELLO	main theme SUB- RITORNELLO solo solo solo (cadentials) (Cadenza) (MAIN THEME)	first subject BRIDGE piano bridge piano second subject (relief subject) cadentials piano climax (CADENTIALS, BRIDGE OR OTHER MATERIAL)	FIRST CONCERTO
Second solo	Middle section: fantasy or devel- opment	Middle section; fantasy or develop- ment	FANTASY
THIRD RITORNELLO Third solo FOURTH RITORNELLO	(MAIN THEME) (OR OTHER MATERIAL) solo can be a reprise of the first solo or can intro- duce new material (SEQUENCES) (CADENTIALS)	FIRST SUBJECT BRIDGE piano section can be the same or reduced, but always a reprise; no new material (BRIDGE) CADENTIALS	REPRISE

2

The Galant Concertos

242 (for three pianos) in F; 246 in C; 413 in F;
449 in E flat; 456 in B flat; 482 in E flat

The new concerto form had already travelled from Potsdam to London via Milan. Through the happy accident of Mozart's visit as an impressionable child of eight to the court of Queen Caroline, it was to be transplanted to Salzburg. Here it was to lie dormant for eleven years (1764–75) until it was brought to life again in the early original concertos which Mozart composed at the age of twenty.

The London meeting with Christian Bach, then a newly arrived 'Italian' German of twenty-nine, was one of Mozart's only two encounters with him, and indeed his only contact with any member of the great Bach family. For in spite of his wide musical travels, he was never to hear Philip Emmanuel perform on the clavier. By the time Mozart left London in 1765 the musical life at King Frederick's court was already in decline. The King had lost his teeth, and with them his ability to play the flute, and consequently, or so it is alleged, his interest in music.

At some time in his life Mozart must, however, have been familiar with Philip Emmanuel's work, for history attributes to him the often-quoted remark, on hearing the news of his death in 1778: 'He is the father, we are the children.'

Where exactly Christian stood in this definition of filial regard it is hard to say. Philip Emmanuel, born twenty-one years before Christian, was old enough to be his father; Mozart, twenty-one years younger again, could have been Christian's son. The relationship between the three men (and between the dates of their concertos) is shown in Table 8.

TABLE 8

Relationships: the Bach family, Mozart and the piano concerto

Year	*C. P. E. Bach*	*Age*	*J. C. Bach*	*Age*	*Mozart*	*Age*
1714	Born					
1735		21	Born			
1738	To Potsdam/Berlin	24		3		
1740	Composes concertos in North German Form for twenty years	26		5		
1750	Father Johann Sebastian dies	36	To Potsdam/Berlin	15		
1754		40	To Italy	19		
1756		42		21	Born	
1762		48	To London	27		6
1763	To Hamburg	49	Concertos Opus 1 published	28		7
1764		50	Meets Mozart	29	Visits London; meets J. C. Bach	8
1765		51		30	107; an arrangement of J. C. Bach's piano sonatas as concertos	9
1767		53	Some time between 1763 and 1777 concertos Opus 7 composed and performed	32	37, 39, 40, 41 Arrangements of sonatas as concertos	11
1773		59		38	175	17
1776		62		41	238, 242, 246	20
1777		63	Concertos Opus 13 published	42		21
1778		64	Meets Mozart in Paris	43	Meeting in Paris	22
1779		65		44	365	23
1780		66	Concertos Opus 7 published (?)	45		24
1782		68	Dies in London	47	413, 414, 415	26
1788	Dies in Hamburg	74			Concertos complete except 595	32

There is remarkable similarity. The two younger men both spent some time *in statu pupillari* with the older when the latter were at the height of their powers as established court musicians, and particularly celebrated for the composition and performance of clavier concertos; both composed some work in the idiom of their teachers; both, after an interval of years and some travel in Italy, went on to develop an individual style. The baton was passed from Philip Emmanuel to Christian in 1750, from Christian to Mozart in 1764, but Mozart did not run with it until 1776.

So far as can be discovered, the London form did not pass through any intermediate hands between the two dates. The Austrians continued in the North German form, the Italians were even further behind, still struggling with clavier concertos in the instrumental forms of Vivaldi and Tartini until Hasse, a frequent visitor from the North, apparently brought the North taste German into favour in Naples and in the Po valley. One Schroeter, it is true, used the London Form in 1772, but then he was a London German, a pupil of Christian, and would naturally follow his master's style.

There is no doubt that Christian influenced Mozart in several forms of composition, but nowhere was imitation more direct than in the piano concertos. Four concertos in Christian's first set of six (Opus 1, published 1763) pioneered the London Galant form; the second set of six, Opus 7, confirmed it. The exact date of the publication of this second set is uncertain (it has been estimated to be 1780) but it is fair to assume that during Mozart's stay in London (which extended over fifteen months) he heard Christian perform some of them, or others similar, for we know that his concertos were in great demand both at the court, where he was a champion of the forte-piano, and perhaps also at Vauxhall Gardens where they may have been performed on 'Mr Tyer's enlarged and improved organ'.

Before examining Mozart's use of the London Form it is worth worth noting two points. First, the forte-piano probably entered his life for the first time in London, and from now on the generic description 'piano' concerto will be adopted in place of the usual 'clavier' concerto. This is simply to avoid switching terms in mid-stream, for during the fourth quarter of the eighteenth century most popular concertos would at one time or another be performed both on the harpsichord and on the piano. After the concerto for two claviers K365, that is after 1779, it is almost certain that all of Mozart's concertos were written with the piano primarily in mind.

Secondly, although Mozart's concertos of 1776 are based precisely on Christian's form, some of the principles in the structure of Philip Emmanuel's (the 'grandfather's') work reappear in the mature concertos and were used by Mozart to resolve certain problems in the construction of his symphonic concertos. These are described in Chapter 4.

To go back to the beginning, however, in childhood Mozart adapted a number of piano sonatas into concertos. These are described in Chapter 5 and they are irrelevant to the London Form, and so, for different reasons, is the first original concerto K175. Thus it is the three little Salzburg concertos of 1776, 238, 242 for three pianos and 246 (the initial K is dropped from now on for brevity) that first show the use of the London form by Mozart. All three coincide very precisely with several of Christian's works, but for purposes of comparison the two Galant concertos 242 and 246 are set against Christian's Opus 7 No. 2 (omitting the Fantasies) in Table 9. 238, the forerunner of the Melodic group, is more relevant to the next chapter.

Table 9 shows how precisely Mozart's early Salzburg Galant form follows the London form of Christian Bach. Indeed there is a far wider variation in structure within Christian's sixteen Galant concertos themselves than between Mozart's six Galant concertos listed at the head of this chapter and the 'standard' or 'average' of Christian's form. (This 'average' is reached by making a judicious summary of the most usual practice over all of Christian's known Galant concertos.)

The nature of the music, too, was at first much the same. As Mozart came to maturity he naturally used his wider technique of composition even when writing in the Galant form, but in these two early concertos several passages could be accepted as the work of Christian Bach.

Closer study, however, reveals minor but significant differences, and these are the first indications of the principles and the methods Mozart was to adopt in developing into one of his greatest and most personal forms of musical expression.

TABLE 9

A comparison between J. C. Bach's concerto Opus 7 No. 2 and Mozart's concertos 242 and 246

(The symbol + is used to indicate sequences following a main subject. NT stands for New Tutti; cd stands for cadenza.

STATEMENT

JCB 7/2	F	B	S	C1	C2	C2
242 246	F F	B B	S S	C1 C1	C2 C2	C3 C3

FIRST CONCERTO

JCB 7/2	f b ps +b s c1 c2 c3 px	C1 C2
242	f bB ps b s c1 c2 px	NT C3
246	f Bb ps +b s+ px	C1

REPRISE

JCB 7/2	Ff bB S c1 c2 px	C2	cd	C1C2C3
242	Ff bB ps +b s c1 c2 px	FB	cd	NT C3
246	Ff Bb ps +b s+ px	C3C2	cd	C1 C3

Two general principles stand out which immediately illuminate Mozart's habit of mind as a composer. The first principle is that 'given' material (that is the subject matter of the Statement and the original piano material in the First Concerto) should be spread evenly and used in such a manner as to ensure that the number of occasions upon which each subject is mentioned is kept in a proper balance. The second is that a concerto should unfold with a sense of natural flow rather than with a jerky succession of one thing tacked on to another.

Let us see how Mozart began to apply the first principle—the even balance of 'mentions'—in 242 and 246. In the two Concerto sections Christian Bach often used two or more of the Cadentials in the piano sequences after the Second subject which led to the piano climax. This was followed by at least two of the Cadentials, often the same ones, in the Ritornello which rounded off the section. The result could be a heavy predominance of the Cadentials over the earlier material. The score of 'mentions' for each subject in the first movement of Opus 7 No. 2 is uneven, particularly since he dropped the piano's second subject in the Reprise:

	First Subject	Bridge	Second Subject	First Caden-tial	Second Caden-tial	Third Caden-tial	Piano Second Subject
Abbreviation	F	B	S	C1	C2	C3	ps
Number of mentions	3	3	3	5	6	3	1

The First and Second Cadentials thus tend to become the dominating elements in the movement, and to make matters worse, since the First is constructed of a repeated phrase, one insistent figure is heard on ten occasions. Mozart realised that after the piano climax the repetition of two cadentials, already becoming well-worn, would not give a sufficiently solid close to the First Concerto or to the Concerto Reprise.

In the First Concerto of 242 he followed Christian's practice of using cadential material before the piano climax. To avoid repeating it, however, he introduced a New Tutti in the subsequent Ritornello. In 246 he adopted a different plan by dropping the piano narration of the Cadentials before the piano climax, and reserving them for the final ritornello. The organisation of the closing part of the two concerto sections is shown in Table

10, also the number of 'mentions' of each piece of material over the whole work. From this it can be seen that Mozart was already more sensitive than Christian to the need for an even spread of mentions and more adroit in achieving it.

TABLE 10

The organisation of material in 242 and 246

The number of subject mentions over the whole movement, compared with Christian Bach's Opus 7 No. 2, is as follows:

SUBJECT	JCB 7/2	242	246
F	3	3+	3
B	3+	3++	3++
S	3	3	3
C1	5	3	3
C2	6	3	2
C3	3	3	2
ps	1	2	2
NT	–	2	–

Note The symbol + in the above table indicates a slight reference, perhaps a bar or two, of the original subject; ++ indicates two references.

The closing sections of the First Concerto and the Reprise are organised as follows:

FIRST CONCERTO

242	s c1 c2	px	NT C3
246	s +	px	C1

REPRISE

242	s c1 c2	px	F B	cd	NT C3
246	s +	px	C3C2	cd	C1 C3

Unless there was some special reason, he aimed to have each subject mentioned at least twice and not more than three times.

From now on this desire to balance the material is evident in every work. A leading subject can be given predominance (271, 449) only if it is done to make a special point; the introduction of new extraneous material (such as the New Tutti in 242) becomes more clearly a second best, and the failure to use all the important material from the statement at some later point in the work was evidently unacceptable, for those experiments in which such a loss occurs (365, 415) were never repeated.

If, however, the idea of Mozart as a good organiser seems to imply a rigid system of planning, nothing, of course, could be further from the truth, for he managed to accommodate the first great principle (that of even balance) within the context of the second—natural progression.

Where Christian's concertos run in an obvious and often jerky succession of one thing after another, Mozart's later concertos unfold with the inevitability of a well-written play. One of the secrets of this organic growth lies within the texture of the music itself, and the way in which Mozart linked his musical thoughts on a subtle but sturdy thread (the 'filo'). This is discussed at greater length in the following chapter on the Melodic concertos which depend more heavily upon it. An inner relationship of themes, however, is evident in the later Galant concertos too, but at the beginning, in the early Salzburg works, there is little or no feeling of consanguinity between subjects. Their greater fluency derives more from a number of devices (some of them imported from the opera house) which break up the repetitive subject matter and vary the insistent beat and rattling pace of the old Galant concerto. Even in these two early works Mozart finds ways and means of softening the Galant pace and mood, of introducing elements of expectancy and surprise, of clinching the moments of supremacy for each of the two partners—in short (to revert for a moment to the origins of the form) of writing a concerto rather in the nature of an operatic aria than in the more declamatory and less flexible style of the oratorio.

The first and most obvious example of this principle is to be found in Mozart's sense of extending the dramatic moment. This is one of the oldest tricks in drama and dramatic music, of which the simplest example is the interrupted cadence. The end is expected: the end is delayed. This 'tension towards finality' was widely used in the arias and duets of operatic music.

The concerto form already had several traditional extensions built into it. There was the duplication or proliferation of Cadential figures, each one final in itself, but not so, because each was succeeded by another, up to the last. Another was the cadenza: the tutti ended the piano narrative, then built towards the expectant 6/4 chord, which suspended time until the soloist had completed his free flight and was joined again by the awaiting orchestra. A third was the piano climax, which was in the nature of one long extension, always nearing the final trill, always postponing the moment. The piano climax of 246 shows how Mozart could seize and exploit dramatic opportunity. The customary delaying tactics are given new impetus in bar 87 where, after a series of agitated figures and a trill which holds out false hopes of conclusion, the piano gives three vigorous octave beats in the bass, and lives again. This quite gratuitous gesture prolongs the tension for a further three bars to the truly final trill. It is a bolder stroke than can be found anywhere in Christian's concertos.

Example 1

bar 86

A common example of another kind of extension—a break in rhythm—is often found in the second or third cadential figure.

In the Statements of the early works, both the Bridges and the Cadentials have the sort of bustling urgency common to the quicker movements of the serenades and cassations of the time. The device Mozart uses to halt and extend the Cadential section is analogous to a caesura or break in the rhythm of a line of verse. In its commonest form it is a suspended and syncopated minim chord resolving into a crotchet (or two quavers), the figure often being repeated. This has also something of the effect of a question which stops the flow of talk. The Caesura (often *forte*) is invariably followed by an answer, usually soft, sometimes building again to a *forte* climax. The two together often make a complete Cadential Figure, as in the Second Cadential of 242.

Example 2
bar 38

Expectancy can, however, be aroused before an entry as well as before an exit. In both of these two concertos the return to the Reprise after the Fantasy is heralded with a new sense of drama. Christian Bach let the Fantasy run to a natural close in the dominant or tonic parallel. Sometimes, with a miniature cadenza, he provided a link for the return of the First Subject in the tonic. More rarely he paused on a long dominant pedal before returning to the tonic. In 242 and 246 Mozart already shows an interest in the potential drama of the return to known places and the home key by turning the end of the Fantasy to an introduction into the Reprise. Thus in 242 the momentum of the Fantasy subsides in bar 166, the rhythm changes and a 'Return' is effected first through a downward scale of trills, and then, after a busier passage, by a unison figure on the three pianos which takes the tonality from C to F in two quick bars.

Example 3
bar 170

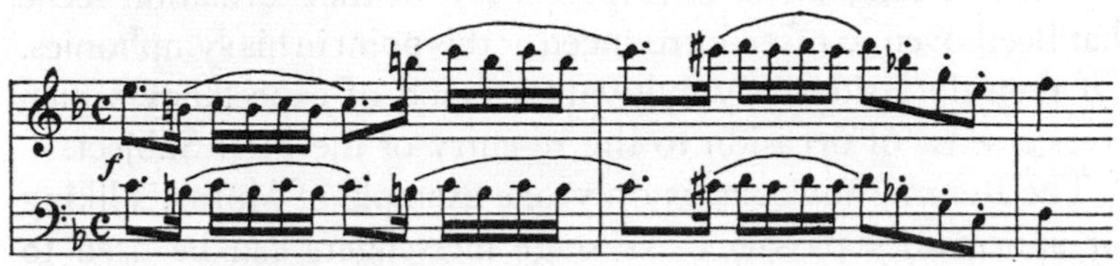

In 246 the Return starts with a dominant pedal and a break in the rhythm six bars before the Fantasy ends.

Example 4
bar 127

A final sketchy little scale confirms that G is no more than the dominant of C.

Example 5
bar 131

In later concertos the true dominant pedal will become insistent up to twelve, sixteen and twenty bars before the Reprise, and always there will be the other characteristic of the Return, a change, or often two or three changes, in the rhythmic pattern. Mozart's Returns never attempt the sort of transformation scene that Beethoven so often introduced at this point in his symphonies, but they do assiduously cultivate a mood of expectancy which gives a sense of occasion to the re-entry of the First Subject.

The Return, however, is only one example of Mozart's liking for anticipatory passages. As stage messengers can be used to build up a situation and to report the approach of a major character, so Mozart would insert little expectant passages, particularly before the Second Subject, to prepare the ear for its arrival. In the later Galant concerto 456, after an incisive end to the Bridge, mysterious chords in the strings (bar 28) introduce a passage of twelve bars which carefully prepares for the entry of the Second Subject, a simple little relief figure played by the oboes. If it had followed directly behind so noisy a Bridge it could scarcely have survived the shock. This extra preparatory material between the main Bridge and the Second Subject was to become common in all three types of concerto.

The opposite of anticipation is retrospect, and Mozart also introduced a retrospective pendant after a main subject to link it by the tail with the next item. Sometimes he combined both. A good example of this is in 482 (bar 13) where the First Subject ends with a long retrospective meditation. This quiet pendant also anticipates one of the main Bridge themes. Although in early Mozart the section would have construed well enough without it, by inserting a link of this kind he softened the abrupt succession of the Galant subjects and the concerto gained a more elegant and leisurely movement from point to point. There are similar pendants after many Second Subjects to link them with the first Cadential.

All of these devices show that the easy succession from one subject or section to the next was as much a part of Mozart's musical rationale as was his sense of balance and proportion, and they are a constant reminder of his unflagging inventiveness as a composer. There is also one more purely technical means by which he made the stream flow more smoothly, namely his peculiar system of slicing one piece of music in half and grafting it to another. To find examples of this device we can turn again to the two early concertos, for this 'slicing and grafting' of material from the Statement is used in 242 and 246 to manipulate the Bridge subjects and the Cadential Figures. As the story unfolds we shall see how widely it was to be exploited in all the concertos.

In the London form the Bridge was used to link the First Subject and the Second in the Statement; to link the first subject to the piano second in the First Concerto; and often to link the piano second and the old Second Subject. It was used similarly in the Reprise. Or, put schematically:

STATEMENT	F *B* S
FIRST CONCERTO	f *Bb* ps *Bb* sS
CONCERTO REPRISE	Ff *Bb* ps *Bb* sS

Thus the total number of mentions would be five, or if the piano second subject were left out of the Reprise, four. So long as the Bridge was a short and unemphatic bustle, this pattern was tolerable, if a little tiresome. But when the Bridge acquired a strong character of its own, then too much of it would disturb the balance. In 242 the Bridge is a section of some personality: it is almost as long as the First Subject and much longer than the Second. It is also repetitive within itself. Thus the use of a large part of the Bridge on five occasions would have distorted the proportions of the work and also, perhaps, have worn the material a little thin. Table 11 shows in detail how Mozart deals with this in 242.

A second and equally ingenious example of slicing and grafting is also to be found in 242 in the use of the Second and Third Cadentials and the New Tutti. On their first appearance in the Statement the two Cadentials seem to form a single piece of music. But in the First Concerto the pianos play only the first part of the sequence (the minim chords in Example 2 above) before they move into the piano climax. The resolution is delayed, and when the final ritornello breaks in it is with entirely

TABLE 11

Slicing: the Bridge material in 242

The Bridge of 242 as it first appears in the Statement goes as follows:

BAR	SUBSECTION	DESCRIPTION
15	B1	Upward bustling figure
17	B2	The urgent answering strain
19	B1	Repeated
21	B2	Repeated
23	B1+	The bustling figures again, but ending in an operatic flourish on the dominant

On its second appearance, after the first subject in the First Concerto:

Bar 64 etc b1 as before
b2 „
b1 „
b2 „
b1 „ but ending with four of the upward bustling figures that switch the tonality *into* the dominant

And on its third appearance between the piano second subject and the Relief Subject:

Bar 87 b1+ — the final set of bustling figures and the operatic flourish only

In the Reprise, after the first subject, where no change into the dominant is wanted:

Bar 186 b1
b2
B1
B2 — ends here: no further bustling figures, no operatic flourish

Finally, between the piano second subject and the Second Subject in the Reprise, the Bridge is used just as in the First Concerto (third appearance, above).

new material. Half-way through its course, however, this new tutti switches, as if in the manner born, into the second half of the original sequence, namely the Third Cadential. Two heads have the same tail: (C2C3) and (NTC3), both form a perfect whole, but the second half of each is identical. The detail of this operation (and the fourth variation in the Reprise) is described in Table 12. Table 13 shows how complete units are switched about in 246. Here, although the treatment of the Bridge material is much the same, the slicing and grafting is generally on a larger scale.

Permutations of musical heads and tails were, of course, performed as a game in Mozart's day, and he himself composed a set of tunes for Musical Dice which would give a fit between a set of heads and tails no matter what numbers came up. Not many composers, however, have used this trick with such genuine art.

Table 12

Grafting

In the Statement of 242 the Second and Third Cadentials are used as follows:

BAR	SUBJECT	DESCRIPTION
38	C2	Slow minim chords: a Caesura (see Example 2)
40	C2	A building climax, leading to –
44	C3	– a typical piece of cadential figuration, the natural complement of C2, with a closing tag to it

In the First Concerto the sequence of events is as follows:

second subject	c1	c2	px	NT	C3

In the Reprise the two Cadentials lie even further apart:

second subject	c1	c2	px	FB	cd	NT	C3

It is interesting to note in passing that the technique of switching units is called by Hutchings 'the system of open ends'. This is a good description of the way in which whole units are switched about, but not perhaps so apt when applied to the slicing and grafting of parts of one to parts of another, for, as we have seen, at the first reading the 'ends' would seem to be anything but 'open'.

TABLE 13

The transposition of Cadentials in 246

BAR	SUBJECT	DESCRIPTION
23	C1	With strong contours: 3 bars. Repeated
29	C2	The Operatic sotto voce; an extension
33	C3	Closing bustle

In the First Concerto the strong C1 provides the closing ritornello. In the Reprise the closing ritornello starts with a reference to C3 (the bustle) at bar 187, then the piano surprisingly introduces the operatic sotto voce (C2) at bar 188, which builds to the cadenza platform. After the cadenza the final tutti is made up of C1 and C3 again.

Overall, as follows:

STATEMENT	C1 C2 C3
FIRST CONCERTO	px C1
REPRISE	px (C3) C2 cadenza C1 C3

Mozart later extended the uses of switching and grafting to make the same units of music read differently in a new context. In 246 the shuffling of the Cadentials did not alter their function: they remained always the signal of approaching finality, and the last one (whichever it might be) provided the end-piece to each section. In the later Galant concerto 413, one unit is not only moved about into the most surprising places but at each move is subjected to a change of character.

The last Cadential of 413 is one of those sad little *envois*, a four-bar cadence which seems about to die away with a sigh (bar 53). Over the third bar, however, the piano enters with an imitation of the little farewell phrase, sticks on the third note and sails out into its solo introduction.

Example 6

bar 53

The closing Ritornello of the First Concerto does not use the farewell Cadential. But wait: at the end of the Fantasy, after an elaborate return with three changes of gear (bars 215—231), the piano's final downward scale, which should deliver us safely back to the First Subject, runs instead into the little Cadential and then once more into the piano introduction.

In this context it is no longer an *envoi* but an *aubade*, and by now the ear no longer trusts its meaning. The four bars have become thoroughly ambivalent, and when they finally turn up again at the end of the closing Ritornello one half expects yet another resurrection from the last dying phrase. Not so, however; three brisk chords put it in its third and final place.

This little witticism shows Mozart's love of mystery, which he could, and did, indulge to the full in the operas. Little passages of this kind are open to at least two readings, and the good performer will incline neither to the one nor to the other but will leave the interpretation open for the listener to take from it what he may. In the original sense of the words, these are *doubles entendres*, and quite unlike the bluff musical jokes of Haydn and Beethoven.

Not all of these several devices in composition are peculiar to the concertos. Mozart's facility as a composer was astonishing and universal, and it is too easy to describe his methods in mathematical or technical terms and thereby perhaps imply that this is how he himself employed them. On this point no one can, of course, be certain, but over the whole range of his more important work he applies a golden touch which conceals the mechanical or technical construction beneath an apparently spontaneous flow of ideas. The music runs with a kind of inevitable logic which carries with it the conviction that it could have been written in no other way and even existed in its own right before Mozart was lucky enough to discover it and put it down on paper.

It is certain, however, that the concertos provided him with the first main proving ground in developing his technique as a composer. 175, 271 and 365 are all major pioneering works unmatched by anything written before 1779 except the Paris symphony and the two concertante works, one for violin and viola and the other for wind ensemble. The great operas and string quartets, the last symphonies, the two big wind serenades and the Requiem were all still to come. It is therefore tempting to regard the concertos, but not so much the Galant group, as Mozart's chosen field for research and development. The choice was probably dictated by his own personal preference and by the fact that he was composing for the instrument he played best.

The Galant form was, however, the starting point of Mozart's development in the concerto form and, as the model studied in childhood, it always remained in his mind. After the first two concertos 242 and 246 the number of concertos in the old form is limited. It became a point of return rather than of advance, and he tended to revert to it only when he was not in the mood for a more ambitious work. There is, however, one more 'first' which occurs before the Galant first subject of 271 and in the passage of 413 already quoted, and which can be mentioned now in the context of the legacy which the Galant works passed on to their more illustrious fellows. This is the piano introduction.

The idea of giving the soloist an opportunity of making a bow in an isolated solo introduction before starting on the main work of the First Concerto would seem at first glance to be similar to the idea of an operatic recitatif.

This may, however, be too simple an analogy. The Galant call sounds richer in the orchestra than on the piano. When played on the keyboard in its traditional place at the opening of the First Concerto, the piano's feeble tone makes a poor effect, especially after the noise and bustle of the Cadentials. A Melodic subject has the necessary feminine and lyrical line to give a well-contrasted entry. So too has the soft answer to the Galant call, the antithesis of the masculine and noisy call itself. Perhaps partly for these reasons Mozart introduced in 271 and 413 the short solo piano passage, introductory in intention, childishly simple in nature, and in the greatest contrast to the Cadentials before it and the Galant Call, which could now follow it given by the orchestra. The piano subsequently took over the soft phrases of the answer.

Alongside these practical considerations there may also have been some vestigial race-memory of the old Aria form behind this innovation. In the Aria the voice had sometimes first entered with a new solo phrase, to be answered by the Main Theme in the orchestra's sub-ritornello. However that may be, the idea of a piano introduction clearly met the need for an entry with a greater degree of dramatic contrast, and there are, in all, nine piano introductions amongst Mozart's twenty-three original concertos.

It is easier to define the nature of the piano introduction in the Galant and Melodic concertos by saying what it is not rather than what it is. It is not a free cadenza, having a definite rhythm and usually a very simple line. It is not an 'Introduction' in the sense of a portentous gathering of tension as in the introduction to some of Beethoven's sonatas. It is not necessarily related to any other material in the work. It is operatic, but neither a true recitatif nor a 'scena'. The best that words can do is perhaps to say that the introduction provides a limpid pool of solo piano tone between two noisy bouts of orchestral texture. Like the relief subjects of old, the contrast is one of volume and quality of sound: the piano is presented in its most frail and feminine role, apparently unequal to the might of its partner. Thus we are amazed when as the First Concerto runs its course it begins to stretch its muscles and gradually outmatches the orchestra in agility and power.

A similar effect is gained, of course, by the piano's solo entry with a simple Melodic First Subject, and in either case it is not too fanciful to say that the piano's gradual ascent to supremacy begins at its first bar of solo, and the smallness of the start makes its final supremacy in the piano climax all the more impressive.

Although many features of the Galant concertos were absorbed into the two main streams of the Melodic and Symphonic works they have nevertheless a distinct character of their own. This can best be seen by looking at the schematic synopses of the Galant form (Tables 14 and 15) and comparing them with those

TABLE 14

The Galant form: the succession of material

(The following synopsis shows the Galant form as it was used by Mozart. The occasional eccentricities, such as the New Tutti in 242 and the piano cadentials in 456, are not taken into account.
Sections in brackets are optional or variable; without brackets constant.)

STATEMENT

F B (B/S) S C1 C2 C3 (C4)

Abbreviation: B/S signifies the anticipatory passage between the Bridge and the Second Subject

FIRST CONCERTO

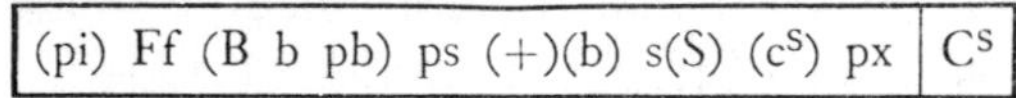

(pi) Ff (B b pb) ps (+)(b) s(S) (c^S) px	C^S

REPRISE

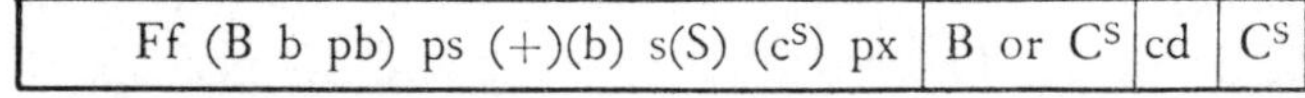

Ff (B b pb) ps (+)(b) s(S) (c^S) px	B or C^S	cd	C^S

Note (*a*) The bridging material after the piano entry in the First Concerto can either develop from the old Bridge (242, 246, 413, 456) or be new (449, 482).

(*b*) The Cadenza was an optional feature in the first movements of Christian Bach's concertos; Mozart always introduces it.

of the Melodic and Symphonic group. The main features can, however, be described as follows:

STATEMENT The First Subject is always a call and answer, although there are many permutations within this formula (Table 16). It is worth noting that most of the Calls are in the common cliché of the day whereas the answers are peculiarly Mozartean in their sweetness and elegance.

The Bridge is always a bustling serenade-type of link with a firm outline and, usually, with more than one subject.

The Second Subject can be of the Relief kind, that is to say it can be insignificant in itself but notable because it provides contrast, as in 246, 449 and 456. Or it can be more lyrical, as in 242, 413 and 482.

There are three or four cadentials, one of them always providing a Caesura, or a contrast in pace.

FIRST CONCERTO The First Concerto follows the regular pattern of Christian Bach (except 482, the sport of the family) with three modifications: the use of the Bridge material diminishes; the cadentials tend to move out of the concerted section; the organisation of the ritornello is more sophisticated.

FANTASY See Chapter 4 where the different types of Fantasy are described. In general the Galant Fantasy uses one of the Cadential phrases as a point of departure. All of them end with a Return.

REPRISE These are regular (again excepting 482) adapting the reprise form of Christian Bach which included both the piano second subject and the Second Subject from the Statement. Until the Ritornello there is little variation from the First Concerto. There is always a Cadenza within the final ritornello, which ends with the last two cadentials (except 246).

The Galant concertos are all scored for the string orchestra with oboes and horns added, except 456 which has flutes and bassoons, and 482 which is given a large wind band made up of flutes, clarinets, bassoons, horns and trumpets (but no drums). Only in later works are the wind instruments given any independent life, and it is true in general to say that the Galant concertos are as unambitious in their orchestration as in their general nature and form.

The six Galant concertos, which cover the span of Mozart's most productive period, form a group that represents not exactly a second eleven but a random collection of less ambitious works with many attractive and endearing features. They lie in the valleys between the spirited experiments of 271, 365 and 415 and the great heights of the mature Melodic and Symphonic concertos. They have the same relationship to the larger works as, for instance, *Il Rè Pastore* has to *The Magic Flute*. The similarity in form of the early works to Christian's concertos is as striking as is their difference in the context of musical history. Christian Bach's work marked the end of one advance; Mozart's Salzburg concertos signalled the beginning of another, which was to translate innocent little salon pieces such as 242 and 246 into such giants of the concert repertory as the two great concertos in D minor and C minor.

TABLE 15

The Galant form: the concertos compared

STATEMENT

242	F		B		S	C1	C2	C3	
246	F		B		S	C1	C2	C3	
413	F		B	(B/S)*	S	C1	C2	C3	
449	F		B	B/S	S	C1	C2	C3	C4
456	F		B	B/S	S	C1	C2	C3	C4
482	F1	F2	B	B/S	S	C1	C2	C3	

* Very short: the first and slender link to introduce the Second Subject after the Bridge

FIRST CONCERTO

242	f	bB	ps	b	s	c1 c2		px	NT C3
246	f	Bb	ps+	b	s+			px	C1
413	pi Ff	pb(b)	ps+	(B/S)S+				px	C2
449	f	pb	ps	b/s	s+			px	C2 C3
456	fF	B pb C4	ps+	B/S	Ss	c1 c2	pc^s †	px	B C3 C4
482	pi Ff1	pb e*+	ps+					px	C1 C2 C3

* Piano episode † The 'piano cadentials'

CONCERTO REPRISE

242	Ff	bB	ps+b	s	c1 c2	px	FB	CADENZA	NT C3
246	Ff	Bb	ps+b	s+		px	C3C2		C1 C3
413	pi Ff	pb(b)	ps+(B/S)	S+		px+	B		C2 C3
449	Ff	pb	ps b/s	s+		px+	B		C3 C4
456	Ff	B	ps+B/S	Ss	c1 c2 pc^s	px(C3)	B		C1C2C3C4
482	Ff1Ff2	Bb b/s		sS+ ps		px	C1		C2 C3

TABLE 16

The Galant First Subject

The Galant First Subject is always a call and an answer. The pattern within this formula is varied, as follows:

	Call	*Answer*	*Subsequently*
242	3 bars	5 bars	Call and answer repeated. Bridge
246	4 bars	4 bars	Answer repeated. Bridge
413	4 bars	8 bars	Bridge
449	4 bars	4 bars	Answer repeated extended and varied: Bridge
456	A double call 4 bars in all	4 bars	Double call and answer repeated: Bridge
482	2 bars+	3 bars+	Call and answer repeated: a pendant to the First Subject (F2) (18 bars): Bridge

3

The Melodic Concertos

238 in B flat; 414 in A; 450 in B flat; 453 in G;
488 in A; 537 in D; 595 in B flat

The Melodic concertos differ from the Galant and Symphonic groups in two ways, one obvious and one more subtle. The obvious difference is one of character. All of them open with a continuous melody of eight bars or more. All of them (except the melancholy 595 in B flat which like many of the late works has a mood of its own) reflect the serene and sunny climate of the serenades. All of them are scored for a small chamber orchestra, always with horns, bassoons (except 238), oboes (except 488 which has clarinets instead), sometimes a flute or flutes, never trumpets and drums (except 537, perhaps added for the celebrations surrounding a Coronation, where trumpets and drums would be apt for the occasion although the music itself, curiously enough, is not). Except in the Fantasies, the Melodic (and the Galant) concertos are unclouded by the minor key. Whereas the Galant concertos prefer the flat keys (perhaps because of the importance of the wind instruments in the Galant call), the Melodic concertos venture also into the sharp keys of A, G, and D.

The second difference (less easy to describe) lies in their greater dependence upon the filo or thread of musical ideas which runs through this movement and imparts to it a sense of organic growth. Later in this chapter the nature of the filo will be examined in greater detail; here it is enough perhaps to indicate why the filo gives the Melodic concertos that special character.

It is, of course, true that some degree of filo working became a universal element in Mozart's method of composition. It was therefore present in the Galant concertos (from 413 onwards), but only incidentally. The construction of the later members of the Galant group still depended upon the strong contours and sharp contrasts of the subjects and sections of the Galant form. The Melodic concertos, on the other hand, although they follow the same succession of subjects, flow more gently and depend greatly upon the ubiquitous filo to give their structure a sense of one thing growing out of another in an extended paragraph, sometimes indeed, as we shall see, from the beginning to the end of a section. The sense of affinity is subtle, as with a poet who uses the overtones of words rather than their surface meaning to relate one thought to another and to extend the same mood over several different ideas.

The Symphonic concertos are different again, for although filo relationships abound, they are no longer the sole or the main binding agent to give the movement its unity. Here Mozart used short themes which are readily recognised by a listener of any musical sensibility as the same piece of music used in various ways. The Symphonic motif lies on the surface and is as recognisable as the subject of a fugue or the opening theme for a set of variations. Perhaps the distinction between the three methods is best illustrated by the opening bars of each of the three early Viennese concertos 413, 414 and 415.

The Galant 413 opens with a traditional loud Galant call:

Example 7

bar 1

The Melodic 414 opens with a soft flowing melody which is the begetter of a great deal of the material to follow, some of it only distantly related:

Example 8

bar 1

The Symphonic 415 opens with an unmistakable theme which is used in several places and in several ways without ever losing its identity:

Example 9

bar 1

It is generally true that the First Subjects are the key to the Melodic method of working. We know that between the years 1782 and 1786, which covered fifteen of the greatest concertos, Mozart formed the habit of writing down beginnings for works some of which he never took any further. These beginnings, which Einstein calls 'incipits', 'springboards', or 'trial runs', imply a fastidious selection of the opening material, because it was from this that the succession of ideas for the whole work would flow. As Einstein says:

> He needed only the beginning: his imagination and unerring taste provided the appropriate continuation, the *filo* of ideas...

The typical First Subject of a Melodic concerto is a single melody opening over a pedal bass and constructed from a number of complementary phrases. Unlike the Galant loud call and soft answer, there is no change in dynamics, the whole First Subject glides by at an even *piano*. One 12-bar pattern (used in 238 and 537) is as follows:

First Sentence (4 bars) (tonic)	Second Sentence (4 bars) tonic IV or tonic V>tonic	Second Sentence (4 bars) Repeated and varied

A second, sixteen-bar, pattern (414, 488) is:

First Sentence (4 bars) tonic-tonic IV-tonic	Second Sentence (4 bars) tonic-tonic V	First Sentence (4 bars) Repeated	Second Sentence (4 bars) Varied & ending in tonic

And the third, an eight-bar pattern (450, 453) is:

First Sentence (2 bars) tonic	Second Sentence (2 bars) tonic-tonic IV- or V	First Sentence (2 bars) tonic IV or V	Second Sentence (2 bars) Return to tonic

These more epigrammatic little subjects are followed by a pendant of four bars (F+) which carries the air of a cadential extension to the First Subject and provides a link with the Bridge. The first part of the Melodic Bridge passage is often related to the First Subject, and nearly always within its course it discloses some filo relationship to what has gone before. It sometimes ends with an emphatic dominant chord, or alternatively there is a further little link (B/S) with the Second Subject. In 453 and 595 these passages assume an importance out of all proportion to their size.

The Second Subjects of the Melodic concertos are usually operatic in nature. The earlier ones (238, 414, 450) are a little tentative, with irregular rhythms and a hesitant step. The later subjects, however, sing out in a strong melodic line; three of them (453, 488, 595) are passionate mezzo-soprano melodies which contrast with the easy beat of the First Subject. The remaining Second Subject (537) has the character of an operatic ritornello and provides a sharp contrast to the less vivacious First Subject. None of these Second Subjects would be out of place in *Figaro*; all of them (after 238) are far removed from the Relief type of Second Subject used in the Galant and most of the Symphonic concertos.

The First Cadentials flow out of the Second Subject, sometimes actually picking it up from closing Tonic V chord (414) and always heightening the tension, sometimes with a Mannheim type of crescendo (414, 450, 595), sometimes a strange conspiratorial sforzando passage (453, 537), always with a strong rhythm to pick up the impetus and push the Statement towards a lively close. The remaining Cadentials are no longer short sequences of Caesuras and answers and the closing serenade-type of bustle. They have developed into characters in their own right. One of them is always slow and elegant in contrast to the vigorous dynamics of the others.

In 414 and 537 this slow cadential is closely related to the Second Subject and reproduces in even rhythm and at greater length a melody which the Second Subject has only sketched out. In both concertos this Melodic Cadential is put in the reprise after the Second Subject and before the piano climax. Another type of Cadential is a sad little *envoi* which gives the statement a coda of its own (450, 488, 595).

Where the closing Cadential has been loud, the First Concerto opens with a simple piano statement of the First Subject. Thus the easy-going melody of the first subject gives just the right dramatic contrast for the piano entry in a melodious feminine role. To call in an analogy from opera, it is as if during a noisy ensemble the heroine has been standing in the wings. Now, as the applause dies down, she enters into the lit area and moves into a clear and easy soprano melody.

This way of launching the piano is used in 238, 414, 453 and 537. In 488 and 595, where the last Cadential is the wistful little *envoi*, the contrast is still preserved by the distinction between the broken-rhythms of the last Cadential and the even flow of the First Subject. In 450, however, where there is a strong filo relationship between the last Cadential and the First Subject, the two are separated by a short virtuoso piano introduction.

Usually the piano repeats the last strain of the First Subject with a *bravura* variation. This coloratura flourish is capped by the tubby tone of the orchestra, always entering at this point with some remnant of the old sub-ritornello (except in the last two concertos, 537 and 595, where the piano bridge springs directly out of the First Subject). This sub-ritornello is not necessarily based on the old Bridge from the Statement, as it is in the Galant form. More often the sub-ritornello seals off the known material and provides a springboard for the piano's own new bridge.

Even in those Melodic concertos where the piano bridge starts with material from the Bridge in the Statement (453, 488), this section soon becomes a fresh adventure which moves forward in a fast pianistic pattern, and in tonality. So far the tonality has, of course, been static. But now there are wide and swift harmonic changes with a greater range than in Galant concertos, and always (after 238) the bridge drives towards the double dominant and thereby establishes a firm dominant tonality for the second group. This wider harmonic sweep has a feeling of greater freedom and movement than the conventional bridge passage of the Galant concertos. The persistent tonic impulse of the statement, however, has prepared the way for this excursion from the narrow compound of the home key. Thus the piano bridge delivers the piano safely into the dominant for its own second subject, and here we come upon one of the most absorbing of all Mozart's problems in concerto form, and it demands a digression.

In symphonies and sonatas the two main subjects (the first and the second) are settled sections within which melodies can have elbow-room to run their course. They are surrounded by passages which are going somewhere (bridges, transitions, developments), or doing something more functional (cadentials, codas, introductions), and which, however tuneful they may be, use tunes for a purpose rather than tunes for their own sake. In Sonata Form the First and Second Subjects are each played three times (if the exposition is repeated) and they may also be used in the development.

In the Melodic concerto form there is no problem about the First Subject. It appears as a complete tune on three occasions only; at the head of the statement, the first concerto, and the Reprise. But the Second Subject is more of an embarrassment, because there are two, one in the Statement and the other the piano second subject in the First Concerto. When both the Second Subjects were a matter of four or six bars each, five little second subjects (one in the Statement, two in each of the concerto sections) could be accommodated, especially since the rest of the work was so full of bustle. There is no sign of strain in the first four Salzburg concertos, where the two second subjects in all their appearances add up to less than one quarter of the whole length of the movement. Indeed there was leisure enough to extend the Second Subject on its subsequent appearances. But when Mozart began to enlarge the form he met with problems. A larger statement demanded a larger Second Subject to keep the balance. And a First Concerto in a richer style demanded something more substantial than a short relief passage after the piano had swung the work dramatically to the double-dominant pedal.

The problem was a simple one of ratio. The First Subject in 238 is 12 bars long. The Second is four bars on its first appearance; so is the piano Second Subject. The ratio of the number of bars of First to Second subject material over the whole work is 36:24. In 453, a typical Melodic concerto, the First Subject had increased to 16 bars, and the Bridge and the Cadentials are on a bigger scale. Hence the Second Subject is extended proportionately to 15 bars. The piano second subject is also 16 bars. Thus the ratio has changed to 56:77. Mozart's dilemma, laid out more fully in Table 17, was that in Concerto form a larger First Subject is multiplied only by three, whereas second subject material is multiplied by five. In Sonata Form both grow equally, because both are multiplied only by three.

By tradition the Second Subjects contrasted with the bustle of the main body of the allegro; they were more languid, more settled and softer. Too much of this and the movement would lose impetus. Over the range of the concertos Mozart tried nearly every possible method of averting this danger. Some concertos, for example, have no Second Subject in the Statement (459, 491), some have no piano second subject (271, 488). By these omissions the Second Subject material was multiplied only by three or four instead of five. All but two of the seven Melodic concertos, however, have the full five 'mentions' of the Second and piano second subjects, and in a Melodic concerto the problem was especially acute.

TABLE 17

The Second Subject equation

The general ratio of First Subject material to Second Subject material in Mozart's concertos is:

First Subject material = F × 3 = 3 F

Second Subject material = (S × 3) + (ps × 2)

which, when the Second Subject is equal in length to the piano second = 5 S

The particular equation in 238 goes as follows:

	Statement	1st Concerto	Concerto Reprise	Total
F	12	12	12	36
S ps	4	6 4	6 4	24

And in 453:

	Statement	1st Concerto	Concerto Reprise	Total
F	16	20	20	56
S ps	15	15 16	15 16	77

We have seen that the First Subject, itself a gentle flowing melody, was followed by a soft and feminine Second Subject (except 537). Thus only the bridges, two or three Cadentials, and the piano climax, had the energy and drive to keep the long concerto first movement rolling forward. There were two further hazards, the slow Cadential which Mozart favoured in the Melodic group, and the limpid second movement, an adagio or andante, lying ahead which would slow down the whole work to a standstill unless the first movement had attained enough momentum.

Whether consciously or not, Mozart was evidently aware of all these factors, and to two of his characteristics already mentioned (his sense of balance and his ability to make a movement 'flow'), we can add a third—a perfect sense of pace. Many of the problems he encountered in the course of expanding concerto form were solved at the first attempt and the solution was absorbed into his general practice, but the awkward second subject equation is treated differently in each concerto.

In 238, as we have seen, the problem does not arise. In 414 both subjects are trimmed back to small proportions and the Second Subject is whirled into a cadential sequence that has first an operatic excitement and then a transformation of the Second Subject itself into a swinging march.

The tentative Second Subject of 450 is dropped from the First Concerto, and when it reappears in the Reprise it is given a lively piano version of the original counterpoint in double-time. The tender Second Subject of 453 is balanced by a piano second subject of great vitality. 488 has methods all of its own which can best be left to a later chapter. 537 has a Second Subject more lively than the first. Only in 595 are both Second Subjects slow and gentle, and this high ratio of Second Subject material coupled with a pensive First Subject gives the movement its peculiarly languid and melancholy nature.

In fact the words 'Second Subject' often carry a different meaning in the Melodic concertos from the sense in which they came to be used in Sonata Form where the term second subject or group is assumed to imply a soft 'feminine' subject in contrast to the strong 'masculine' first subject. Mozart's method of dealing with the concerto problem was not only to omit mentions and cut back in size, but sometimes to introduce lively piano second subjects of a kind unknown in the concertos of his contemporaries.

These offered the possibility of a combination of subjects which together gave the right balance of pace over the whole movement. To take two examples:

	F	S	ps
450	Gentle, whimsical	Operatic, syncopated	Relief, caesura and decoration
453	Easy and light	Cantabile; aria	Lively and rhythmical

In dealing with the Second Subject problem Mozart can be seen to be probing, experimenting and adjusting his methods. Such was his talent, however, that the listener accepts each solution as a part of the inevitable logic of the work.

A less noticeable development in Mozart's practice is his treatment of the passages which join and follow the second subjects in the First Concerto. Here there is no 'problem' to be solved, only a strengthening of two potentially weak spots where, unless precautions were taken, the fabric of the movement would sag.

To see this danger in perspective let us look back to the end of the Statement. First there is the piano's quiet entry with the First Subject which passes through its later decorations to the point where it is sealed off with a short ritornello; next the adventurous piano bridge thrusting forward and outward until it reaches the double dominant. Here the piano second subject is launched by a bar or two of orchestral introduction. In the earliest concertos the repeat of the sonatina piano subject had an extended tail, or a bar or two of loose consequences which led to a part of the old Bridge (242, 246) or directly to the Second Subject (238). As the scale of the movement grew larger, there was a need for something more substantial to insulate the two second subjects, often still very short, for the reasons which we have seen. What was wanted was something that gave enough momentum to avoid a relapse but not so much as to spoil the contrast with the piano bridge which had gone before and the piano climax which was to follow. Mozart therefore developed a section of more purposeful consequences after the piano second subject which grew in size from 8 bars in 414 (begins bar 106) to 12 bars in 453 (bar 122) and 28 bars in 537 (bar 136). These passages usually stay in the dominant, but in other respects have the character of a purposeful link leading out of the piano subject and moving forward on their own chosen path until they reach their destination, which is the entry of the Second Subject.

Similarly the passage following the Second Subject grows in consequence. In 238 the little four-bar second subject is simply stretched out by a further two bars (71 and 72) leading to a Cadential and the piano climax; in 414 there is a five-bar extension of the material (bar 119); in 453 the two second subjects are so long that the piano climax follows at once; in 537 there are fifteen bars of sequences (bar 178) during which the piano becomes absorbed in its own contrapuntal line of thought.

The piano climaxes vary in length from 25 bars (537) to an average in the high teens; they are not so highly pitched as the great climax of the early concertante work for two pianos (365) nor of the symphonic concertos, being fast and pretty rather than powerful, and this, of course, is in keeping with the Melodic character. The tuttis which end the First Concerto are drawn from the Bridge material in five concertos out of the seven, often with the addition of a Cadential. The Fantasies, which are described more fully in Chapter 4, are more independent than those of the Symphonic and Galant groups, seldom being related to the rest of the work.

In general, Mozart's principle of reprise in the Melodic concertos is to follow the lines of the First Concerto. If any 'given' material from the Statement was not contained within the First Concerto, there were still plenty of positions available where it could be popped in to make up an even number of 'mentions'. If, for instance, there was no reference to the old Bridge in the First Concerto up to the climax, it could be used in the closing ritornello. Nevertheless there is one Bridge which disappears without trace after its first and only entry (414) and in every concerto except 453 and 595 some of the later Bridge material is not repeated. After 238 and 414 the Cadentials are distributed very evenly, never appearing less than twice, seldom more than three times.

The real problem of reprise, however, was to arise, as we shall see, with the Symphonic concertos, yet even in the Melodic concertos Mozart was too original a composer to be content with an exact reprise of what had gone before by merely changing only the few bars necessary to keep the tonality in the tonic throughout. Thus after 238 there is not one Reprise that does not have its surprises, greater or less, of omission, insertion or extension.

The First Subject always opens the Reprise in the orchestra, but the piano's methods of entering the texture and taking command are various. There is always some change in the nature of the Sub-Ritornello or the piano bridge; the piano's subject and its sequences remain the same, but the expectant passages (B/S) may be thrown in before the Second Subject (which is always present). The piano climax is the most variable; in 414 and 537 the long melodic cadentials appear unexpectedly within the climax; in nearly every concerto the climax is reworked and sometimes rewritten to balance in length and power with the other adjustments already made. The Cadenza ritornello and the final tutti are made up mainly of Cadentials often unheard since their first appearance in the Statement. Two concertos (453, 488) have short codas.

The Melodic form is tabulated at the end of the chapter. It is not, however, by making tables or studying patterns of symbols that the chief characteristics of the Melodic concerto can be grasped. The secret of their serene unity and effortless progress lies beneath the surface. Mozart's method was not different in kind from the methods of other composers, but he acquired a degree of skill and subtlety that justifies perhaps a special study and the use of a special term—the filo.

Let us start with the Mozart family's own use of the word. Leopold wrote persuasively to Mozart during his trip to Paris, begging him to compose for the Parisian taste:

> What is slight can also be great if it is written in a natural, flowing and easy style, and at the same time bears the marks of sound composition. Such works are more difficult to compose than all those harmonic progressions which most people cannot follow… Good composition, sound construction, *il filo*, these distinguish the professional from the amateur even in small things.

What exactly Leopold meant by the word we can only guess. It could have been a technical term which had a precise meaning to the Mozart family, or it could have been no more than a chance use of a handy Italian expression. Einstein, however, has chosen to fix upon it a special meaning, namely Mozart's peculiar ability to string music together without seeming to do so. This quality is described (more vaguely) by Girdlestone as follows:

> Mozart gives his succession of phrases an internal unity which is felt but cannot be analysed, and binds together, with a single flow of emotion, themes whose outlines are very different. However changeful their shape and however clear-cut the separation between them, the continuity of the emotion is not broken; we grasp it intuitively when analysis reveals but a series of apparently independent subjects.

Although the filo is much more susceptible to analysis than Girdlestone suggests, it is a subjective quality and therefore can only be given a subjective examination. The most obvious filo relationships all will recognise, but there will be some shadowy associations which seem real to some, and to others an illusion. Some pictures in the fire are only seen by those who want to see them.

Let us first of all distinguish again between the directly identifiable use of themes on the one hand, and the filo on the other. The former gives clear signals to the ear (and, on paper, to the eye) that there is a logical and conscious association or relationship between one passage and another. When listening to a canon something happens in that delicate adjustment between the mind and the ear which directs attention to an identical pattern in sound moving in two different planes of time. Similarly in a symphony the mind accepts thematic shapes, hears them change, combine, develop, and always recognises their identity. There are three passages in which the First Subject of 271 is varied by the piano and, through all the changes in the form of the theme, identification is clear; the listener knows it is the First Subject he is hearing. Similarly, in 415 the First Subject and the first Cadential have a relationship which is open and evident. In deploying filo relationships, most of the work is done behind the scenes.

Only the learned ear can follow at first hearing the intricacies of symphonic and contrapuntal working. Few of us listening to a complex fugue for the first time can aspire to the level of understanding reached, say, by reading Tovey's *Art of the Fugue*, which dissects and sifts the mass until every component is put in order. The filo, however, demands a quick ear rather than a learned one, and a child can be as accurate as a professor. To recognise the degree of filo relationships is not unlike detecting family likenesses in people and animals. Some have the knack of it, others have not.

First it will be as well to deal with an old red herring. This is the view that Mozart wrote intuitively; he did not himself work out the mechanics of his music; because of his great genius and unerring taste his music came out like a sort of divine fart, involuntary and unpremeditated. It is doubtful if this can be entirely true.

There are three methods of working out a composition which may overlap or may be distinct:

1. On paper. So far as we know, Mozart made sketches only for contrapuntal passages. But perhaps for elaborate working he needed an *aide-memoire*. Many people destroy their rough working out of vanity, some out of tidiness.

2. At an instrument. There is no direct evidence of what Mozart actually did at the clavier. Certainly he worked at it, but there is a great difference between originating through the fingers at the keyboard and trying out something already three parts complete.

3. In the head. Mozart's ability to carry music in his head was certainly phenomenal and the evidence suggests that the main substance of a work existed in his head before he set pen to paper.

Einstein, from his study of the manuscripts, defines his method of composition as follows:

> The *filo*, the 'thread' that Mozart follows, is so dependent upon the right beginning; the beginning must be 'the very best'. Mozart has this *filo* in his head before he starts to write: all witnesses of Mozart at work agree that he put a composition down on paper as one writes a letter, without allowing any disturbance or interruption to annoy him – the writing down, the 'fixing' was nothing more than that – the fixing of the completed work, a mechanical act. Mozart's procedure during this process is easily followed, thanks to his frequent changes to fresh-cut quills and the varying colours of his ink, which evidently thickened quickly and had to be thinned out or freshened very often. Mozart never writes out parts or sections of a movement, complete in all voices, but always a *whole*. Sketch and final form blend into one act of writing; he does not make rough drafts... In a work of chamber music, or a symphony, he fixes first the principal voices, the melodic threads, from beginning to end, leaping as it were from line to line, and inserting the subordinate voices only when he 'goes over' or 'overhauls' the movement in a second stage of the procedure.

A reasonable deduction, therefore, might be as follows. Mozart thought out the subjects of a concerto and its shape at least up to the Fantasy, before sitting down to fix it on paper. The piano bridges and the piano climax might not be formed. The Fantasy might be a fresh or a separate inspiration. The Reprise would almost certainly be constructed at the desk with the sight of the Statement and the First Concerto already on the page, except perhaps in those concertos where it takes an original form (271) or has to solve some special problem of integration (365, 488).

There may therefore be an element of truth in the theory of the 'divine fart'. The generation of the filo from tune to tune could well have been a subconscious act based upon reflexes conditioned by the long and gruelling course of instruction applied by Leopold during his childhood. The important point, however, is that whether Mozart's filo came about by intuition or by conscious thought, it exists. It is no less subject to analysis because it passes from his subconscious to ours.

Let us take first an example from 414. The First Subject starts:

Example 10

bar 1

The Second Subject has no direct filo relationship, but it does carry an air of belonging to the First.

Example 11

bar 32

The questioning Caesura which ends the first phrase has an answer headed by a downward semiquaver run:

Example 12

bar 36

The second phrase itself runs into a Caesura, from which the downward run rescues it and builds into a Mannheim crescendo (the first Cadential):

Example 13

bar 40

The Cadential ends with a full close. The second Cadential swings out with a direct filo relative of the Second Subject, this time a third lower, with a firmer step, and with the Caesura removed:

Example 14

bar 50

And the Second Subject thus transformed now seems even more like an extended version of the First.

The sense of kinship between the First Subject and each successive link in the chain is often nebulous, but sometimes it can be pinned down. Thus the First Subject of 453 has an extra phrase (F+) which ends:

Example 15

bar 13

and the first phrase of the Bridge answers it:

Example 16

bar 16

One test of the power of the filo is to hum the First and Second subjects of each Melodic concerto one after the other, and it will be seen that they form a couple united always by a similarity in feeling, sometimes by a common harmonic pattern, sometimes by affinities of rhythm. The influence of the First Subject can, however, reach right out to the last Cadentials, as in 450:

First Subject:

Example 17

bar 1

Third Cadential:

Example 18

bar 53

The filo relationship in the Statement may be direct, as in the above example, or it may be more complex, as in the example from 414. In this latter kind of working the themes have a father-to-son relationship rather than a fraternal one. The parent theme lays its impression on the mind, the next generation keeps certain characteristics but acquires new ones as well. The third generation may inherit the new characteristics (the First Cadential of 414) or it may revert back to the character of the founder member of the family (the Second Cadential of 414).

Selective breeding through the filo stops short, however, at the end of the Statement. After this point the material is either entirely new or only one generation away from a statement theme. Thus a piano bridge or a climax might relate to a piece of the statement. But a climax never derives from a piano bridge. Nor does the piano second subject have any offspring, except, of course, in its own sequences and in the Cadenza.

Thus the Statement is the power-house of the entire movement, generating the original impulses which pass on to what follows. Within the Statement, the First Subject is the greatest generator of all. All that has been written about the importance of Mozart's first subjects in deciding the character of a work is indeed true, but its influence goes further than that, for, particularly in a work constructed on the lines of a Melodic concerto, the whole movement can be littered with its direct and indirect progeny.

The unifying force in the Melodic concertos is therefore based on continuing similarity of *feeling*, often oblique and perceptible only to the listeners' subconscious. The symphonic way of working depended upon a direct and clear association of *shape*. In terms of literature, the Melodic concertos use the methods of analogy and simile, the Symphonic method those of logical argument. The Melodic concertos are not, however, smaller or less in any way than the Symphonic group; a Melodic concerto can be compared to a comedy, to *Cosi Fan Tutte* or to *Figaro*, whereas the Symphonic concerto has the more serious ambition of a *Don Giovanni*, or a *Magic Flute*.

In conclusion, however, to return to the outward appearance of the Melodic form, Table 18 shows first a 'standard' or synthesis of all the concertos (excluding 595) and then the detail of each concerto in a comparative table. From this it will be seen that, generally speaking, the only formal differences between the Melodic and the Galant concertos are:

STATEMENT — The F+ passage occurs in four, and the B/S passage in two concertos out of seven.

FIRST CONCERTO — The first subject is usually sealed off by a sub-ritornello made up from the Cadentials (three times) or the Bridge (twice). The piano bridge is new material. The closing ritornello is made up from Bridge material (five out of seven) usually followed by one Cadential or more.

FANTASY — Unlike the Galant Fantasy the Melodic middle section does not usually pick up the last cadential of the preceding ritornello and use it as a subject for development. The Fantasy is independent—except 595 which develops the First Subject, 537 which does use the Galant form, and 450 which opens with a variant of the last Cadential.

REPRISE

The Reprise is more varied: cadentials are introduced before the piano climax in 414 and 537; a return to the old Bridging sequence of the Statement appears in 450 and 453; the extra Second Subject is inserted into 488.

TABLE 18

The Melodic form

A general synthesis:

Statement	F (+) B (B/S) S C1 C2 C3(C4)			
First Concerto	f (+) (C or B) pb ps + (b/s) sS(+) (Cs) px	B(+Cs)		
Reprise	Ff (B or C) pb ps + (b/s) sS(+) (Cs) px	Cs or B	cd	Cs

The construction of each concerto:

STATEMENT

238	F		B		S	C1	C2	C3	C4
414	F		B		S	C1	C2	C3	
450	F	+	B		S	C1	C2	C3	
453	F	+	B	B/S	S	C1	C2	C3	C4
488	F		B		S1	C1	C2		
537	F		B		S	C1	C2	C3	
595	F		B	B/S	S	C1	C2	C3	C4

FIRST CONCERTO

238	f	C3	pb	ps+		Ss+	C1	c1	px	B C2C3C4
414	f c3	C3	pb	ps+		Ss+			px	C3
450	pi f		pb	ps+					px	B C2C3
453	f	Bb	pb	ps+	B/S	sS			px	B C4
488	f	B	pb			sS1		c1	px	B S2
537	f+	C1	pb	ps+		sS+			px	B C3
595	fF		pb	ps+	b b/s	Ss	c1	C1+	px	NT C2

REPRISE

										CADENZA	
238	Ff	C3	pb	ps+		Ss+	C1 c1	px	C3		BC2C3C4
414	Ff c3	C3	pb	ps		Ss+	C2 c2	px	C1		C3
450	Ff	B	pb	ps+		Ss		px	C1 C2		C2C3
453	Ff	B b/s		ps+	B/S	sS		px	C1		C2C3C4B/S
488	Ff	B	pb			sS1	c1 sS2	px	B S2		C1C2CODA
537	Ff		pb	ps+		s+	px C2 c2	px	B		C3
595	F		pb	ps+b b/s		Ss	c1 C1+	px	C2c2c3		NT C4

4

The Symphonic Concertos

415 in C; 451 in D; 459 in F;
466 in D minor; 467 in C; 491 in C minor;
503 in C

Mozart gained his reputation as a child prodigy through his remarkable ability at the keyboard and his precocity as a composer. This second reason for his celebrity, however, needs some qualification. There is no doubt that from the age of seven or eight he worked with the grammar and prosody of music in the way that a golden youth of eighteenth-century England might have handled Greek prose and Latin verse. His first truly original works were in the field of opera and light entertainment, and some of them show the technical facility and the happiness of invention which often mark the first stage of success in the career of a composer of genius. In another way, however, he was slow to mature, certainly no faster than some of his contemporaries and many of the most famous of his successors. This was in the art of composing absolute music in a style that could express the full range of his complex, many-sided and often intensely serious musical personality.

This maturity came suddenly; the difference between his symphony in C (338, 'Beecham's favourite') and the Linz symphony (425), and between the piano concerto 415 in C and the D minor concerto (466) is amazing, yet they lie only three years apart. These years were the watershed between the happy, tender music of his youth and the passionate and jubilant music of his maturity.

The great works of this last period reflect three characteristic moods. The first a sort of apotheosis of his youth, and these include the Melodic concertos. The last was more sombre and reflective, of which the Requiem, the Clarinet concerto and the piano concerto 595 are examples. Between these two lie the works of passion and power; the later operas, some of the Haydn string quartets, the last three symphonies and the four great Symphonic piano concertos 466, 467, 491 and 503.

Three earlier concertos blaze the trail, 415, 451 and 459; these, however, are still emerging from the Galant/Melodic method. In them, the symphonic idea gradually extends its influence, and the last four Symphonic concertos reach an absolute distinction from the Galant and Melodic works. The word 'Symphonic' requires perhaps some explanation as a label for these works, because it is applied generally and equally to Mozart's early symphonies (which are Galant, and quite 'unsymphonic' in this sense) and to the later ones. It was, however, Haydn and Mozart himself who elevated the word 'symphony' to mean something more than the light Cassation, the Italian Overture or the serenade-type of orchestral work of his early days, and in the next century Beethoven and Brahms secured the position of the symphony as one of the highest forms of endeavour for the serious composer. It is in this sense that the word is used to describe the larger concertos, which stand apart from the simpler and less ambitious Galant and Melodic works. The distinction is great, for they differ in scale, texture and structure, and they employ a different method of treating thematic material.

The last symphonic concertos are big works, the shortest first movement playing for just under 400 bars (466), the longest 523 bars (491). The early Galant concertos were as short as 200 bars; the melodic often between 300 and 350. Even this comparison does not reflect the massive change in the scale of work which is shown better, perhaps, by the increased complexity of their composition, by the emancipation of the inner parts, by the extensive use of counterpoint, and by the many originalities of scoring and invention throughout the whole movement. It is broadly true to say that for every original bar composed in 175 (that is to say a bar neither repeated nor transposed from an earlier section of the work) there are ten in each of the four last Symphonic concertos.

All the Symphonic concertos (except 415, and 459, which is an interesting hybrid between the Melodic and Symphonic styles) are scored for a large orchestra. A flute, trumpets and drums were added to the usual wind section, and 491 has a pair of clarinets too. The piano itself is *primus inter pares* rather than soloist. The contrast of the simple piano tone in its slender feminine role with the string chorus is seldom used except in the piano introductions; the two climaxes are built not by the soloist alone but by the combined forces of the partnership (although the more powerful piano part is written in such a way as to leave no doubt about which is the leader).

This sense of unity, which applies equally to the form and the texture of the movement, marks one of the differences between the Symphonic concertos and the others. The Galant and Melodic works arc based broadly on the concept of the operatic works or the early church music which conceives matters in terms of ritornello and solo, of one single melodic line followed by another, of tunes which belong to one party or the other, on vertical harmonic support for the melody, on a system of succession, the whole being bound together by the subtle influence of the filo. The symphonic idea was entirely different: it was to select a short theme or series of themes which were not melodies or complete subjects but basic units of music, never more than four bars and sometimes less than one bar in length, and to use these themes as a central 'motif' in a system of symphonic working. These short units are used by both partners, and introduced in one form or another again and again, and so provide the movement with the central idea that it had lacked since the Main Theme of Emmanuel Bach. This new use of thematic material is another decisive element in distinguishing between the Symphonic concertos and their Galant and Melodic fellows.

The use of short musical units ran alongside other features in Mozart's symphonic advance, a new breadth of plan, the use of counterpoint, the final emancipation of the lower strings and the wind band, in fact the concept of an orchestra as an instrument which could be used both vertically and horizontally at the same time. The Baroque composers had looked mainly along the lines in terms of canon, fugue or other forms of counterpoint. The Galant school tended to look along one line only (the melody); for the rest they worked up and down when writing in the necessary support. Even Mozart himself, until this time, had habitually first written out only the melody and bass in his orchestral works. Now he (and Haydn) added a new dimension to music by judiciously uniting the two approaches so that counterpoint broke in at will, but only when it was wanted to make its effect. Thus the symphonists drew on the power of counterpoint while at the same time liberating it from the strict rules of the old 'learned' music.

In his youth Mozart had shown little sympathy for the masters of the old contrapuntal Establishment, Telemann, Fux and even Sebastian Bach. His return to counterpoint, however, is well documented and well known. It occurred in 1782 at the age of twenty-six through the exercise of re-arranging some of Sebastian Bach's works for performance in Vienna. Over the same period of time he was playing the works of Handel and Sebastian Bach in Baron van Swieten's 'amateur' string quartet. It seems that he saw the power of polyphony afresh, and, like any ambitious composer, he wanted to use it for his own purposes. His strict academic essays were often unfinished, and all but a few seem to have been little more than exercises. He began, however (and amongst the first movements of the concertos the first real example is 415), to experiment with simple elements of canon. This technique he developed until he could manipulate a sophisticated texture which read both as homophony and polyphony, two good examples of the final stages of the art being the finale of the Jupiter Symphony and certain sections of the C minor mass. At the same time he developed the system of relating different passages in the same work by means of a recurrent motif. Add to these two a third ingredient, a widened harmonic range, and a fourth, a more subtle and at the same time a more powerful use of the orchestra, and the sum of these parts explains Mozart's quite sudden advance as a symphonic composer. Let us start by looking at the ultimate expression of the Symphonic form as it is to be seen in the last four concertos (466, 467, 491 and 503).

The Statements all open with an introductory gesture. 503 has a fully grown 'Introduction' before and outside the First Subject which is a separate little section on its own, the very first example in the concertos of a symphonic tradition that was favoured by Haydn and Beethoven. 466 and 467 open with a *sotto voce* sentence built on the main motif which is both a premonition and a prelude. The whispered sentence is followed by a sudden blaze of sound in which the preliminary theme is transformed into the shape of a First Subject. 491 follows the same dynamic pattern but the First Subject serves as its own usher, appearing first in a mysterious *piano* and then immediately in loud defiance.

The motif or motifs which play so large a part in the whole movement are always embodied in these one or two opening sentences, which (to avoid fresh terms) can continue to be called the First Subject, although First Group would now be a better description. Thus, after an uneasy opening, the forte section of 466 has three elements which are destined to be used symphonically:

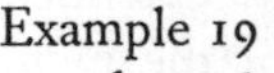
Example 19
bar 16

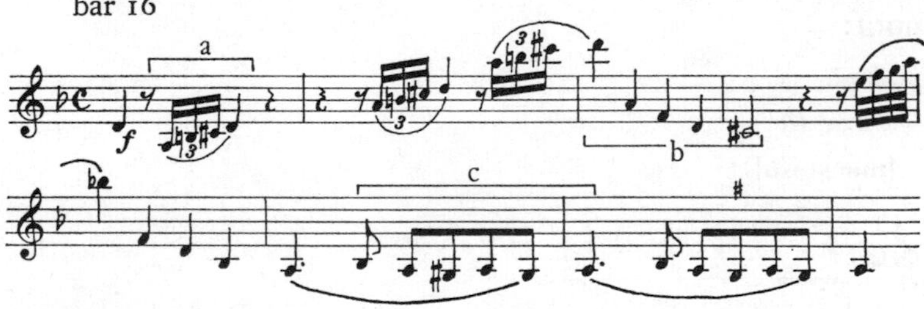

First there is the upward triplet sweep, 'a', second the emphatic downward arpeggio, 'b', and third the grinding semitone on the dominant, 'c'.

467 spreads its net wider, but the opening military air is used as a 'First Subject' throughout the movement and is the originator of many variants:

Example 20
bar 1

491 is more concise:

Example 21
bar 13

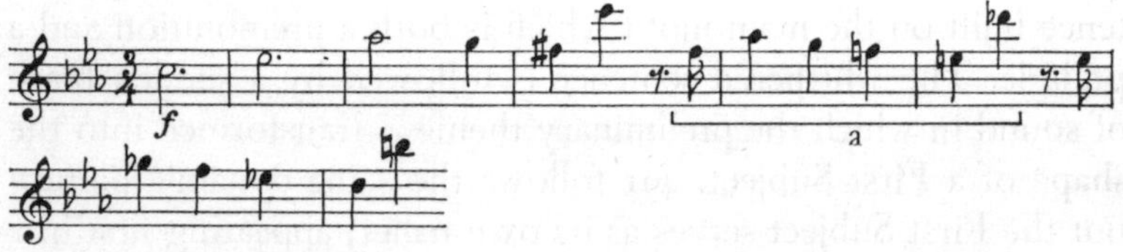

The complete theme is used throughout as a First Subject but it is in the second phrase (marked 'a') which holds three units that will generate much of the later material. They are:

1 The iambic beat at the start
2 The three crotchet strokes in the centre bar
3 The final leap

The final example, 503, has a most elaborate and extended *forte* section growing from the first quiet mention of the main motif:

Example 22
bar 18

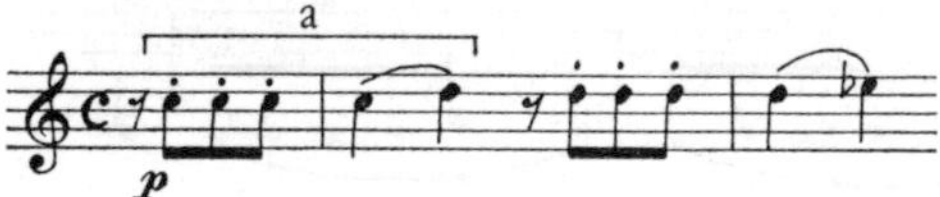

Here 'a' first pushes upwards; then downwards;

Example 23
bar 22

then it is accompanied by an antiphonal scale 'b'—

Example 24

bar 26

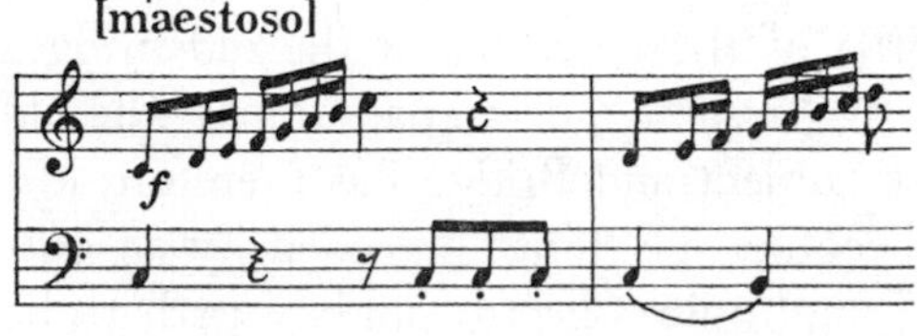

—builds to a climax (bars 36–41) and comes out of it with a wider downward interval between the crotchets.

Example 25

bar 40

These units of music within the first subject which act as agents to build and bind together the movement are described more fully in the analysis of each concerto in the second part of this book. They are mentioned here to explain a change of method. Where the Galant and Melodic concertos have a succession of *subjects* the Symphonic concerto has a succession of *sections*, some with themes of their own, others fulfilling the same function as before (Cadential, piano bridge, etc) but using again the basic units from the opening section. The way in which the Symphonic idea was first introduced in 415 is compared to its final deployment in 503 in Chapter 7, p. 150. There it can be seen that in 415 the symphonic idea was used tentatively; in 503 it is all-pervasive.

The second structural change in the Statement can only be seen by stepping back from such close quarters and seeing how the music flows from its introductory sentence to the point of entry of the Second, or Relief Subject. The old distinction between the First subject and the bridge has gone. There is an opening or introduction that can be called 'separate', but once the *forte* passage begins, it flows without let or hindrance until it reaches and rests on the dominant chord. The later material, it is true, sometimes has a little of the character of the old bridges but it is essentially a part of the same musical paragraph. The old distinction between First Subject and Bridge has therefore lost its meaning, they have become one thing, preceded by an outrider. The opening of a Symphonic concerto can best perhaps be described as an introductory First Subject followed by the First Subject/Transition, or in the case of 503 a separate introduction followed by a First Subject/Transition.

A longer and more Sonata-like Second Subject might seem to be the natural consequence of the more powerful first section and the greater size of the Symphonic works. Instead Mozart reverts (except in 503) to a slender Relief passage only twelve bars long in 466 and 467 and a little longer in 491. These Relief subjects are scored lightly for wind instruments and provide a contrast in tone and pace; they are not so strong in character as the string Second Subjects of the Melodic concertos and their role is passive—to provide a genuine 'relief' from the surrounding tumult. Their brevity and small structure were to be helpful in solving the second subject equation which, as we have seen, would otherwise have cropped up in the two concerto sections.

The closing section of the Statement, too, is very different from the easy string of Cadentials which rounded off the Melodic or the Galant Statement. As soon as the Relief subject is over, the orchestra plunges again into a full symphonic passage, a continuation as it were of the first opening *forte* and based (except in 503 which holds its fire a little longer) on the working out of the motif. Somewhere, as the Statement draws to an end, there will be a slower Cadential, expressed with elegance or yearning, and the Statement generally ends with a dying fall instead of the bustle and buzz of the Galant form.

This new form of Statement, massive and unified, has therefore only two checks in its vigorous course, the Relief passage and one of the Cadentials. Now, at the close, the orchestra hesitates, and then ushers in the piano, in one of the few remaining operatic gestures, to make its bow in an extended introduction. Once launched, the piano first sails out alone, usually in its fragile feminine role; soon, however, the orchestra may join in and round off a concerted introduction by taking over the start of the First Subject. All four First Concertos start in this way, as indeed they must, because the character of the opening sentence of the First Subject is essentially orchestral. The piano could not convey the same musical idea merely by playing the same notes. It can and will work with the same thematic material, but since the effect of the opening sentence depends so much on orchestral sound and texture it must stand down from its traditional role and allow the orchestra to open the solo section with the First Subject.

Thus the introductory sentence of the First Concerto is given by the orchestra and this is followed, as in the statement, by the *forte* passage. Now the piano will usually climb into the texture and, with growing persistence, develop its own line of thought which quickly smothers the orchestra (still working with the motif) and leads into a piano bridge of its own. Except for 466, the most sparingly constructed of the four, each piano bridge is long and inventive, sometimes extending to the sort of episodes that belong to the more discursive type of Concertante bridge, first used in the concerto for two pianos, 365. Once in the new key the second subjects unfold, the piano's own subject supplying all the strength of character that was missing from the mild Relief passage in the Statement. The way in which the second group is handled is as flexible as in the other concertos; once the Relief comes first (466), three times it is dropped (467, 491, 503), and once (491) there is a substantial new Second Subject from the orchestra.

After the second group, instead of the customary sequences leading to the start of the piano climax, there is a concerted treatment of the motif which invigorates the pulse of the movement and forms the first section of the piano climax. Some 'given' thematic material is usually introduced at this point. The succeeding piano passages which form the pinnacle of the climax are both more athletic and more muscular than those of the Melodic concertos—the staves being filled with double arpeggios and octave passages rather than scales or runs. The final ritornello of the First Concerto brings back the main units once more, this time in the form of the first *forte* passage in the statement.

The third section of the concerto movement, the Fantasy, has not so far been discussed in any detail, and for two reasons. First, because Mozart's ways of handling the fantasy are so various as to allow only the broadest generalisations. They are therefore better left to the latter part of this book where each one can be seen in the context of the whole movement. Secondly, because in the Melodic and Galant concertos the Fantasies are usually only lightly related to the main musical subjects of the movement.

A traditional shape for the keyboard and concerto fantasy, often used by Christian Bach, was as follows. The piano would play an eight or twelve bar sequence twice or three times, passing through a different key at each repetition. Next there would be a separate harmonic development of a fresh musical idea, usually resting for a little while on the tonic parallel (a vestigial race memory of the North Germans' more rigid rules of key structure); next perhaps some fast arpeggios modulating back towards the dominant pedal.

This pattern (with wide variations) was used by Mozart in the little Salzburg concertos. But an interesting and mysterious difference developed between the fantasy for the Galant and that for the Melodic concerto. The Galant concerto tended to pick up a phrase from the last Cadential in the ritornello of the First Concerto and to open the Fantasy with this (or a variation of it) almost as if it were a theme given out for improvisation (246, 449, 482), or else to use 'given' material in the later development (449, 413). The Melodic fantasy, however, usually started with an entirely new musical idea (238, 414, 453, 488). Only 450 and 537 open with a 'pick-up' from the ritornello. This difference goes beyond the likelihood of chance, since both families cover the full span of composition from 1776 to 1790 and lie scattered indiscriminately amongst each other and the symphonic works. One can only speculate that Mozart, whether consciously or not, felt that the Melodic style needed a fresh beginning to the fantasy whereas the more epigrammatic Galant style benefited from a musical pun to set the third act going.

The more significant point, however, is not in the distinction between the Galant and Melodic fantasies, however intriguing that may be, but in the much greater distinction between both of these and the Fantasies of the Symphonic concertos. In no Fantasy of a Melodic or a Galant concerto (excepting 595) is there any development of First or Second subject material from the statement (although, as in 488, there is development of new material). The Symphonic concertos, however (looking for a moment beyond the last four to the full span from 415 to 503), are true to their principle of unity and tend to use one of the motifs either in a full symphonic development (459, 503), or in snatches of development which occur in a more loosely constructed Fantasy (415, 466, 491). Only 451 and 467 follow the Galant pattern of a 'pick-up' from the orchestra's last Cadential and then go on to a free fantasia. The reason for uniting the Symphonic Fantasy with the rest of the work through the use of one or more of the main units is, of course, a natural extension of the symphonic idea. The Symphonic Fantasies are also different in stature, some of them being of nearly equal weight to the other sections of the movement. Many Galant and Melodic Fantasies leave the impression of an almost extempore excursion outside the frame of reference of the other three parts, providing something more like an entr' acte than a symphonic development. The Fantasies of 466, 491 and 503 are no diversion from the main line of the movement; they continue it by directing the flow of the music into a swifter channel which moves from point to point until it reaches the Return, with its ambivalent sense both of being the finale to one act (the Development) and the prelude to the next (the Reprise).

The Reprise itself had become an increasing test of Mozart's ability to do two things—to recall everything of importance that had occurred both in the Statement and the First Concerto and at the same time to provide a properly balanced final section for the movement. Clearly he felt a strong compulsion towards total recall, towards the tidiness, the logic and the musical necessity of tying up all loose ends in the Reprise, but he felt an even stronger impulse towards the exact balance of the parts, that is to say that the Reprise, from First Subject to Cadenza ritornello, should approximately balance in length with the First Concerto. This was always achieved to within a matter of plus or minus 10 per cent.

The problem of reconciling these two principles grew with the complexity of the concerto form. Originally there had been no problem at all. The *da capo* Aria had repeated the whole of the First Ritornello and the First Solo after the Middle Section. The Extended Aria showed an easy disregard for total recall and so did the North German Concerto. Christian Bach had, however, restored the position by introducing all of the subjects of the Statement into the First Concerto. Thus the material of the Statement was 'recalled' twice, both in the First Concerto and in the Reprise (Table 19, Stage 1).

Mozart continued in this tradition with his early Salzburg concertos, save for one refinement. Where Christian had played some or all of the Cadentials with the solo itself and then repeated them in the closing ritornello, Mozart tended to avoid this repetitive pattern and to use the cadentials only within the ritornellos. The result, as we have seen, was that often two Cadentials out of four did not appear in the First Concerto at all. The situation could easily be restored, however, by using the two missing Cadentials at the very end of the Reprise after the Cadenza (Table 19, Stage 2). It was still possible to recall all original material easily and sweetly into a Reprise which balanced exactly in length with the First Concerto from its First Subject to the Cadenza platform. (The Cadenza and the final ritornello are taken to lie outside the main balance. They form a separate appendage, a free solo display rounded off by familiar material.)

TABLE 19

The problem of Reprise

Stage 1 – Christian Bach

STATEMENT	F	B								C1	C2	C3	C4
FIRST CONCERTO	f	Bb	ps +	B	S	c1	c2	c3	px	C1	C2	C3	C4

All the material of the Statement is contained in the First Concerto. Therefore a Reprise of the First Concerto serves as a Reprise of the Statement material as well.

Stage 2 – early Mozart

STATEMENT	F	B					C1	C2	C3	C4
FIRST CONCERTO	f	Bpb	ps +	(B)	S +	px	C1	C2		
REPRISE	Ff	Bpb	ps +	(B)	S +	px	C1	C2/cd/	C3	C4

Only two of the Cadentials are left out of the First Concerto; therefore if they follow the Cadenza in the Reprise all given material is recalled. (*Note*: the Cadentials can of course be used in any order and in any combination.)

Stage 3 – later Galant and Melodic

STATEMENT	F	B		S			C1	C2	C3	C4
FIRST CONCERTO	f	pb	ps +	(S)	+ px	B	C1			
REPRISE	Ff	pb	ps +	S	+ px	B	C1/cd/	C2	C3	C4

None of the material of the Statement except the First and usually the Second Subjects are contained in the solo section of the First Concerto. The Ritornellos carry the remainder.

(*Note* The above tables are, of course, broad and schematic. Mozart used many devices to introduce Statement material into the First Concerto, such as the sub-ritornello of Cadential material to close the First Subject and the insertion of Cadentials into the piano climax.)

As the concerto form expanded, however, a problem arose. Increasingly Mozart began to give the First Concerto a character of its own. More and more he discarded the sequence of the Statement and introduced new material where old material had previously stood. The piano bridge no longer joined the end of the old Bridge to the piano second subject: it could spring out of the first subject itself and assume a character of its own (450), sometimes with interpolations and episodes (365). The sequences after the piano second subject expanded in length and gained a new importance (271) as, too, did the sequences after the Second Subject (413, 414). The Second Subject itself might be dropped (450). There might be no mention of any material from the Statement between the beginning of the First Concerto to the end of the piano climax (Table 19, Stage 3).

These omissions could still, however, be countered by a shorter reference to the Bridge and a more sparing use of the Cadentials within the ritornellos. But total recall was by now very difficult. In Part Two of this book the first encounters with this problem in the two Salzburg experiments 271 and 365 are fully described. The latter demonstrates that the concertante principle of giving one stream of material to the orchestra and another to the soloists is irreconcilable with a complete reprise.

The Symphonic idea finally led to a solution which has never been used, and therefore perhaps never properly appreciated, by any composer in the concerto form since Mozart. Let us pause to look afresh at what Mozart was striving to achieve, and let us first, by way of comparison, look at the two different problems of reprise as posed by Sonata Form and Concerto Form.

Sonata Form has only one section to recapitulate—the Exposition. The only problem here is to give freshness to what has already been heard twice before (if the exposition has been repeated) and in particular to avoid a sense of flatness at the point of entry of the Second Subject in the tonic instead of in the more dramatic dominant. The problem of the Reprise in the later concertos, however, is to reconcile two widely differing sections, the Statement and the First Concerto, into a single Reprise which will give a conclusive affirmation of all the important musical ideas of both and at the same time not be over-long. All good dramatists prefer a short last act.

Until he tried the Symphonic form Mozart had managed by jobbing, switching, grafting and cutting to recall all original material into the Reprise, albeit at a reduced length and in a different sequence. The new difficulty the Symphonic idea seemed to pose was simply this. If there were two quite different 'expositions', one a substantial orchestral statement and the other a piano 'exposition', how could both be welded into a single reprise?

This indeed is the problem in 415, the first Symphonic essay. Here a fragment of the Bridge is thrown in after the piano climax in the Reprise. In this way the degree of recall is improved, but only at the expense of omitting a final statement of the main theme at this point. This concerto suffers too from a further problem of reprise, for Mozart wrote a brilliant and highly pianistic First Concerto which (save for a passing nod in the piano climax) omitted the Second or Relief subject of the Statement.

It is impossible to say, of course, whether the problem of reprise caused Mozart to reorganise the Statements of his later concertos or whether, because Mozart instinctively designed a different form of statement, the problem of reprise disappeared. All seems inevitable and right when devised by genius, and even in the earliest concertos, where the symphonic idea was in the process of being hammered out, the frustrations and maladjustments do not seem (except perhaps in 415 and 459) to detract from the validity and wholeness of the works.

But let us see how the final form of the Symphonic Statement helped to solve the problem of Reprise. Instead of a separate First Subject and a Bridge Mozart devised the single long paragraph described earlier in this chapter—an opening sentence; the *forte* passage; and then the Transition continuing in an unbroken run on to the dominant chord. All of these were linked together and all were dominated by association with the motif or motifs. A reprise of a part of this paragraph at the head of the First Concerto and the Reprise served both to signal the start of the cycle and to recall the motif. A reprise of the central or later part of the paragraph in the closing ritornellos of the two concerted sections both gave a sense of reprise and again introduced the unifying influence of the motif.

To return to the Statement again, after the Relief Subject the work with the motif continues, forming a central symphonic section, which, although called the 'Transition/Cadential', reads very differently from the Cadentials of the Galant days. In 415 the motif was transformed at this point into a vivid *forte* passage, and, although one of the most memorable incidents in the work, this separate and independent passage proved impossible to recall. In 466 the central passage continues with the end of the First Subject/Transition material and moves late in its course towards a cadential mood. In 467 and 491 the central passage starts again with the opening sentence, the premonition of the motif. 503 has a new central passage, a filo relative but not a restatement of the motif.

Because this weighty central passage ran to a cadential close, the statement could now end with fewer 'independent' cadentials; 466 has only one more, 467, 491 and 503 two each. Thus it became possible to recall both this Transition/Cadential section and the true cadentials after the cadenza at the end of the Reprise.

The broad pattern of the way in which the symphonic material in the Statement came to be deployed, to be used in the First Concerto and to be recalled in the Reprise, can be described as follows:

	OPENING SECTION	CENTRAL SECTION	CLOSING SECTION		
STATEMENT	F/T (m)	S T/C (m)	C^s (m?)		
FIRST CONCERTO	Ff/Tt (part) (m)	(S) and piano material including (m)	F/T (Con.) (m)		
CONCERTO REPRISE	Ff/Tt (part) (m)	S and piano material including (m)	F/T (Con) (m)	cd	T/C Cs (m)

m stands for the main units or motifs; F/T for the First Subject/Transition; T/C for the continuation of the Transition which leads to a cadential close. (A description of the structure of each Symphonic concerto is given in Table 20).

TABLE 20

The structure of Symphonic concertos

Notes

1 The following table is intended to give no more than a comparative guide to the main structure of the Symphonic concertos. Each concerto is analysed in detail in the later part of this book.

2 Since the symphonic method uses a number of short units, the labels no longer always imply a 'subject' but often a section of music which has within it several units. Again this is broken down in the individual analyses.

3 These units are often used in counterpoint to the piano part (and sometimes to each other). The method of description adopted here is to mention the thematic material used in counterpoint, say in a piano climax, only when it plays a leading part. Thus the piano bridge of 459 is marked pb(f) because it involves both piano and orchestra in a clear statement of the main theme.

4 To make the table as clear as possible the practice of repeating a symbol in upper and lower case when played in turn by the piano and orchestra (Ss) is dropped where there is an almost invariable pattern of interchange, e.g. the piano second subject is shown as ps on each appearance, not psPs.

5 Thematic material used within a piano climax is shown in brackets between the beginning and end of the climax, thus: px(C3) px.

6 The following new or unfamiliar symbols are used.

T Transition
F/T First subject – transition combined
T/C Transition passage ending with a cadential close
I Orchestral introduction
e Piano episode

Summary: the Symphonic concertos

STATEMENT

	OPENING SECTION	RELIEF SECTION	CONTINUATION	CADENTIALS
415	F T	S	C1	C2 C3 C4
451	F T	T/S S	C1 C2	C3 C4
459	F T		T/C	C1 C2 C3
466	F/T	S	T/C	C
467	F	S	T/C	C1 C2
491	F/T	S1	T/C	C1 C2
503	I F/T	S	T	C1 C2

FIRST CONCERTO

	OPENING	TRANSITION	SECOND SUBJECT & CLIMAX	RITORNELLO
415	pi Ff	pb	ps px (c3) px	F C4
451	fF	pb e t/s	Ss+ px (C1 C2) px	F C3
459	fF	t1 e pb(f)	Ss px (t/c) px	F
466	pi Ff/Tt Ss	pb	ps px (t/c) px	F/T C
467	pi Ff	e1 e2 pb	ps px (f) px	F C1
491	pi Ff	pb	ps px (Ss2) px	F/T
503	pi Ii FfTt	pb e	ps px (f/t) px	F/T

CONCERTO REPRISE

	OPENING AND EARLY REPRISE	LATER REPRISE AND CLIMAX	RITORNELLOS		
415	pi Ff pb	ps px (c3) px	T		C2 C3 C4
451	Ff T/t t/s	Ss+ px (C1C2C3) px	FT		C4
459	fF t1 pb(f)	Ss px (tc/ c1) px	F		C2 C3
466	Ff/Tt Ss pb	ps px (t/c) px	F/T	CADENZA	T/C C Coda
467	Ff pb(f)	ps px Ss px	F		T/C C1C2 Coda
491	Ff pb tT1 Ss2	ps px (t) Ss1 px	F		C1C2 Coda
503	Ii Ff/Tt pb e	ps S px (f/t) px	F/T		T C1 C2

Thus it can be seen that the opening symphonic group (F/T) can be recalled in its entirety, but in two separate places. The continuation of the Transition (T/C) section can be recalled after the Cadenza. The above table takes count only of the 'verbatim' repetitions of the symphonic material, for the units or motifs were also used, either contrapuntally or in the melodic line at one or all of the following points:

(1) A Cadential in the Statement
(2) The piano bridging area in the First Concerto and Reprise
(3) The piano climaxes
(4) The Development
(5) The Coda (where present)

And so total recall became possible and Mozart suited his methods to each occasion. There is no formula for a Symphonic Reprise, nor is it any longer predictable from a study of the earlier sections. It is the final act of a Symphonic drama and each one is separately created to hold appropriate surprises and to raise the level of the movement to a dramatic conclusion. It has become an act of composition, no longer merely of rearrangement.

There are two final points concerning the Symphonic Reprise. First, the golden rules of proportion are always observed; from the start of the Reprise to the cadenza platform the variation never exceeds 10 per cent (except 491) when compared with the length of the First Concerto (excluding of course the piano introduction). In 491 the Reprise is shorter by some forty bars, but this is compensated by a much longer closing tutti after the cadenzas, including the most elaborate coda in the concertos (fifteen bars).

The second and last point is one of feeling for tonality. The Symphonic concertos exploit an ambivalence between the major and the minor modes which was one of Mozart's most favoured techniques (and which was perhaps one of his greatest achievements in widening the range of feeling in music). 503, a triumphal work in C major, has shadows of the minor key clouding over the majestic introduction in the eighth bar. Both the concertos in the minor key exploit the transforming effect of a change of mode on their main subject-matter. This is nowhere more effective than in the Reprise, where the customary transformation of, for instance, the piano second subject from first appearance in the dominant to the tonic usually lacked excitement and often caused problems of register. A change of mode could give the Reprise a twist towards either a more buoyant or a more melancholy reading of known material and thus affect the impact of the whole last act. In 466, for instance, the piano second subject appears in the first concerto in the major (the tonic parallel). In the Reprise it is in the tonic minor and so gives the last act a downward thrust towards the mood of resigned melancholy with which the work ends. In 503 the lively march, the Second Subject from the Statement which had first appeared to be in two minds whether it was in C major or C minor, is recalled only in the major mode, and thus strengthens an already jubilant conclusion.

The story of Mozart's Symphonic advance from 271, an essay favouring the Sonata style, through 415, 451 and 459 to the last four great concertos, is told in Part Two. It is worth noting now, however, that, unlike Christian Bach and Joseph Haydn, Mozart did not attempt to write a concerto in Sonata Form. Christian Bach, after two essays in writing 'symphonies' in his Opus 1 set, abandoned the idea; Joseph Haydn never found in the concerto a vehicle to suit his adventurous and impulsive mood in composition. Mozart adapted the old form and then created a new one within it, for a far wider gap lies between the last Symphonic concertos and his own early work than between the early Salzburg concertos and those of Christian Bach.

PART TWO

The First Movements Examined

5

Early Salzburg

Arrangements: 107; 37 in F; 39 in B flat; 40 in D; 41 in G;
Original Concertos: 175 in D; 238 in B flat;
242 in F for three pianos; 246 in C.

The construction of each concerto is summarised, with musical examples, in the tables at the end of the book.

Mozart's first acquaintance with the piano concerto was as a performer. As early as 1763 when he was seven years old the word 'concerto' began to appear on the bills of the public concerts which Leopold arranged for his two prodigies in the capital cities of Europe. It is clear that both at court and in public the younger child was the star attraction. He must have played almost entirely on the harpsichord (a forte-piano is mentioned once) and no doubt the concertos he played would sometimes be supported by no more than a string bass, two violins and perhaps a viola. What concertos he played we do not know. There is a record of a performance by Wolfgang of one of Wagenseil's concertos with the composer himself turning the pages. In Paris the Germans Raupach, Honauer, Schobert and others may well have provided him with music, in London probably Christian Bach. It would be surprising indeed had he not become acquainted with much of the keyboard work of the London Bach. The Mozarts lodged first in Hare Court off Charing Cross Road, later in Westminster and Soho. Three times they visited the Court where Christian Bach was the Music Master to Queen Charlotte and Wolfgang evidently formed an attachment to him which lasted until he died in 1782.

Christian Bach's Opus 1 set of six piano concertos had been published in 1763, two years before the Mozarts' visit. It is likely that Leopold would have copied a set, and Wolfgang could well have performed some of them at his concerts at Hulford's Great Rooms in Brewer Street and in the pavilion in the Spring Gardens near St James's Park.

It is difficult to realise today, when music in all its forms is a very available commodity, that in the eighteenth century a performing troupe like the Mozarts could easily run short in their repertoire, not for lack of ability, but because their limited travelling library of music was exhausted. Mozart's first alleged essays in the composition of concertos may well have been prompted by the sudden need for a piece. In 1765 Leopold and he 'arranged' three of Christian Bach's sonatas as concertos (107) and two years later a similar and more interesting conversion took place in Salzburg when the father and son jointly arranged some piano music written by the Paris Germans (no doubt acquired during the tour) into four clavier concertos 37, 39, 40 and 41.

How much Wolfgang was involved in these two events is uncertain. He was nine and eleven years old respectively when the work was done and the manuscript shows the hands of both father and son working alternately. He is likely to have been more of a copyist than a composer, and the 'composition' consisted at most of inserting orchestral ritornellos and arranging light accompaniments to transform the piano solo into a 'concerto'. The very small part of the finished score that is original lacks any sort of character or inspiration. It could be from the pen of Leopold, who had written plenty of dull music, some of it still extant, or by a talented child given a task to complete in a hurry.

Wyzewa and Saint-Foix have painstakingly identified the original piano music. Two of the First Movements of the later set are by Raupach, two by Honauer. Having listened to one of each, it seems doubtful whether their conversion into a 'concerto' was an advantage. The Mozarts did little more than arrange a Statement, mainly from given material but sometimes with an interpolated orchestral bridge and cadentials, and then insert further ritornellos at judicious intervals. The details of their conversion of the first movement of a sonata (by Raupach) into the first movement of 39 in B flat is given in Table 21.

It was not until 1773 that Mozart, at the age of seventeen, composed his first original piano concerto. Before examining this truly surprising work it may be useful to review some of those aspects of his wide-ranging musical life which had influenced him as a composer of this first concerto, and indeed of later works too.

TABLE 21

The Mozarts' method of conversion: 39 in B flat

Honauer's movement originally read as follows:

EXPOSITION	First Subject: Bridge: Second Subject: Sequences: Cadentials
FANTASY	Free
REPRISE	End of Bridge: Main Cadentials. Close

The Mozarts used this sonata Exposition as their First Concerto. They constructed a statement by orchestrating (for two oboes, two horns and a string quartet) the first subject; by writing an orchestral Bridge that used elements of the sonata bridge; by converting the main Cadential into a Second or Relief Subject; and by inserting one new Cadential.

Then followed the First Concerto as described above, followed by a ritornello of the First Subject in the dominant; the fantasy of the original sonata ending with a New Tutti; a part of the Bridge; the Relief/cadential, one of the original piano cadentials, another few bars of New Tutti; the cadenza, and finally the Mozarts' own orchestral Cadential.

The following table shows the converted sonata set out as a concerto. New material added by the Mozarts is put in brackets, ritornellos inserted by them are printed in italics.

STATEMENT	F	(B)	R	(C1)	C2	
FIRST CONCERTO	f	pb	ps+	C2 r	C2	*F*
FANTASY	Free	(*NT*)				
REPRISE	Bb	Rr c2	(*NT*)	(Cadenza)	*C1*	

First, Mozart had reached the end of his career as a child prodigy. At the age of six he played before kings and princes in Munich and Vienna, at the age of seven he performed in Munich again, Augsburg, Heidelberg, Frankfurt, Cologne and other

German cities; at the age of eight at Versailles in the presence of Louis XV; in the same year at the court of George III, and at public and private gatherings in London. At the age of nine, on the return journey, there were concerts in Amsterdam and the Hague, the next year at Versailles again and at Dijon, Ghent, Geneva, Zurich and again in Munich. At the age of twelve he was both composing and performing in Vienna. At thirteen (in 1769) he made the first Italian tour to Verona, Mantua, Milan, Parma, Bologna, Florence, Rome, Naples, Venice and Turin, returning home after one year and three months on the road only to set out again five months later to fulfil a commission to put on an opera at Milan. He returned to Salzburg in December 1771 for a stay of nine months, returning to Milan in October of the next year for another opera (*Lucio Silla*) and finally reached Salzburg in March of 1773. His seventeenth birthday was on 29 January, and he composed the concerto 175 towards the end of the summer. The shift in emphasis between earning a living as a performing child and as a brilliant young composer/virtuoso had probably occurred during the first Italian tour.

As a prodigy he must have had his full share of petting and adulation from ladies in high society. As a clever little boy composer he had probably received help from Christian Bach and certainly from Padre Martini. This was in addition to the constant slogging imposed on him by Leopold. From Christian Bach he may have picked up a new method of writing for the keyboard and a new taste in performance; from Padre Martini a respect for counterpoint, but not, if we are to look at the evidence of his narrowly gained election to the Philharmonic Society of Bologna, any great proficiency. From Leopold he learned the habit of constant practice, hard work and consequently the facility to write music quickly. In addition to these three he met the leading composers, instrumentalists, singers and impresarios of the day and developed a sharp critical sense which he did not hesitate to express with a pen dipped in acid.

Leopold was the architect of Wolfgang's success, and his method of exploiting the boy's precocity resulted in what must have been the most cosmopolitan musical education acquired by any composer of that time, or previously. From this world of experience in music, Mozart formed definite tastes.

He liked a good audience, and enjoyed applause. No wonder, because a professional musician in his day was as precariously placed as a music-hall artist in Edwardian England. Unless 'they' applauded, the act was cut, unless a reputation could be built and protected there was no work. A child's lifetime of performing left him with a strong performer's temperament. Secondly, he liked the new fashion. The musical world was split (as it often is) between a professional regard for what was academic ('learned' music, counterpoint, 'the old style') and what pleased the public and the patron (the Galant style, the Italian taste). Mozart's strong preference lay with the Italian style and we can distinguish very early between works composed with a genuflection towards 'learned music' (the early string quartets 155–160) and the more natural and happy cassations, serenades and divertimenti of his youth.

Finally, he was enchanted by the theatre. The Italian opera house stood for all he loved best in the world, the nature of the music, the sense of theatre, the chat and gossip of rehearsal, the professional pleasure of adapting an aria to suit a good voice, the personal pleasure of conducting the performance and standing up to receive the applause of a brilliant audience. All his life Mozart longed to be commissioned to write opera (without a commission no composer of that period would have dreamed of putting pen to paper, for the idea of music as a thing which must be expressed at the dictation of the composer's soul was not to arrive until Beethoven), and the vaguest prospect of the pleasures of composition, rehearsal and performance would always excite him into a sort of theatrical fever.

If, however, this wish were denied, as so often it was, then the next best thing perhaps was to sit at the keyboard before a good house and perform a brilliant concerto of his own composition. After the operas there is no doubt that Mozart's own *persona* was poured more generously into the piano concertos than into any other category of his work, for as he composed them he had in his mind the vision of performance. The happy accident that Mozart was a great composer writing for his own hands makes the piano concertos his most personal legacy.

175 *in D major*

The little concerto in D major, 175, was certainly designed to raise an audience to its feet. It was not 'little' by contemporary standards, being longer than most of Christian Bach's Opus 1 concertos, and it was scored for oboes, horns, trumpets and drums, the first time—so far as is known—that a clavier concerto had been given so robust an orchestra. The exact occasion of its composition and first performance is not recorded. It may have been written for the Grand Concert in Dr Mesmer's garden on 18 August 1773, or more likely perhaps, in view of the origins of 242, 246 and 271, as an offering for performance by the pianist Marianne Martinez (a pupil of Joseph Haydn and a friend of the poet Metastasio) when the Mozart family visited Vienna in late September or early October.

The first movement is a dashing allegro which inherits the forms of the past but breathes the spirit of the future. It is the work of a young man who, because he has not yet even recognised the complex problems of concerto form, writes as if there were none.

During his lifetime it was of all the concertos his greatest popular success, perhaps due to the archaic flavour which may have helped to bridge the gap between the old taste and the new, also because its youthful exuberance is very hard to resist. As a vehicle for a virtuoso pianist it must have seemed a phenomenon. With its full orchestra and its noisy progress, it was no longer a piece for a chamber player. This is perhaps the first 'concert' piano concerto, the first that demands a large hall, a packed house and a pianist with a good sense of audience to get the most from its mood of reckless excitement.

The chief interest of the work centres around the nature and use of the First Subject, which, for the first and last time, has the character of the Aria ritornello.

Example 26

The first strain with its firm outline following the common chord, supported by a busy orchestra, could belong to a North German composer. The second strain, although Mozartean in outline, is supported by a texture which sounds archaic. Only the third is of a kind that has something in common with his later work. Nor does any other concerto have a first subject of the same inner structure, nine-plus bars, three strains, none of them repeated and with no continuing melody.

So much for the First Subject on its first appearance. Let us follow its career throughout the movement. In the First Concerto the piano plays straight through the three strains and then a noisy extra bar of tutti allows the strings to turn back to the dominant and the piano gives a gracefully ornamented version of the third strain once again. This is capped by the first strain played by the orchestra, and sounding unmistakably like the sub-ritornello of the old North German concerto. The piano then runs its course, interrupted three times by the First Subject and the equally ritornellic Bridge, until its final trill. It has, however, thrown in a reference to the First Subject as a complement to the Second. The final ritornello is made up of the First

Subject's second strain, which runs into the Cadentials. This too is reminiscent of a mid-ritornello of the old school.

In the Fantasy the piano opens with a derivative of the First Subject's first strain and is interrupted by a ritornello of the original. This sequence is worked through a parallel cycle in the tonic and rounded off again with the First Subject as ritornello. We hear no more of the First Subject (for fourteen bars) until the start of the Reprise, where the pattern is much the same as the First Concerto except that the Bridge provides the tutti after the piano climax. The second strain of the First Subject and the string of Cadentials are saved until after the Cadenza. All in all, there are twenty-two mentions of one or other of the three strains of the First Subject, counting the piano development in the Fantasy as only two, and the sequences to the Second Subject as one on each appearance, as follows:

	F1	F2	F3
Tutti/ritornello	6	3	1
Piano	2+(4)	2	4
	12	5	5

Finally, the First Subject grows bigger each time it appears as the Main Theme:

STATEMENT	F1 F2 F3
FIRST CONCERTO	f1 f2 f3 (extra bar) f3 (varied) F1
REPRISE	F1 f1 f2 f3 („ „) f3 („) F1

By the time the First Subject had become double-headed in the Reprise, whether he intended it or not, Mozart has firmly implanted upon it the sense and function of an Aria ritornello. The same air of ritornello also hangs about the Bridge with its old-fashioned even groups of four semiquavers. This figure was firmly in Mozart's mind throughout the movement, and the filo depends almost equally upon this and on the First Subject.

But to return to an account of the course of the movement, the two busy opening passages, the First Subject and the Bridge, are followed by a tricky Mozartean Second Subject (bar 16). This is a delicious fragment; here, on its first appearance, it passes by in an instant and leads directly into the First Cadential, a hesitant opening phrase followed by a neat answer. The Second Cadential (bar 29) opens with the same phrase as the first, but caps it with a portentous reply leading up to a diminished seventh, of which we will hear more later. The Third and last Cadential consists of three bars of figuration round the common chord of D.

The piano's voice is not distinguished when it opens the First Concerto, the left hand simulating the busy orchestral accompaniment with thick Alberti figuring. The decorated repeat of the third strain (apparently an original idea, and one which Mozart was to use many times again) is more pianistic, so too is the piano bridge which spins out of a variation of the old Bridging material. The piano second subject (bar 59) is no more than two perky little phrases (related to the First Subject) and their answers, and it is not until the Second Subject that the piano is given a chance to sing.

It is worth pausing to look at the ingenious handling of this section. The original Second Subject consists of three sprightly violin phrases. Four would have made a complete cycle, but the fourth turns into the First Cadential. In the First Concerto the Second Subject is played by the piano, this time with all four phrases complete. Then follow four bars of suspended animation with thirds and sixths on the piano derived from the First Subject drifting over a dominant pedal. Next, quite naturally as if it had always been there, the piano provides a lyrical answer to the Second Subject, a sweet flowing cadential figure (bar 76). This answer (four bars, equal in length to the second subject) is then repeated.

This is not the end of the story. In the Reprise when the same point is reached, the second subject is followed at once by the answer and the suspended passage follows only after the whole of the second subject and its answer are completed. The slight puzzle of the First Concerto is resolved in the Reprise (Table 22).

TABLE 22

175—the consequences to the Second Subject

In the Statement the last phrase of the Second Subject runs straight into the First Cadential (bar 20). In the First Concerto all four phrases are complete (bars 68–71). They are followed by a four-bar extension on the dominant pedal of A (bars 72–75) (s+). Then the piano gives its lyrical answer (four bars), which is repeated (bars 76–83) (s++). As follows:

4 bars	4 bars	8 bars
s	extension (s+)	lyrical answer (twice) (s++)

In the Reprise, the fourth phrase of the second subject runs straight into the piano's answer (bar 188) and the extension over the dominant pedal comes last, as follows:

3 bars	8 bars	4 bars
s	lyrical answer (twice) (s++)	extension (s+)

This device neatly serves two purposes. First it allows for an aria-like extension of the Second Subject in its second and third appearance. Secondly, it introduces a new lyrical tune belonging solely to the piano. The same idea lies behind the treatment of the Second Subject in 271 where the piano is given an enhanced role to compensate for the lack of a piano second subject. Mozart did not, however, develop such possibilities after Salzburg. As we have seen, the second subject equation was to face him with problems of compression which ruled out leisurely extensions of this kind.

To return to the First Concerto, after the second group there are four bars of concertante treatment of the earlier Bridge material followed by a remote version of the Second Cadential. The piano sticks to the diminished seventh with four heavy beats (bar 90) and runs out to the trill in bar 94. Although constructed from apparently random material, this short passage does achieve the effect of a true piano climax.

The Fantasy starts as if it were to be a considerable affair, but after two cycles based on the First Subject it loses its impetus and ends with a half-close. No cadenza is marked, and there is no sign of a Return. In terms of harmonic progression and of form, it corresponds to the simpler Fantasies of Christian Bach.

The sequence of events in the Reprise follows the pattern of the First Concerto, but this treatment gives the first signals of Mozart's deft craftsmanship in switching, adapting and cutting given material to make the whole section hold together and to spice it with novelty and surprise. The Reprise treatment of the First and Second subjects has already been mentioned: in addition there is an adroit adjustment of the piano bridge to meet the need to deliver the piano second subject in the tonic instead of the dominant, and, happiest touch of all, at the end of the climax, the four heavy beats on the sub-dominant chord do not resolve but return a second time to extend the dramatic moment of the piano's exit (bar 209).

The cadenza platform is made up from the Bridge, and the final ritornello from the First Subject followed by all three Cadentials. But here again the Second Cadential, although initially restored to its original form, takes its cue from the piano and delays the movement's end by failing to resolve its caesura on the diminished seventh at the first attempt.

Seen in perspective this concerto is of particular interest because it shows Mozart at the beginning of his career as an original composer writing a work which adopts the form and many of the habits of Christian Bach, but whose texture and subject-matter often sound more like the work of the North Germans. He never visited Potsdam or Berlin, and so far as we know he escaped the direct influence of King Frederick's composers. Some of their work, however, was likely to be available to him in print, and he must have heard a great deal about them through his many encounters with musicians who knew them personally and admired their work. It is likely that Leopold held them in high esteem, and Wolfgang was not yet by any means emancipated from his influence. It is unlikely that Christian Bach's second (Opus 7) set of concertos had been published in which he developed the piano climax and initiated the idea of a more dramatic return from the Fantasy to the Reprise. Mozart may well have seen some of them in manuscript, however, during his London visit. Taken all in all, therefore, this movement would seem to be a young man's attempt to assume the grand manner of the North Germans within the more modern structure used by Christian Bach. In the event, however, it was his native ingenuity and high spirits that were to carry the work into popular favour, where it has every right to remain.

The second movement, a slow andante, has some pleasant moments, and the final allegro with its lip-service to counterpoint and its fiery little piano tunes is the most interesting and, to a present-day audience, probably the most enjoyable of all. Mozart, however, apparently did not consider it suitable for the Viennese audience of 1772, for he withdrew it and substituted the insipid little rondo 382 in its place. It went well. Mozart probably performed this concerto in public more often than any other; it was one of the six concertos published during his lifetime (the others were 413, 414, 415, 453, 595, and also the rondo mentioned above, 382).

During the years 1773 to 1777 Mozart spent more time at Salzburg than he had done during any equivalent period since the first four years of his infancy. There was one trip to Munich in the winter of 1774/5 to mount the opera buffa *La Finta Giardiniera,* but with this exception he was confined to the musical circle of Archbishop Colloredo's court.

From his eighteenth to his twenty-second year Mozart, fresh from his experience in the finest musical centres in the world, felt increasingly frustrated by provincial life. It would be wrong, however, to think that the resources of the court were small or that his employer was an indifferent patron of the art. Charles Burney, that observant eighteenth-century Londoner, writes in his *Present State of Music in Germany* (published in 1773):

> ... the Archbishop and sovereign of Salzburg is very magnificent in his support of music, having usually near a hundred performers, vocal and instrumentalists in his service. The Prince is himself a dilettante and a good performer on the violin; he has lately been at great pains to reform his band which has been accused of being more remarkable for coarseness and noise than delicacy and high-finishing.

The Abbot of St Peter's in Salzburg, Beda Seeauer, writes in his diary on 24 April 1775, perhaps with more than a touch of sycophancy:

> ... In the evening, at the party, the Prince himself condescended to fiddle *violino* 2 *do* and many of the high nobility *utriusque sexus*, with the gracious Lord himself *in capite*, as happens almost every day, proved their skill in the art of music.

The leading figures amongst the Archbishop's one hundred at this time were Domenico Fischietti, second Kapellmeister (engaged because the first, Giuseppe Lolli was old and incapable), Leopold himself as Vice Kapellmeister, Michael Haydn (Joseph's brother) as Konzertmeister, and Anton Adlgasser as court organist. It is interesting that Colloredo should have preferred Italians for the top posts, and although little is known about either of them (save that Fischietti composed a large number of *opera buffa*), they must have had their influence on the style and taste of the court's musical life. Leopold was a man with a considerable reputation, as the author of a standard work on violin instruction, as the father of a prodigy, and as a composer, although his employer and colleagues may have found his work as pedestrian as we do today. He was, however, a notable diplomat and skilled in the intrigue and power politics of court musical life, a hard man to discredit or dislodge. Michael Haydn was considered 'learned' and efficient but evidently he lacked the personality and talent of his elder brother. Adlgasser is described as 'very learned' and to the Mozarts his name was synonymous with the old style of composition.

All of these men wrote and performed music daily, organised

church services, open-air concerts, informal musical evenings, and occasionally greater events. Mozart's own assignment was that of assistant Konzertmeister to Michael Haydn. He would compose or conduct to order but clearly had the free licence due to a young man with a world-wide reputation. Although the stimulus to write for a provincial court must have been less than the prospect of an opera for Milan, he had ample opportunity to compose, and technically he made progress. Evidently he was pleased with a motet (222) which he wrote for the Cathedral and sent to his friend and master Padre Martini, who replied:

> ... I can tell you with all sincerity that I was singularly pleased with it, finding in it all that is required by Modern Music: good harmony, mature modulation, a moderate pace in the violins, a natural connection of the parts and good taste ... you have made great strides in composition ...

We can see from the diaries and letters of the time that Mozart's incidental music for the 'heroic drama' (*Thamos*), his serenades and the musical play *Il Rè Pastore* all won acclaim in Salzburg. For the rest he wrote divertimenti, symphonies, masses, a bassoon concerto, violin concertos and in the year 1776 when he was twenty years of age, the three piano concertos, 238, 242 and 246. We know nothing of the occasions for which 238 was composed: we do, however, know that 242 was written for Countess Lodron, wife of a court dignitary, whose salon was a centre of Salzburg's musical life. It is written for three pianos, two of the parts being moderately easy and one quite elementary. Perhaps Countess Lodron had two daughters. 246 was written for Colloredo's niece, Antoine, Countess Lutzow, probably one of Leopold's pupils. She and her brother were members of the musical and artistic Czernin family whose home also seems to have provided another of the musical and social centres of Salzburg.

238 *in B flat*

The first concerto 175, for all its lively characteristics, could have been written by a stranger; the second, this cheerful little work in

B flat, could only have been written by Mozart himself. It is the founder of the Melodic line, and it is the prototype for the later and more elaborate works. The scale is small and the structure precise. The first subject is truly melodic, a first phrase answered by a second which is repeated with a new ending, twelve bars in all. The short Bridge (bar 12) has an individuality of its own and the Second Subject the authentic pleading voice and hesitant step that were to mark the character of the Second Subjects in the melodic family. Only the later Cadentials revert to the conventional type.

The piano sings out the melody at the opening of the First Concerto and prettily decorates the two answering strains of the First Subject. A short side-ritornello made up from the Third Cadential seals off the 'given' material and then the piano moves out in a new melodic line.

This is the most original moment in the movement. There is no reference to the old Bridge nor does the piano indulge in the busy scale passages usually associated with the piano bridge of the day whether in a sonata or a concerto. Instead, the bridge itself is more lyrical and memorable (the kind of passage that many pianists would select for a cadenza) than the piano second subject, two perfunctory pairs of phrases, four bars in all. It is followed by sequences which move forward elegantly to a trill on the double dominant.

The orchestra starts the Second Subject, and after two bars the piano starts it again, thus slightly extending the length of the second group. Then the orchestra and piano each give a version of the First Cadential, the piano running on into its diminutive climax (eleven bars) and the section ends with a ritornello made up from Bridge material and the later Cadentials.

The middle section, too, is a fair harbinger of Melodic Fantasies to come. It is quite unrelated to any subject-matter in the rest of the work and flows easily along in the style of a solo piano fantasia with mild modulations and an occasional bar or two of tutti. There is, however, a definite, though miniature, Return (bar 125). The Reprise is an exact repetition of the First Concerto with only the smallest changes—a different distribution of the First Subject between piano and orchestra, an extra two bars in the climax and a Cadenza platform built on the Third Cadential. The Bridge and the other Cadentials follow the Cadenza.

This bright and amiable little movement is the strongest in the work; in the second movement the occasional felicities scarcely balance the tedium of slender thoughts slowly expressed, and the rondo finale, although brisk enough, is neither so inventive nor so well sustained as the first movement.

242 *in F major (for three pianos)*

Unlike the boisterous 175 this concerto, and its fellow 246, are chamber works, and they provide the closest link with the concertos of Christian Bach. They are scored for a string quartet with optional parts for oboes and horns, and in their pleasant and unambitious desire to please they reflect the manners of his second set (Opus 7). The comparison with Opus 7 No. 2 given in Table 9 (Chapter 2, p.51) shows that both composers were using virtually the same form. (Several points concerning these two concertos, such as the treatment of the Bridge material in 242, have, of course, already been discussed in the earlier chapter.)

242 opens with a typical if rather stiff Galant call followed by a soft legato answer, the whole repeated. Then a busy Bridge, a formal Second Subject of serenade type with a more lyrical last strain, a First Cadential, a sharp Caesura in the Second, and a conventional close to the Statement.

The three pianos open the First Concerto in unison with the call, decorate the answer and continue with the bridge material, which leads straight into their own second subject (bar 74). Here they play in turn a florid figure more like the early piano bridge material of 175 and 238 than their piano second subjects. After some appropriate sequences and a short tutti reference to the Bridge, they take over the Second Subject, repeating the last lyrical phrase. Then a piano version of the First and Second Cadentials and a short piano climax, followed by a New Tutti and the Third Cadential.

The Fantasy is again an entirely free piano piece in which the orchestra has little to do. It has a well-developed return, for the first time, with two changes in rhythm.

In the Reprise, there are few changes; the First Subject is given more ornament, the piano's second subject is played twice, the piano climax has one bar less and the following ritornello is botched together from the opening call and two bars of the Bridge leading straight to the usual platform on the 6/4 chord, perhaps the clumsiest ritornello in the concertos, and probably a device to avoid too much use of the Cadentials. The final ritornello uses the New Tutti with its Cadential tail (described in Chapter 2, p. 47).

The pianos work together as a team, for they constantly seem to be handing over the baton of the main melodic line to each other. There is little give and take in duet or trio, they form instead as it were one instrument with six hands, two of them less assiduous than the other four. There will be more to say about Mozart's method of writing for concerted pianos when we come to look at 365—the point here is that this concerto could almost as well have been written for one.

This little movement, although it lacks the vigour of 175 and the charm of 238, nevertheless has many felicities. The second movement is much more successful, if a trifle over-long. The whole work suffers, however, from a languid Minuet finale which fails to hold the interest.

246 *in C*

Again, except for two truly Mozartean moments, the whole of this movement could have been written by Christian Bach. The First Subject is neither a true Galant call nor a melody, it harks back to something older, not perhaps so archaic as the opening of 175, but its square shape and its rubbing bass make it sound old-fashioned. The solid opening phrase has an answer, which is repeated and leads to a conventional opening of the Bridge. The Bridge ends with the first truly Mozartean phrase (bar 17). The

Second or Relief Subject is a weak thing, and the Cadentials are unremarkable except that one of them (the Second) has an unusual conspiratorial air about it.

The First Concerto runs on the same course as that of 242, the piano and orchestra sharing the bridge. The second moment of delight arrives with the piano second subject, which at the start sounds as if it would sing out like an aria, but which is followed, alas, by sequences which are more reminiscent of the schoolroom than the theatre. Again the Bridge material (this time the Mozartean second strain alone) is called back to introduce the Second Subject which is enhanced by a concerted treatment between the piano and orchestra and capped by a long new liquid strain from the piano (cf. 175). The short piano climax is kept alive by a vigorous extension (bar 87). Since no cadentials have been used so far, the closing ritornello is made up of the First Cadential, but with a strange new Cadential attached.

This new morsel (a filo relative of the Second Cadential) is seized by the piano as the opening subject for the fantasy, which again is free, and more lyrical than its predecessors. It goes at a gallop until it is brought to a halt by the same new phrase (bar 118), whence it runs again up to a six-bar Return on a busy dominant pedal.

The Reprise is virtually unchanged and unremarkable save for one thing. The eagerly awaited entry of the piano second subject disappoints because it is in too low a register (starting on the E above middle C instead of the B: one-fifth lower). It attempts to improve matters by making its repeat entry an octave higher. This, however, sets it too high and the original mezzo-soprano effect is lost. The cadenza ritornello and the final tutti are made up from two Cadentials. Both this concerto and 175 have two rudimentary cadenzas.

The second movement of the concerto is not so attractive as that of 242 and the final Minuet is again repetitious.

There are two general points that apply to all three concertos of 1776, and they relate to Christian Bach. The first is that Mozart was breaking with Christian's tradition of playing the Cadentials within the piano section of the First Concerto. In 246 he kept them entirely within the ritornellos, and their number of mentions dropped accordingly. From now on he was to shuffle the pack of ritornello material with increasing dexterity, and evidently only when he so organised the movement that the closing ritornellos began with the First Subject and Bridge material did he feel free to revert to the older tradition of playing cadential material within the piano section.

The second point is the interesting question of whether Mozart or Christian Bach was the first to exploit the Return and the fully developed piano climax into the concerto form. Christian's Opus 1 set published in 1763 had neither. The third set, Opus 13, was probably published in 1777 and had both. The date of the publication of the second set (Opus 7) is set as late as 1780. They have two full piano climaxes and a premonition of the Return. On balance, the evidence favours Christian. Date of publication may have no relation to the date of composition; his first set, for instance, was published within a year of his arrival in London and may well have been written in Italy. Furthermore, a concerto of his pupil, Schroeter, was published in 1772 and this has both a distinct Return and a full climax for the piano.

Before dismissing the two Galant concertos of 1776 as two of the weaker brethren amongst the twenty-three, it is salutory to compare them with the six violin concertos, five written in 1775 and one in 1777. If Mozart had been a virtuoso on the violin instead of the piano, and if he had given up the composition of piano concertos in 1776 and gone on in his most productive years to write a further nineteen violin concertos, then there is little doubt that these four little piano concertos would today be in the repertory of every concert pianist and would hold as high a place in the concert hall and the record catalogues as do the six violin concertos. For it could be claimed that these four almost wholly neglected piano concertos are in no way inferior to the companion and contemporary works for the violin.

Two Experiments

271 in E flat and 365 in E flat

Mozart's next two concertos were to be experiments in different forms on a grander scale. 271 was to favour the Sonata style, 365 the Concertante. They are both of the élite, not only amongst the concertos but in any estimation of the complete catalogue of Mozart's work. 271 was again a leader amongst his contemporary compositions, for it outshines any other work of 1776 and 1777 in ingenuity, in brilliance and in the courageous size of its endeavour. Both concertos raise the same problem, namely how to reconcile an original and more pianistic First Concerto with the traditional type of Statement. For all their individual success, they failed to give Mozart a permanent and satisfactory solution. They were, however, a reconnaissance in force that left the safe little base camp of Christian Bach's concerto form far behind and made a bold excursion into *terra incognita*.

We do not know what happened late in 1776 to stimulate Mozart to write his first great concerto. Perhaps the desire came from within, or perhaps it was the visit of the French pianist, Mlle Jeunehomme, that gave him an opportunity to show Salzburg that he was a composer capable of writing for the world of music that lay beyond Countess Lodron and Countess Lutzow. In the same month, on 29 January 1777, he was twenty-one years old.

271 in E flat

Let us begin by looking closely at the First Subject. So far, concertos in the Galant tradition had opened with a loud call, followed by a soft answer. The whole first subject could read—Call: Answer: Call: Answer (e.g. 242); or Call: Answer: Answer (246); the whole sequence running perhaps twelve bars. Here Mozart opens with an epigram. The first half is loud call:

Example 27

bar 1

This is complemented by a loud reply (played furthermore by the piano, a point to which we will return later):

Example 28

bar 2

The call and reply are then repeated, the whole thing taking only seven bars. The complete epigram can be called F1, and is so short and sharp that, although complete in itself, it can be followed quite naturally by the true Galant type of soft legato answer (F2), itself a filo relative of the second half of the epigram.

Example 29

bar 7

This merges (a new departure) into the opening of the Bridge, whose main feature is a strong staccato figure in the lower strings, a unit longer and more purposeful than has been used before (bar 14). The main characteristic of the Bridge is a strong sense of movement, from the First Subject to the Second. This makes it less susceptible than previous bridges to Mozart's usual practice of chopping and slicing Bridge material for insertion into the static ritornellos at the end of the two concerto sections.

After the bridge comes a little operatic introduction (again for the first time); a slight hesitation on the dominant by the oboes in thirds (bar 22), resolved by a run down the scale back to tonic and the Second Subject.

This is the longest and most sonata-like Second Subject in all the concertos. It is a strong sweet melody in two strains, the second running straight to the First Cadential, a noisy symphonic piece. After a Caesura comes a filo relative of the Second Subject (bar 46), a sad little *envoi* (C2), almost a Mannheim sigh, and another *locus classicus*. Then comes a more conventional Third Cadential (bar 56), and finally a staccato little closing cadence over which the piano enters with a trill (C4).

So that we may understand Mozart's intentions, let us pause here and look forward and back. Evidently he had three complementary ideas in mind. First, to use the epigram as a micro-Main Theme to bind the work together. Secondly, from this intention came the plan to use the epigram as the subject-matter for the piano bridges in the two concerto sections and for development in the Fantasy. Thirdly, he decided to design the movement with only one Second Subject. Two of these ideas were in the symphonic or sonata tradition.

It was becoming common in Sonata Form to take a fragment of the First Subject and to use it in a transition to throw the bridge across to the dominant key and the entry of the Second Subject. Haydn, in particular, was fond of this device. Similarly, of course, a single second group instead of two separate second subjects, one in the Statement, and one in the First Concerto, would bring the concerto nearer to Sonata form, though it is doubtful whether this decision was motivated by thoughts of Sonata Form or by a more practical consideration. The hard fact of the second subject equation (described in Chapter 3, page 75 onwards, and in Table 17) must have faced Mozart for the first time, and if he were to give more preponderance to the First Subject and its development, something had to go. Perhaps he decided it should be the piano second subject; at any rate, for whatever reason, it was jettisoned.

Returning to the First Concerto, perhaps to counteract the missing piano second subject, he gives the piano a limpid and affecting little introduction (again, for the first time). This establishes the piano as a character in its own right, and in a gentle mood, which is to contrast with its character as an earnest worker in the passages just ahead. Next comes the epigram, shared between the piano and the orchestra as before. The piano immediately develops the call, and then runs into a free bridge; gives the operatic introduction (bar 83), and plays the Second Subject, the second strain being repeated by the oboes (bar 104) with a delicious piano and violin accompaniment (another new departure, this time in scoring). The piano takes up the end, and after a pair of caesuras (bars 109 and 110) supplies yet another lyrical strain to round off the Second Group.

Next there are more caesuras, a great deal of stopping and starting, a short piano climax, and the closing tutti. This is made up from the first three Cadentials, and the piano again strays into orchestral territory by giving its own version of the 'Mannheim sigh' Cadential. The First Concerto has taken on more of the shape of a Sonata Form Exposition with a second group in the dominant which is all of a piece, and no shorter (30 bars) than the combined piano second and Second Subject of previous concertos.

So far, however, there has been no second mention of F2 nor of the Bridge. The First Concerto appears to have ended (bar 148). But now f2 follows the closing ritornello, played by the piano. It has no business to be there, but it makes its appearance quite naturally and with quiet assurance. At the sixth bar it is diverted from its original shape into a neat closed cadence. Then follows F1 unaltered but in the dominant key, and the piano moves off into a dashing development of the call. This is the middle section, for the first time a Development in place of a Fantasy.

Again in this most experimental of all concertos, it is worth pausing to see how this bizarre sequence of events has struck other critics. There is one attractive theory which is hazardous but interesting. Let us first review the sequence of events:

FIRST CONCERTO	DEVELOPMENT
... px C1 C2 C3	f(2) Closed Cadence. Ff1 f1 developed...

The idea is advanced that Mozart, relying on the shortness of Fantasies of the day, dropped in the tiny variant of F2 and then, as a bluff, returned to F1 as if it were the start of the Reprise. (The Haydnesque joke of a 'false recapitulation'.) The idea is intriguing because the bluff can be pushed further, for the development of F1 begins almost on the same line as the piano bridge in the First Concerto.

It is more likely, however, that Mozart felt compelled to find a place for a second mention of F2 and found the best he could. The incident has an effrontery that matches the pert demeanour of the opening epigram and indeed of the whole work.

The Development is a spirited affair, running in a direct line for fifteen bars, where it slackens off. There is an indication of a Return (bar 180). The Return leads, however, not to the First Subject but to the Bridge, followed by the operatic introduction and yet another Return back to the beginning of the Reprise. This way of finding a place for the second mention of the Bridge is ingenious, for, because of its transitional nature, the only alternative to using it in the customary places is to give it this role as a Bridge/Return from the middle section.

The Reprise starts again with the epigram, the piano and orchestra exchanging parts. This seems an almost gratuitous piece of impudence, for here the orchestra has always had the right at least to begin the Reprise with the First Subject. The piano's transition/bridge this time uses the answer for subject-matter in a completely fresh passage. The second group passes off as before, with the horn joining the piano in the first strain (bar 216); after the Second Subject comes the stopping and starting before the piano climax, just as in the First Concerto. Suddenly, however, F2 appears again (bar 251), first in the orchestra and then taken over by the piano and whirled into the closing section of the piano climax. The ritornello is made up of the First and Second Cadentials, a final appearance of the epigram, piano and all, and a cadenza platform built on the call. In Mozart's own Cadenza he uses the Second Subject and cunningly builds in the missing third mention of the Bridge, and the movement ends with the Third Cadential, followed by the Fourth (the staccato figure) still acting as a hinge to bring in the piano's trill and final appearance in a coda (again the first) of six bars, a cascade of arpeggios dropping from the orchestra's final chords.

The movement is a great success. It does not have quite the swagger of 175 but it is humorous, charming, and at the same time it has strength, particularly in the Development. There are a number of felicities: the staccato Cadential which begins life as a hinge between the Statement and the piano introduction and ends as a link for the last cadential cascades of piano arpeggios; the elegant violin accompaniment to the Second Subject; the oboes' fragile repeat of the second strain with the piano now filling in; the unexpected piece of leadership from the horn. The weakest links are the two piano climaxes, which seem to stumble and halt at the start and fail to finish well. Many of the techniques Mozart introduced in 271 were to pass into his repertory of composition and to be used again and again.

The introduction of the piano at the beginning of the Statement and elsewhere within the orchestral reserves is not structurally important, but it adds piquancy to the work's already impudent character. In opera Mozart always composed carefully for his cast, and he may have suited the general posture of this concerto to the personality of Mlle Jeunehomme. She was, after all, a visiting celebrity and must have caused some small stir at the Salzburg court. If there is anything in this fancy, the reflection of her personality left by this work would indicate a pretty young woman; dashing, witty, and with a good sense of theatre.

The second movement of the concerto is again revolutionary, a long and sombre Andantino in C minor; the third movement, perhaps the most novel of the three, a fast-moving rondo of the kind that Beethoven favoured, with a Minuet section embedded in the centre. For the first time, the three movements form a trinity, and the complete work is on a majestic scale, being more than double the length of the Galant concertos.

This concerto has internal evidence to show that it was the first to be written for the forte-piano rather than the harpsichord. The cantabile second subject would not sustain on the older instrument, and in particular bars 96 to 100 demand a singing tone for the melody, in the right hand, which is virtually unaccompanied. Broder in his informative article 'Mozart and the "clavier" ' (*Musical Quarterly*, 1941) does not agree, putting 413 as the first 'piano' concerto. There is no doubt that 365, the next concerto after 271, was written for two harpsichords, perhaps because of the difficulty of finding a matched pair of forte-pianos in Salzburg. But we know from Schubert's *Deutsche Chronik* for 1775 that 'last winter' he had heard Mozart perform on the forte-piano. This, of course, was two winters before that in which 271 was composed. More convincing than this, however, is the evidence of the 'piano' part itself. Anyone who sits down and tries out the passage mentioned above on a harpsichord will form his own conclusions.

In the autumn of 1777 Mozart and his mother made the tour to Munich, Augsburg, Mannheim and Paris. Four events amongst many may have had some special relevance to the piano concertos.

The first was Mozart's introduction to Stein's pianofortes. His long excited letter to Leopold, written on 18 October 1777, is full of an artist's appreciation of a new opportunity. There is no doubt that the improvements in the instrument made during his lifetime gave the piano an aura of novelty—it was the new and progressive instrument, and any technical development would naturally attract the interest of a young and ambitious composer who was also in the top flight as a performer.

Secondly, he heard the Mannheim orchestra, probably the finest ensemble in Europe, for the first time. He writes to his father on 4 November:

> The orchestra is excellent and very strong. On either side there are ten or eleven violins, four violas, two oboes, two flutes and two clarinets, two horns, four violoncellos, four bassoons and four double basses, also trumpets and drums.

If this (say about forty players) was 'very strong', one wonders what was his basis of comparison, that is what numbers would make up a 'strong' orchestra and an 'average' orchestra, i.e. the one at Salzburg. Perhaps between twenty and thirty. (In Adam Carse's book *The Orchestra in the XVIIIth Century*, the Salzburg orchestra is quoted at a strength of twenty-six in the year 1757.)

Mozart would have heard the remarkable precision and dynamic range of this orchestra; have heard, too, clarinets, and the compositions of the Stamitz family and the composers of the Mannheim school, from whom he was to borrow freely, with his usual discrimination. Some direct legacies from this visit were his subsequent use of the Mannheim Full Close at the end of a Bridge passage, of the Mannheim Crescendo, the Mannheim Rocket, and, perhaps more indirectly, his awakening interest in the clarinet.

The third event was his meeting with Christian Bach in Paris in August 1778. His pleasure is warmly expressed in his letter to Leopold of 27 August. It is likely that they discussed, amongst other things, their work as composers and performers of piano concertos, and, if they met around an instrument, perhaps with musical illustration.

The fourth was Mozart's activity in writing music for wind solo and ensemble which arose from the chance of falling in with three players from the Mannheim orchestra, Wendling the flautist, Ramm the oboeist, and Punto who played the horn. The wind Symphonie Concertante (Anh 9) was written for these three and an unknown bassoonist (Ritter). Although it was never given any performance in Paris that year, the act of composition may, as we shall see, have a bearing on the form of 365.

It is unlikely, however, that any of these happenings affected Mozart so much as the deepening of his emotional maturity caused by his mother's death, his first serious humiliation in love, and the liberty of travelling the world for the first time without Leopold's managerial presence. Soon after his return to Salzburg in the middle of January 1799 he wrote that dark-hued and beautiful work, the Sinfonia Concertante for violin and viola (364), and a few months later the concerto for two pianos (365), for performance by Nannerl and himself.

365 *in E flat major for two pianos*

Before looking in detail at this concerto it is interesting to compare the three concertante works—for wind quartet (Anh 9), for violin and viola (364), and this one for two pianos (365)—all of which he composed within a period of eighteen months. There is no doubt that in 365 he was making his second large-scale experiment in the form of the piano concerto, and that the experiment leaned towards a concertante treatment of the two pianos.

The Wind Concertante is a mild leisurely work padded out to give every member of the quartet a chance to show his paces and perhaps to meet the instructions of Le Gros, the organiser of the *Concerts Spirituels*, who may have wanted a work to suit 'the long taste'. It has the usual four main sections and curious false start after the Statement, a beginning which peters out after 31 bars and which is followed immediately by the First Concerto proper. This may have been written by Mozart to fill time, but it is more likely to be the mistake of a copyist or arranger, for Le Gros lost the score and it did not turn up until many years later. When it was rediscovered the original flute and oboe parts had been rearranged for oboe and clarinet.

The Sinfonia Concertante for violin and viola needs no detailed description to show the contrast. The Statement is spacious but of regular construction. From the last Cadential the two solo strings spin out an introductory figure, and the concertante section opens with a new First Subject followed by a succession of violin tunes. This section does not refer to anything that has been heard in the Statement. Even a side ritornello and the closing tutti are new.

The Fantasy opens with a reference to the Second Cadential, but again the two soloists provide their own material right through to the start of the Reprise. This last is a little more compromising. The Statement's First Subject, at half its original length, is interrupted by the solo string introduction, followed by the same stream of solo melody. After the solo second subject, however, the orchestra's Second Subject returns and the movement ends with the two New Tuttis and two of the original Cadentials. Table 23 shows the difference in the construction of the two concertante works and it also shows that Mozart's starting point in the design of 365 lay approximately half-way between the two.

The relevant point is that Mozart had an additional decision to make when writing a concerto for more than a single instrument. Some part of the duetting between the orchestra and the solo could be transformed into sections of duetting between the soloists. The question was, how much? If virtually the whole of the concerto sections were given up to interplay between the soloists, then the relationship between the orchestra and the soloists would be lost, and the work would become an accompanied duet rather than a 'concerto'. If the soloists had no more to do than in a concerto for a single instrument, then there was little point in having a second piano at all. Let us see how Mozart dealt with this matter.

The First Subject is the purest Galant call and answer. The answer links into the first part of the Bridge; the second part of the Bridge starts softly and builds up to a half close on the dominant (as it does in the Wind Concertante). There is no true

Table 23

The Wind Concertante, the Sinfonia Concertante and 365 compared

The following comparison shows the difference between the use of given material in the three concertante works. Neither the Fantasies nor the false start in the Wind Concertante are shown: nor is there a distinction between 'given' material repeated or 'given' material developed – the purpose being simply to show how much subject matter each section has in common.

STATEMENT

Wind Concertante	F1 F2 F3 B1 B2 B/S S C1 C2 C3
365	F1 F2 B1 B2 S C1 C2
Sinfonia Concertante	F1 F2 B B/S S C1 C2 C3

FIRST CONCERTO

Wind Concertante	f1 f2 f3 new B/S S new F2 F3 B1 C1 C2 C3
365	f1 f2 c2 C2 new C1
Sinfonia Concertante	new

REPRISE

Wind Concertante	Ff1 Ff2 Ff3 new B/S S new C1	CADENZA	C2 C3
365	Ff1 f2 new Ff2 new(B2)		C1. C2
Sinfonia Concertante	F1 new S new		C2 C3

The amount of significant material 'given' in the Statement and *not* used in the First Concerto is as follows:

Wind Concertante		None omitted
365	B1 B2 S	C2 Omitted
Sinfonia Concertante		All omitted

and in the whole work after the Statement:

Wind Concertante		None
365	B1(B2)	
Sinfonia Concertante		F2 B B/S C1

Second Subject; in its place there is an unusual figure in the lower strings which has a strong filo connection with F2 and has the characteristics of a Relief subject (bar 30). A not dissimilar passage in the Wind Concertante leads to a full Second Subject, but this one, after three repeats, within a crescendo of the Mannheim type, leads straight into the First Cadential (bar 42). The Second Cadential, a filo relative of the Bridge, ends the statement.

The two pianos make a mighty opening with the call and then decorate and play with the answer in a leisurely dialogue. This section is sealed off with a side-ritornello (the Second Cadential, the pianos playing the first two bars and the orchestra finishing it off). Now the pianos have an uninterrupted run until the closing trill of the climax.

In the First Concerto the usual terms (piano bridge, episode, piano second subject, etc.) carry different meanings, for, as in the Sinfonia Concertante, there is a stream of melody from the two pianos with sequences and connecting passages between. The usual landmarks are there—a move to the dominant, a piano second subject, a set of consequences, a piano climax—but all except one bar of tutti are played by the two pianos and all are composed of new material.

The first concertante bridging tune/episode (bar 84) is similar to the most memorable of the string subjects in the last movement of the Sinfonia Concertante. It has wide leaps, is unlike any other piano subject in the concertos, and sounds almost like a string tune transposed for the keyboard. A second little subject (ps 1) (which also has a counterpart in the Sinfonia Concertante) is reached in bar 96. It is in the dominant and followed by the true piano second subject (ps 2, bar 104), 16 bars long and within which the lead is taken in turn by the soloists. A few bars of free consequences lead to the piano climax (bar 120) which is prodigious, matching the string climaxes of the Sinfonia Concertante in its power and virtuosity. The short closing ritornello is supplied by the First Cadential.

The Fantasy starts with the second part of the Bridge played in a dialogue between the two pianos. At the seventh bar it moves into a fantasia in the grand manner (the pianos alternating and not playing in duet). The rhythmic pattern of the Relief-type Second Subject forms a powerful bass figure answered by configurations from the piano bridge in the treble. This material is developed until a striding octave figure (also derived from the Bridge) takes command. Then with a sequence of delicate scales (still related to what has gone before) it reaches a rousing return. But as in 271 the Return does not lead to the Reprise. Instead we have the unusual Relief-type passage (bar 192) followed by a new and somewhat abrupt return leading back to the delayed First Subject.

The Reprise follows the outline of the First Concerto. F2 is given some varied treatment in the minor (a prophetic moment). The side-ritornello (C2) has gone, and so has the first leaping piano bridge/episode. The other two (the piano second subjects) follow, but where the piano climax should start (bar 252), F2 appears once more (again as in 271). Some heavy caesuras bring the momentum to a halt, and a fresh start is made (bar 264) to bring the piano climax up to the sticking point. In the final bars the pianos give a slight reminder of F1 by tripping down the arpeggios of the Call before leaping on to the final trill. A small section of the end of the Bridge makes up the ritornello before the Cadenza, which is a short final duet/display starting with the First Subject's call and then using material mainly from the central section of the Fantasy. The two Cadentials make up the final tutti.

In this compromise between a piano duet with orchestral backing and a piano concerto there are both gains and losses. The pianos are given a holiday from some of the restrictions of concerto form, and it is in one sense true to say that the piano climax in the First Concerto starts at the piano passage after the sealing-off ritornello (bar 84) and has an uninterrupted run for some 70 bars up to the final tutti. The piano tunes, the first with the big leaps (piano bridge/episode), the second little one with its swinging thirds (ps 1), and the last with its strong shape (ps 2) all keep the momentum going with never a pause for any slow, lyrical or static second group material. The result is a powerful accumulation of nervous energy which is released in the blazing pianistic display of the climax. The style of the work suited Mozart's performer's temperament, for we know that it was one of his favourite pieces in the concert hall. It is full of opportunities for the two players, as, for instance, when F2 is dropped into the piano climax in the Reprise after the big second subject tune (exactly as in 271) thus giving the performers a chance to exploit a high dramatic contrast. Although it may improve the moment, however, this pause in the race does perhaps do something to destroy the dashing *perpetuum mobile* of the first time out.

There are other penalties. Most of the Bridge, an attractive passage with plenty of potential use ahead of it, disappears after its first and only appearance. There is no room in the Reprise for the first piano tune (pb/episode), which is also worthy of more than a single outing. There is something unhappy about the Relief-type subject. On first hearing it seems designed for some development or ingenious transformation later in the work. But when it returns after the Fantasy, it does not construe as well as the similar passages in 271, where the Bridge and the operatic introduction were thrown in. This was successful because both were anticipatory. This Relief passage is the opposite; both static and repetitious.

The great and successful predominance of the pianos in this work is gained, of course, at the expense of the relationship between the pianos and the orchestra. Outside of the Statement the ritornellos are compressed into a total of less than forty-five bars in all—the lowest figure in any concerto. Nor do the pianos show any marked affection for the orchestral material except F2, and there is none of the happy instrumentation of 271, nor are the pianos ever invited inside the orchestra as accompanists.

Although Mozart the performer favoured this work, Mozart the composer evidently did not, for he never wrote a concertante work again for two pianos and orchestra. This style was reserved instead for the two-piano sonatas.

Today the work has a further deficiency for which Mozart

cannot wholly be blamed. In that dark and elegiac work, the Symphonie Concertante, the two soloists speak with different voices. Thus when one entry follows another, the effect is unmistakably that of a duet. Pianists say there is great pleasure in the duet work in 365 but they have the advantage of knowing when they are playing and when they are not. This knowledge is denied to the gramophone or radio listener, and the duet writing is of such a kind that, without a score, it is impossible to know which piano is playing. In the concert hall, with the slight separation of sound and the visual aid of the performers at work, the concerto is noticeably more effective; but even so one suspects that it is the performers who have the best of it.

Before leaving this concerto, the big piano tune (ps 2) deserves notice. This tune is far removed from the florid four-bar little piano subjects of Christian Bach and of 175, 238, 242 and 246. Although it has grace, it is not lyrical, and although it is a firm melody, it is not static. It has a lot of movement, and its energy builds the momentum towards the climax rather than allowing it to slacken. When there was no second subject in the Statement, Mozart was to use tunes of this type again (415, 467), and once (453) he used a near relative of this tune to counterbalance a slow and true second subject which, without a fillip in the earlier part of the second group, might have brought the momentum of the movement to a standstill.

There are one or two general points to be drawn from a valedictory review of these two great experiments, the last of the Salzburg line. First, in 271 and to a lesser extent in 365, Mozart formed a vocabulary or repertoire of quite personal concerto techniques which he was to draw upon over and over again. The concentration needed for pioneer work of this kind must have been very great and it would be reasonable to think that not until he became deeply involved in the Symphonic form did he expend so much sheer effort in the composition of a concerto. Perhaps the first challenge to equal that of 271 was the composition of the D minor (466) five years and twelve concertos later.

At the same time he probably learnt as much from his failures as from his successes. The central problem of concerto form was now staring him in the face. A traditional Statement contained a certain amount of given material. If he were to write a fresh and original kind of First Concerto giving full scope to the piano and with plenty of freedom for new invention, then he would lose touch with the 'given' material, lose symmetry in the balance of 'mentions', and, above all, destroy the unity of the movement. It is a problem not uncommon amongst playwrights who write one play in the first act, another in the second and only then contemplate the sad possibility that the two cannot easily be brought together in the third. In one sense, when writing the First Concerto Mozart was also writing (or not writing) the Reprise. A first concerto containing virtually all 'given' material can be converted easily into a universal reprise; a First Concerto which turns its back on 'given' material poses the question, when it comes to the reprise, of either/or.

Mozart begged this question in 271 by using his wonderfully adroit sense of jobbing about with the surplus material from the Statement which was left out of the First Concerto. The Bridge and the operatic introduction, it will be recalled, he dropped in at the end of the Fantasy, the one piece of Bridge left over he recalled in the Cadenza. The Answer (F2) went into the last piano climax. (This expedient, as we saw in 365, is only a qualified success.) But the Concertante nature of 365 made such a comprehensive recall impossible.

These two points (the end of the Fantasy and the start of the final climax) continued to be the most receptive areas for surplus material. It was the Bridge passages in particular that continued to pose the most brutal problem. An orchestral Bridge in the Statement—a new piano bridge in the First Concerto—which in the Reprise? One solution was to use the orchestral Bridge as ritornello elsewhere (the Melodic concertos). The final solution came only with the later Symphonic concertos, and it was achieved by the most radical change of all, the transformation of the Statement from a sequence of short subjects into a unified whole, of which the first long paragraph included a Transition partly made up from the same material as the First Subject.

The two concertos illustrate one general point about the nature of First Subjects. It is broadly true that the First Subject is an index to the character of the whole movement. The old Main Theme has in it an element of rondo (which is expressed in the word ritornello). It was the 'given' tune which supplied the sense of return to a known place between variables. It could be a recurring chorus which marked off sections of solo, and this indeed was its function in the North German concertos, which was partly retained in 175. In Christian Bach's form, however, the character of the First Subject changed slightly and became the first item of a stream of material, which on each appearance signalled that the whole cycle was starting off again. This is nearer to its role in Sonata Form, and it is the function it fulfils in 242 and 246. Now Mozart was looking for a new quality in the First Subject, namely plasticity. In 271 he started with a short subject that could be used for development throughout the work. Soon he would want to push the idea of a 'motif' much further.

Such a subject or 'motif' must have two qualities: it must be short, and it must be instantly recognisable. The long tubby openings of 175 and of 246 were too wooden, the opening of 242 too nondescript. The epigram of 271 was suitable. But here we come to a practical point that must always be in the thoughts of those people who, like Mozart, have constant experience of working with an audience. The First Subject must stop people from talking. Court audiences at Salzburg were presumably no quicker to settle down than audiences today. Rousseau, in his *Dictionary of Music*, shows that he was aware of the problem. In debating the merits of a French *grave* opening to an overture, as opposed to the Italian allegro, he gives this point to Italy: 'a big audience makes much noise, and to constrain them to silence a loud and striking opening is necessary.'

If 271 were played today at any fashionable or social gathering, the first pair of epigrams would probably be lost. Perhaps this is one reason why Mozart repeated them. But louder and longer calls simply asserting the key, as in 365, were the best insurance. Such an opening serves the same purpose as the chord which is given today in certain circumstances when a lady or a gentleman wishes to say a few words.

Such a tonic/dominant assertion does not provide good material for development. It is possible, therefore, that a 'call' opening like that of 365 was followed by a subject with a rhythmic short motif for two different practical reasons: to get the house settled, and to provide material that could be worked upon symphonically. If there is anything in this theory, we can only assume that the paying audiences in Vienna were more attentive, for many of the later concertos open quietly.

But to return to the opening of 365. Not only is the slow tonic/dominant assertion a new item for the repertory, but the F2 is even more of a *locus*. The rhythmic pattern of this phrase, an entry on the last three quavers of a bar followed by four (or two) crotchets, is a most useful formula. The same feeling is already there in 242 and 246, but the rhythm is not. In 271 it is complete, except that the three quavers have rests between them and give an even beat with the smooth crotchets of the second bar. But 365 strikes the formula that is used again in the statement of 456, and, above all, in 503, and which is first cousin of phrases used extensively in 413, 482, and 488. This is perhaps the most characteristic 'motto' in all of the concertos.

7

Early Vienna

413 in F; 414 in A; 415 in C

Between the composition of the concerto for two pianos in 1779 and of the first three Vienna concertos in January 1782 Mozart experienced the elation of presenting *Idomeneo* at the court in Munich, and of popular success in Vienna: he also went through two of the most traumatic experiences of his life—the breach with his employer Archbishop Colloredo, and the mortifying entanglement with the Weber family which lead to his marriage with Constanze.

There has been a tradition of reading the history of genius in such a manner as to justify the artist's often ignoble behaviour. Today we are much more aware that great talent often implies a waywardness, a vanity and a concentration upon selfish interests that frequently cut across the prevailing rules of social behaviour. And so it is true that Mozart, when unprotected from the world by the careful statesmanship of his father, was imprudent, untruthful and notably unsuccessful in arranging his financial and personal affairs.

In March 1781, Colloredo, piqued by Mozart's frequent absences, insisted that he return to Vienna. He expected him to continue with the routine of court service and it may be that he even had some intention of putting the young man in his place, for he was lodged with the court entourage, and not in a separate house as were some of the other leading musicians, and his fees for performance were kept down to a reasonable minimum. Nor was he given leave to freelance outside the terms of his contract. Mozart felt this regime to be an intolerable restriction upon his ability to earn money and fame in a society where he was, at the time, much in demand. This was indeed the classic situation in which a young man's talent had outrun the terms of his contract. He wrote 'How much do you suppose I could make . . . now the public has got to know me? But this Arch-Idiot of ours will not let me.' And again, 'If I were free I should give a grand concert, take four pupils, and in a year I should have got on so well that I could make at least a thousand thalers.' It is, however, quite likely that he also had qualms, for his friends had warned him of the fickleness of the Vienna public and throughout his correspondence he can often be heard to be whistling to keep both his own and his father's spirits up.

After a final confrontation on 9 May 1781 Mozart left, or was turned out from, the Archduke's household and he resorted to another, the home of the widow Weber where she lived with her three unmarried daughters. This was a name of ill-omen to Leopold who had been scared half out of his wits by Mozart's earlier romance with Aloysia Weber in 1777. He regarded the Webers as a shiftless disreputable lot and feared that the mother would entice his son into marriage with one or other of the daughters. He was right. In spite of Mozart's continued denial of the allegations of a liaison between himself and Constanze (the second daughter) and his assurances that he did not contemplate marriage and that he had been and remained entirely continent, Leopold urged him to find other lodgings. He procrastinated until the gossip and scandal became sufficient grounds for the girl's guardian and her mother to move in and blackmail him into signing a document which bound him either to marry Constanze or alternatively to pay her alimony of 300 gulden a year.

Mozart was sorely tried by these two episodes. He had to face the total displeasure of Leopold with whom he still did not wish to make a break, and in doing this he displayed some of his more unpleasing characteristics. His letters alternate between a hollow bravado to justify his 'honour' and 'true love' and whining entreaties designed to arouse his father's compassion, of which, as he should have known. there was very little to be had. He also must have suffered intensely from the ribald gossip that surrounded his affair with Constanze and have been embarrassingly aware of the pathetic and ridiculous part he was forced to play in the confrontation with her guardian and mother.

All of these worries combined to make composition difficult. During the nervous turmoil of his crisis with the Archbishop, Mozart says that he had to leave the opera in the middle of the first act and go home to lie down. A month later he begs his father to stop sending such stern letters, 'for they only irritate my mind and disturb my heart and spirit; and I, who must keep on composing, need a cheerful mind and a calm disposition.' It is no wonder that during this period (January 1781–June 1782) his output was limited. He had not yet acquired the fortitude of his later years which enabled him to withdraw from the distresses of the world into the serenity of his private life as a composer.

Chief amongst his worries was the question whether or not he could succeed as a freelance musician in Vienna. Quite apart from his vanity, which was wholly committed, there was the simple question of earning a living. In a letter to his father in January 1782 he assesses his prospects with a little more realism, and sets out the four main sources of his prospective income:

> I have three pupils now, which brings me in some eighteen ducats a month;...I really need only one more, because four pupils are quite enough. With four I should have twenty-four ducats, or 102 gulden, 24 kreuzer. With this sum a man and his wife can manage in Vienna if they live quietly and in the retired way which we desire; but, of course, if I were to fall ill, we should not make a farthing. I can write, it is true, at least one opera a year, give a concert annually and have some things engraved and published by subscription. There are other concerts too where one can make money, particularly if one has been living in a place for a long time and has a good reputation.

The music lessons were a recognised routine; he approached

the production of an opera with an excitement and a certainty of touch that never deserted him. As a performer, too, it is likely that his virtuoso temperament and sense of audience would carry him through any occasion. It was in composing for the 'carriage trade' of Viennese musical life that he evidently had of take thought and adjust his style to a taste different from that to the family and court circle in Salzburg.

The three piano concertos, 413, 414 and 415, were composed in 1782 and 1783 with the primary purpose of raising subscriptions for their publication. The history of this transaction throws some light on Mozart's business methods. By December 1782 he had written one of the set (414) and intended to offer them at a subscription of six ducats: in January subscriptions were solicited in the *Wiener Zeitung* at four ducats, which his father thought was still too dear. The printed scores were to be available at his house 'in April'. In February he wrote to Baroness Waldstadten asking for a loan and mentioning that the subscriptions were coming in very slowly. In April he wrote to the Paris publisher Sieber offering to sell him the set at thirty louis d'or, and finally they were published by Artaria nearly two years later in March 1775. How many subscriptions he raised and how many of the subscribers had the pertinacity to collect their edition, we shall never know.

Subscription publication was a common practice in Vienna at that time, and in the case of these concertos it must have carried with it certain obvious restrictions. If the editions were to sell, the piano part must be suitable either for a harpsichord or a fortepiano. The orchestral parts, too, should be such as to allow the work to be performed either in the chamber with only a string quartet in support, or in the concert hall with a larger orchestra. Thus the wind parts in the set are all 'optional', though 415 must surely have lost some of its character without its trumpets, drums and wind band.

He wrote to Leopold on 28 December 1782:

> These concertos are a happy medium between what is too easy and too difficult; they are very brilliant, pleasing to the ear and

natural without being vapid. There are passages here and there from which the connoisseurs alone can derive satisfaction; but these passages are written in such a way that the less learned cannot fail to be pleased, though without knowing why.

This group of three concertos, despite emotional and editorial difficulties surrounding their composition, form a fascinating entity. One is written in each style, Galant, Melodic and Symphonic (a point that Hutchings makes in his study of the concertos, using the first two adjectives); the first two show considerable advances in technique; and the third is a milestone in Mozart's own development and in the whole history of the concerto. In 415 he first applied the symphonic idea (as described in Chapter 4) to the concerto form. It is true that when compared with the later symphonic giants the symphonic element in 415 appears to be tentative and incomplete, but this did not prevent him from writing a successful movement in a hybrid form. In dismissing 415 as a failure Hutchings is doubly wrong; if given the right performance it is a success in its own right; but, more important, it is the first step towards Mozart's more mature methods of composition.

413 *in F major*

This concerto was mentioned in Chapter 3 as a typical example of the Galant style. Seen in perspective within the Galant family it lies between 246 written some six years before and 449 written two years later. It marks a distinct advance over the earlier work, for in 246 each subject and each section was largely independent, and the movement was held together by the impetus of the music and by one natural consequence following another. In 413 there is a new binding agent at work, a form of the filo, but a form based more on rhythm than on melody. This was to become a characteristic both of the symphonic and the later Galant concertos.

The movement is in 3/4 time (449 and 491 are the only other two such first movements) and from the start we are made aware of the triple beat. The Galant call (F1) begins with three crotchet beats and a minim, and this pattern crops up again and again:

Example 30

bar 1

the sweet answer (F2) has a variation of it:

Example 31

bar 5

and after the opening bustle of the Bridge (B1) another variant appears (B2):

Example 32

bar 16

The last two bars (22–23) of this short Bridge switch suddenly into C major, but in an off-hand manner that clearly leads to a passage *on* the dominant rather than *in* it.

In the next two bars (24–25) there is a new figure which is part neither of the Bridge nor of the Second Subject proper. It is, rather, a diminutive introduction to the Second Subject, and, as so often in Mozart, the nature of the introduction indicates with delicate assurance the nature of what is to come next.

Its rhythm is an epigrammatic elision of the pattern of the call with the last bar of the answer and emerges as:

Example 33
bar 24

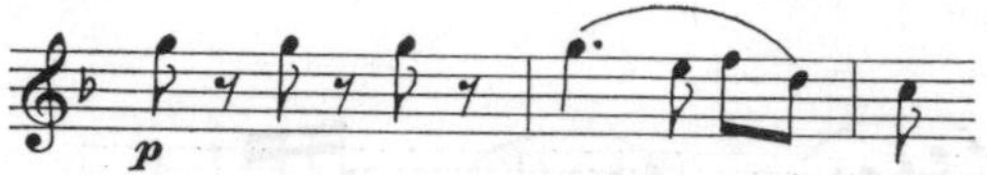

On its first appearance it seems innocent enough, but as the movement unfolds we shall see what an important part it is to play.

The Second Subject, in spite of its trill and semiquavers, is still recognisably in the rhythmic pattern of the answer:

Example 34
bar 26

After its first outing it slips back with a sense of relief into its proper key, the tonic (bar 34), and runs into the First Cadential, a thoroughly unremarkable closing flourish. The opening of the Second Cadential, however, provides something of a caesura with a new jerky rhythmic beat, only to resolve into the same little introductory passage (B/S), now transformed into the Third Cadential, extended and with each new entry echoing the one before. It appears to be conclusive until the piano enters over the last bars and uses the same opening three notes to herald its own introduction.

The piano introduction proper carries the rhythmic patterns of both the call and the answer within it, but with the first beat missing:

Example 35
bar 59

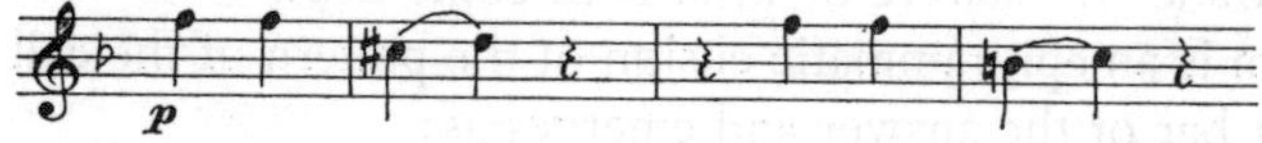

The First Concerto opens with the notably unpianistic call played by the orchestra, and the answer by the piano with the ending, as usual, repeated and varied. A vestigial sub-ritornello seals off the known material, and the piano moves into one of the rare static and banal piano passages in the concertos. The piano bridge proper sings out in bar 90—a variant of the later Bridge material and still with the rhythmic patterns of the answer.

The bridge runs quickly to the dominant and to the piano second subject (bar 102), again an unremarkable passage, but destined to appear again in the Fantasy. This subject can be read as an episode (as in 365) because it is still in the transitional area and the double dominant has only been touched in passing. Next comes a caesura (bar 110) which leads to the little introduction to the Second Subject. This time, although the notes are the same, the Second Subject is firmly *in* the dominant and not *on* it. Nor does it slide towards the tonic on its second outing: instead the piano arrests its course and with a new closing Cadence ending with two distinct caesuras, and then runs into the opening of the piano climax. This incorporates some of the earlier arpeggio and scale passages, but in the context of the run up to the climax they have more sense of purpose and pass off well enough.

A slight touch of magic appears (bars 157–159) which can be traced back to the caesura in bar 110. Here a series of extensions/caesuras in the rhythm of the answer screw up the tension for the final trill. The closing tutti is made up of the Second Cadential.

The Fantasy is not outstanding: the piano takes a variant of the Second Subject through two cycles in C minor and G minor. Then the piano second subject (or episode) appears in D minor. Modulatory sequences follow, the dominant pedal is reached in bar 213, and in bar 220 the first Return is sounded. This Return figure derives from the bass octaves in the second half of the original piano second subject, and on its fourth appearance the Return breaks tempo and almost slumps towards a full stop (bar 224). The piano picks up this impetus with a second Return figure based on the opening phrase of the Fantasy and leads back to the favoured Bridge–Second Subject link, or Third Cadential, now quite definitely an invitation to the piano to introduce the Concerto Reprise.

This follows its natural course with a few extra bars from the piano after the Second Subject and seven extra bars inserted to heighten the climax. The cadenza ritornello is made up from the old Bridge, and the cadenza itself (a good one) employs yet again in its central melodic patch the same little hinging phrase (B/S). The final ritornello consists of the Second Cadential and ends with the now thoroughly ambivalent Third Cadential (B/S). For a moment it seems inevitable that the whole affair is going to start again. But no—it is a true Cadential at last, and put firmly in its place with three sharp chords.

This movement is not in the top flight even of the Galant first movements, but it is agreeable and easy-going. By using the little link passages both in its first form and as the last Cadential six times in all, Mozart makes it the hero of the piece, albeit a diminutive one. This is an early example of the art of ambivalence which was one of his favourite devices. There is nothing in the little phrase itself that clamours for attention, but by the end of the movement it has thoroughly intrigued the ear with its qualities of epigram, imitation and surprise. He failed to find a place for the First Cadential after its first appearance, but otherwise the material is neatly organised and maintains interest by the subtle and continuing development of the opening rhythmic patterns.

The two subsequent movements do not enhance the concerto's appeal as a concert piece. The second, although pleasing enough, is a Larghetto of a simplicity bordering on the insipid. There are lengthy piano passages with a single melodic line over an Alberti bass and the orchestra has so insignificant a part that the movement would lose little in an arrangement for piano solo. The final rondo is marked Tempo di Menuetto, and the minuet subject, ordinary enough in itself, does not lead to any episode of interest, save one, where for a moment (bars 149–169) the movement rises above its general level of 'ordinary' Mozart. But even so, it would be extraordinary if it came from any other composer.

414 *in A Major*

From its first bar this concerto points the difference between the Galant and the Melodic style. In place of the crude call and sweet answer of 413, the first subject of 414 is an eight-bar melody, the first four over a pedal bass. The second strain holds up the flow with a series of syncopations: the melody is then repeated and the syncopations are resolved in the second half of the second outing. These sixteen bars contain ideas which form the basis of the great bulk of what is to come, but this time, unlike 413, the filo will be spun with melody as well as with rhythm.

The first Bridge subject is conventional, and breaks entirely from the filo, but at bar 25 there is a second syncopated passage, at least a distant cousin of the first one. The bridge ends with a flourish (bars 29–32) which is less an introduction to what is to come than a small-scale cadential to what has gone by.

The Second Subject is related to the First in two ways: it owes its shape to the melody and its rhythm to the syncopation. Because of this halting rhythm the Second Subject leaves the ear unsatisfied: it is all stop-start and appears to be an introduction to something that never arrives. This impression is strengthened by the First Cadential which grows out of it (bar 41) on an expectant pedal point in a series of tense little phrases. Out of its final flourish a free-running version of the Second Subject (now the Second Cadential) flows smoothly through to the Third and final cadential, which ends with a tag which is soon to be given a new role. (see pages 84-86)

The shift of emphasis and shift of interest between the Second Subject and the later cadential material is a technique that Mozart was to use later on within the bigger structure of the symphonic concerto, but in this early example it is a particularly happy and neat little plot. The First Subject itself has its binding syncopations which are resolved in its second outing: the Second Subject (based on the first) runs into similar heavy weather and then reappears triumphantly (a third lower and with the melody thrusting outwards and upwards) as a cadential thus reflecting the first subject's own progress from first to second appearance. There is one last refinement: the latter part of the transformed Second Subject (bars 53–54) is very close to the latter part of the First (bars 13–16).

As we shall see, the Second Cadential is later given a special importance. As in 413, where the little introduction to the Second Subject (which became the last cadential), lives on in the ear when the more orthodox passages are forgotten, so in this concerto the Second Cadential with its epigrammatic summary of the main ideas of the filo becomes the touchstone or index of the whole movement. It is worth noting that Mozart, as well as giving the cadential pride of place in the reprise, returned to it in one of the cadenzas.

The First Concerto opens in true melodic style with the solo piano playing the First Subject. This gains a light orchestral support on the repeat, but the solo takes over again to vary the second ending. The last bar (79), however, runs straight into a solo version of the Third Cadential, which is repeated by the orchestra as the sealing-off ritornello.

Now the piano picks up the closing tag and uses it to modulate towards the double dominant. This is established by a bar of side-ritornello (96). The piano's second subject is neither strong nor melodic, being rather a series of pianistic figures, the whole played twice and leading to some elegant sequences which duly introduce the Second Subject. The piano takes over the strain and again, after some caesuras, leads on with more urbane sequences to the piano climax (bar 131). Here there is a surprise; instead of the generally smooth-flowing melodic climax there is a series of triplets in the right hand with an insistent hammering figure in the left which is derived from a scrap of the second subject. This produces the tension not so much of competing in a race as of battering against a brick wall. After a false trill, the same passage is repeated. The climax ends with a scale passage that is close both to the piano's own ending to the First Subject and to the opening of the Third Cadential, which duly follows the trill as the closing ritornello.

The Fantasy starts with a phrase that might or might not be related to the tag of the last cadential, or even to the opening two bars of the First Subject itself. It is repeated, not in a different key as is the usual cyclic opening, but merely an octave lower. It is then varied and runs into the free modulating passage which reaches a full stop on the dominant chord in bar 194. Then with only the slightest cadenza it returns to the First Subject and the reprise.

This is true to type, to begin with. The orchestra plays the First Subject the first time, then the piano takes up the repeat and all goes on as before until the piano bridge. This is shortened by six bars, and after the piano second subject the sequences too are cut down, this time by eight bars. The reason is not far to seek, for after the Second Subject the piano follows the same course as in the First Concerto until suddenly it calls back the sequences that had been lost and uses them to lead to what now reads as a stronger and more substantial Second Subject, and it is in fact the Second Cadential.

This is the surprise and the triumph of the movement. As in its first appearance this Cadential had resolved and released the hesitation of the second subject, so now it appears as the melodic climax to the movement. So much so that if a critic new to the work were to hear the reprise first and were asked to job backwards and to name the main subjects he would surely define this tune as the main Second Subject from the Statement. It is true that the Galant tradition had often used cadential material in the later stages of the two concerted sections, but this time Mozart gives the original Second Cadential a new meaning and a central importance.

This section is followed by an entirely new piano climax of nineteen bars. It has a different return, and this time it runs unimpeded to the trill. The cadenza ritornello is made up from the First Cadential, and of the two cadenzas, the first simply extends the Second Cadential to a final flurry of arpeggios, while the second (which is more elaborate) refers back to the First Subject and the piano's original and varied ending to it. The Third

Cadential provides the closing ritornello.

This charming and ingenious movement is played frequently and is well known to most pianists who specialise in Mozart. It demands an understanding of the basic idea of tension and release which it does not always receive. The two piano climaxes must be approached quite differently, as must the Second Subject and the Second Cadential in order to give the sense of climax and to bring out the full flavour of the plot.

The balance of mentions suffers from the special treatment accorded to the favoured Cadential, for the vigorous little bridge, which has plenty of running in it, disappears from view after its first appearance. A similar plot was to be handled in a different way in the larger A major Melodic concerto, 488.

The later movements of the concerto help to explain its popularity with Mozart himself (it is known to have been one of his favourites and he left two cadenzas for each movement) and in the concert repertoire today. The second movement is an elegant and superior Andante whose somewhat ordinary main subject is adorned by variations which sweep the movement along in a stream of fresh invention. The rondo, marked Allegretto, is cheerful, neat and does not outstay its welcome. All of the cadenzas are interesting.

415 *in C major*

Like the first two concertos in this group, which announce their nature at once, 415 opens with a two-bar phrase that cannot be mistaken for anything but the main unit, or motif, that is the hallmark of a symphonic concerto. Since this is the first appearance of the symphonic form, 415 marks perhaps the most decisive step forward in the whole story of the concerto. Christian Bach had written only in the Galant and Melodic forms; the single experiments of 175, 271 and 365 did not lead to any lasting development. Here, however, is a new kind of movement which was to prepare the way for others, including the great concertos 466 in D minor, 491 in C minor, and the later C major, 503.

To take the most significant advance first, let us look at the use of the symphonic unit and how it is beginning to transform the structure of the movement.

The main unit is first introduced as the First Subject; it returns again in the First Cadential, at the head of the First Concerto (naturally enough), and as the closing ritornello to the First Concerto; it is developed briefly in the Fantasy; and its final mention is in the opening of the Concerto Reprise. In order to see how this scheme was to be extended, it is interesting to compare the extent to which a main unit or main units (M) were used in this prototype C major concerto with their use in the great C major 503:

	415	503
STATEMENT		
Introduction	—	
First Group/Subject	M	M
Bridge/Transition		M
Relief/Second Subject		(M) Filo relative
Cadentials	M	M
FIRST CONCERTO		
Introduction	—	
First Group	M	M
Piano Bridge		M
Piano Climax		M
Closing Ritornello	M	M
FANTASY	(M)	M
CONCERTO REPRISE		
Introduction	—	
First Group/Subject	M	M
Piano Bridge		M
Piano Climax		M
Cadenza Ritornello		M
Closing Ritornello		M

In 415, the symphonic idea, although quite clearly in Mozart's mind, is not yet fully deployed; there are, for instance, only four bars incorporating the main unit in the whole of the reprise. He had not yet reconciled the old with the new, for the piano climaxes are not yet supported by the main unit in orchestral counterpoint beneath them. Nor does it appear in its proper conclusive position before the Cadenza. But the decisive steps were taken: the nature of the main unit is short and symphonic; it reappears at key points to assert its dominance as a Main Theme; on its reappearance, although varied it is no longer a filo relation of the original but definitely the same thing albeit in a more developed form.

A comparison between the filo relationship in the Statement of the Melodic 414 and the symphonic treatment of 415 clearly shows the difference:

Example 36

And so the movement starts with a soft statement of the main unit in a three-part canon. This is completed in nine-plus bars and a new type of Transition follows over a tonic pedal for eight bars. It continues to echo the rhythm of the main unit and is more a steady gathering of tension than the sequence of discursive Bridge-type figures to which we are accustomed. It has, in fact, the nature of a true Transition passage for the first time. In bar 18 a powerful figure in the bass switches the pedal on to the dominant, and there follows another surprise. When we expect a true second subject, there is instead something more like a Relief passage on the dominant pedal (bar 24) over which the first violins introduce a series of upward runs, which are to become another important point of reference:

Example 37

bar 32

The effect of these two sustained pedal points is to build a sense of considerable anticipation which is realised by the return of the main unit (bar 36) now in a more definitive shape. This (the First Cadential) begins as a part of the central section of the Statement, but it ends with an air of cadential finality.

The First Cadential leads to a caesura; the impetus is picked up by the Second Cadential (bar 47), a stock figure which is nevertheless still reminiscent of the main unit. The Third Cadential (bar 52) is derived from the 'upward runs' in the relief passage, and the scale that follows its fifth repetition ends in another caesura, one that is to enhance an important moment later in the movement. The Statement ends with a closing flourish—the Fourth Cadential.

The First Concerto opens with a piano introduction which has the tinkling sonatina-like quality of the introduction in 413, yet it too has an echo of the rhythm of the main unit. The orchestra enters with the main unit itself, which the piano adorns with a trill and an extended closing figure. Then the piano's true voice takes the lead, and it remains fully in command through the next sixty to seventy bars of the concerto.

The piano bridge opens with free arpeggios (bar 78) which lead brilliantly but more cursorily than usual to the dominant, and here, after a slight gesture from the orchestra, the piano second subject sails out (bar 93). This is a complete eight-bar melody, a descendant of the memorable piano subject of 365 and precursor of the one to come in 503. Its effect is perhaps greater because there was no true Second Subject in the statement and because there has been, as yet, except for the diminutive piano introduction, no lyrical relief from the orchestra's symphonic voice and the flashing arpeggios from the piano.

This notable tune is played twice and is followed at once by another rapid pianistic passage (bar 108), the start of the piano climax, which soon sets to work on the 'upward runs' pulled out from the Relief passage (bar 32) and played in counterpoint first above and then below another rapid little figure belonging to the piano itself. Between these two bouts of activity there is a slower progression (bar 121) which has some relevance to the opening of the Fantasy. After more fireworks the piano reaches a false trill in bar 132. But the climax is not over, for the piano (not the orchestra) caps the trill with the triplet Cadential (C3) and with the orchestra's help it runs up to the point of its caesura. And here is one of the happiest moments of the movement: the sticking point of the little climax is pushed up a semitone a second and third time, and only then is it released by the piano in another four bars of gymnastics which lead at last to the real trill and the end of a piano climax thirty-eight bars in length.

With the benefit of hindsight from the later concertos it is not perhaps too fanciful to hear beneath the piano passages in the bridge and the climax the unwritten echoes of the main unit, and thus to anticipate Mozart's later discovery that a substream of this material would strengthen and support the symphonic unity of the movement. As it is we have to wait for the closing ritornello to introduce the main unit (followed by the Fourth Cadential) to round off the section.

The piano opens the Fantasy with four powerful minim chords, related perhaps to the caesura in the Third Cadential. After the four minim beats the piano runs into a rapid little canon which is rounded off by the orchestra. This is repeated a fourth higher (bar 168) and the main unit enters under the piano's independent embellishments (bar 176), and after a brief development of six bars it dies away to leave the field clear for further arpeggios until the first Return is sounded in bar 188. There is a second Return, a tiny cadenza in free tempo, and the piano introduction heralds the start of the Concerto Reprise. This, with only the variation of two or three bars, follows the course of the First Concerto until the final ritornello, which is made up from the original Transition passage.

The Cadenza starts by picking up the vigorous bass figure from the close of the Transition, and in its lyrical section turns naturally to the piano second subject. It returns, too, to the 'upward runs' used in the Relief passages and so extensively in the two piano climaxes. The closing ritornello consists of the Second, Third and final Cadentials.

Of all the concertos 415 is perhaps the most undervalued by pianists, conductors and managers. Quite apart from its historical importance, it is an invigorating movement to play and to hear, and it offers the performer a challenge greater than any previous concerto, or indeed of any of the concertos to come until 466. It displays Mozart's piano style in its most brilliant early contrapuntal form (which Hutchings, alas, describes as 'pretentious rubble') and it offers the pianist a chance to dominate almost the whole of the first movement after the Statement. It is a paradox that in this first essay in the symphonic form the piano should lead so independent a life, yet the result, if performed with the right sort of vigour and attack, can be supremely successful. The perfect synthesis of the two voices in the symphonic material is not yet there, but instead there is an equally satisfactory but entirely different balance of contrast, the piano speaking in one voice and the orchestra in another.

The second movement of 415 is one of those Mozartean Andantes of the second order which depend largely upon performance for their success or failure. Unless the 'andante' is taken at a light and easy pace, the soufflé can sink. In particular the frequent repetitions of the long opening theme demand a clear tone and a light accompaniment if they are not to drag. In the last movement, however, we find another major essay, a suitable match to the first. This is a rondo, with a typically cheeky first subject, but which unfolds upon a scale more extensive than we have met before. There is an adagio piano episode (which appears twice) and another big episode in the symphonic style (bars 148–187). Instead of a cadenza and a final statement of the rondo theme the movement ends with an elaborate and highly successful coda. In the last movement as well as in the first the concerto discloses its ambition.

8

The Six Concertos of 1784

449 in E flat; 450 in B flat; 451 in D; 453 in G;
456 in B flat; 459 in F

In the year 1784 Mozart composed more great music than many other well-respected composers have written in a decade. In addition to the six piano concertos listed at the head of this chapter he also produced a sonata for the piano (457), two sets of variations (455 and 460), a violin and piano sonata (454), a string quartet (458) and the quintet for piano and wind (452), besides a considerable output of dance music.

Nor did he lock himself away from the world for long spells in order to compose this vast body of work. His performing diary for the month of March went something as follows. He played at Count Esterhazy's on the 1st, 5th, 8th, 12th, 15th, 19th, 22nd, 26th, and 29th (every Monday and Friday). He performed a concerto at his sister-in-law's concert on the 11th. On Wednesday the 17th, the 24th and 31st he gave subscription concerts in a room in the Trattnerhof. On Saturday the 20th he played at Count Zichy's—and one further concert was postponed because it clashed with Prince Lichtenstein's opera. In all, fourteen performances in twenty-one days. Many pianists today would regard a programme of this kind as heavy enough in itself without the additional burden of composing a series of masterpieces.

This extraordinary bout of creative and artistic activity had several causes. First Mozart had come to terms with a new public, as sophisticated and as critical as any in the musical world of the day. On a good night his public concerts 'went magnifique' and the leading amateurs such as Count Esterhazy and Baron van Swieten showed their admiration for him through their patronage. For an artist of Mozart's temperament there is no stimulus equal to success.

During this year he poured out his talent to please his audiences, and to please himself, for the two were still compatible. The tuneful, vivacious and gay works of 1784 (perhaps with the exception of 449) were suited to the Viennese taste: as yet there were no disturbing shadows to darken the mood of the music, and few new and discordant progressions to offend ears accustomed to the simple system of harmony used by the contemporary Viennese composers.

A second reason for this creative spurt lay in Mozart's development as a composer. Certainly he had never stood still for long, but in this year he made an unparalleled leap forward. In the negative sense Mozart's advance depended partly upon his abandoning proven formulae and methods of composition which used the clichés from his own and other people's repertory. The stock cadential figure, for instance, begins to disappear; the old tubby bridge with its predictable contours becomes more of an individual piece to suit each different work; each new composition aims higher, is never content to repeat the pattern of an older one, nor, in the more carefully composed works, to repeat itself. On the more positive side, Mozart's new interest in counterpoint spread like a flame across the pages of his scores, liberating the inner parts and the wind band from their subservient roles and allowing them to enrich the texture with their individual voices.

A third reason for the fertility of this year lay in Mozart's liberation from the confines of a small and tedious court circle and his entry into cosmopolitan life where he worked in a musical society whose standards were international. No more the backstairs gossip about Michael Haydn and Adlgasser, instead a chance to discuss with equals the work of Gluck and Joseph Haydn. His spirits had recovered from the personal mortifications of 1782 and now he was ready to accept any challenge. His competitive nature drove him to prove that he was the most popular performer and composer in Vienna, and, in this year at least, perhaps he succeeded. Even a year earlier he had written to Leopold:

> ... I played a concerto [probably 175]. The theatre was very full and I was again received by the Viennese public so cordially that I really ought to feel delighted. I had already left the platform but the audience would not stop clapping and so I had to repeat the rondo, upon which there was a regular torrent of applause.

The first three of the mature Viennese concertos (449, 450 and 451) were performed at the three subscription concerts in March. The first had been written for his pupil Barbara Ployer, and Mozart wrote about them to Leopold two months later:

> I really cannot choose between the two of them [450, 451] but I regard them both as concertos which are bound to make the performer sweat. From the point of view of difficulty the one in B flat beats the one in D... The one in E flat does not belong at all to the same category. It is one of a quite peculiar kind, composed for a small orchestra rather than a large one.

453 was given its first performance on 13 June at a private concert at the house of Herr Ployer, the agent of the Salzburg court in Vienna. Mozart had again written it for the daughter of the house, Barbara. 456 was written for Maria Theresa Paradis, a German pianist who had been blind from birth. We know from Leopold that at a subsequent performance by Mozart himself the Emperor waved his hat and called out 'Bravo Mozart!' There is no record of the first performance of 459. It has the nature of work written for a pupil or a visiting pianist rather than one by Mozart for himself, but such speculation can only rest on internal evidence.

449 *in E flat*

The structure of this movement stands somewhere between the Galant and the Symphonic idea, but decidedly nearer to the former. Quite apart from its thoroughly operatic flavour, it must be classed as Galant because the germinal phrase that runs through much of the movement does not keep its identity on its several appearances. Each version is a relative of the original (often a very close one), but its kinship depends upon variations of a phrase snatched out of the opening call. This is no more than a trill on a dotted crotchet (which has the effect of making the weak second beat emphatic), two semiquavers—and into the next bar. (It is interesting to compare the Statements of 449 and 415, for there is some similarity in the subsequent treatment of the opening theme; in 449 this depends upon the filo, whereas in 415 of course, the relationship is symphonic.)

The movement begins with a first subject which embodies, as well as the pregnant phrase, two characteristics of the whole movement: an unconventional and sometimes harsh tonal progression, and a pithy concentration of ideas, sometimes following closely one after the other, sometimes overlaid in counterpoint. The call is in unison and appears to strike C minor in the second bar, modulating to B flat in the third, and it is in these last two bars (3 and 4) that the 'germinal phrase' lies. This last phrase of the call (bars 5 and 6) is picked up as the first phrase of the answer (bars 5 and 6) and thereby subtly changes its character. The answer is repeated with a descant above it. The descant ends in a two-bar figure which runs on three times over and under the last two bars of the answer.

Example 38

bar 11

This is the most epigrammatic opening of any in the Galant concertos and by the time it is over yet another index of the movement has shown itself—the rhythm of six quavers in the bar which is to beat like a pulse throughout the greater part of the Statement.

From the sweet and easy close to the First Subject, the Bridge plunges darkly into C minor and leads through fragmentary figures in the violins to a close in F major. Here, with a new and dynamic flourish which puts a stop to the steady quaver beat in the bass, there is a link passage (B/S) to the Second Subject.

This is firmly in the dominant, and a filo relative of a phrase in the First Subject. It is reinforced by the pedal of B flat, and could well be described as a relief passage. In its third phrase (bar 46) it runs on more easily and includes a happy reference to the little cadential descant of the First Subject (bar 50). Next comes a larger pedal passage (the First Cadential) which gathers tension in much the same way as the Relief subject of 415 and, continuing the parallel, leads to a remote but more affirmative version of the First Subject (the Second Cadential). The Third Cadential too has an inversion of the First Subject's trill phrase, a powerful canon with the foreshortening effect of *stretto*. The first time out the trill is in the bass and another voice in the treble gives a diminished inversion of the last bars of the answer; the second time the roles are reversed. The last and Fourth Cadential is a conventional closing flourish.

The First Concerto, too, has an unusual opening, for instead of the orchestra giving the call and the piano chiming in with the answer, the piano manages the whole business on its own. Not quite the whole, however, for the descant is played by the piano alone and the orchestra provides the closing notes of the answer beneath it. The piano bridge provides only a negative surprise, for in a movement of such rapid tonal shifts its bubbling scales linger in the region of E flat and finally perfunctorily drop into B flat without moving through the double dominant. At this point it seems as if the transition of the Statement and the First Concerto had been switched around for no purpose. But the piano second subject, a plaintive little tune of some charm (bar 121), jumps almost immediately into C minor, thus achieving a startling remoteness without the help of the conventional long way round to the dominant key. Next comes the link passage (B/S) and the Second Subject, both still played by the piano, and a short but effective piano climax. The piano, indeed, plays almost as dominant a part in this First Concerto as in those of 365 and 415, for it is not silent for one single bar from its entry right up to the final trill. This is a true 'piano solo', and it demonstrates that the days of sub-ritornellos sandwiched between piano passages are gone forever, and also that an equal partnership between the two voices in the concerted sections has still not arrived. The closing ritornello is made up of the Second and Third Cadentials.

The Fantasy is replaced by a Development, which is short (some forty bars) and confined to a vigorous working out of the 'trill phrase', the version plucked from the Third Cadential. Both voices have a share of the subject and again the closing section before the Return is reached, again with an effect of compactness through *stretto.* The first return, a smooth complement to the roughness of the final trills, begins at bar 212; the dominant pedal is reached at bar 219. Here there are two changes of gear (from semiquavers to quavers—from quavers to crotchets)—the first fully composed ritenuto in the concertos. The crotchets deliver us back to the Reprise through a rising chromatic link. This is another milestone of the early Vienna Concertos: a cadenza at this point would be unthinkable.

In the Reprise of the First Subject, the orchestra takes the call and the first answer, the piano picking up the descant, the strings supplying the counterpoint as before. The piano bridge starts by duly repeating the same passages, but at bar 260 it embarks on a new adventure with florid passages in the right hand over a fragment of the canon subject of the Third Cadential in the left. Then all goes according to custom, with an extension of seven bars to heighten the reprise of the piano climax. The cadenza platform is made up from the C minor Bridge passage and after a thin cadenza (which begins with a figure from the Bridge and otherwise only mentions the Second Cadential) the movement is ended with the powerful Third and the conventional Fourth Cadential.

At first hearing this is not a prepossessing movement, but with familiarity its manner of direct attack seems to reflect a spontaneous burst of power rather than a lack of grace. It is much more in the nature of a work by Beethoven, and quite unlike the gay, elegant Mozart of 450 and 453, and equally unlike the sad eloquent Mozart of 466. It represents not so much a lapse in taste as a piece composed compulsively, driven out by one of Mozart's less familiar daemons. With its succinct methods of expression, and its compression of ideas, the movement must have taken him longer to write than the usual Galant or Melodic work. We know that counterpoint was one thing that Mozart could not carry in his head. Nor is there a great margin for interpretation: the intention of the work is clearly set down, and between fairly narrow limits, and can only be performed in one way.

The Andantino is not in the first rank. It has a long and intense main subject, and the piano's treatment of it does not seem to flower. The movement ends (unusually, for a Mozartean slow movement) before it has found its full expression. There is again something a little weird in its tone of voice, a graceless intensity that is unfamiliar. The finale is quite the most successful movement of the concerto, a fast rondo that is constantly surprising us with its ingenuity in the treatment of its staccato little main subject. Here again the piano takes an heroic part, selecting from the repertory of Rondo devices to keep its own voice more than usually insistent. In particular it has a number of contrapuntal passages in the same style as the first movement of 415 with the orchestra often providing it with no more than a semi-audible harmonic base. Yet the rondo too has the same slightly dotty intensity of the other movements; its speed and dash are not spontaneous, and there is a feverish beat in its pulse. Perhaps some lover of Mozart with a compendious knowledge of all his works could find a work, or even a movement, parallel to this strange wanderer amongst the concertos. Whether or not a fellow exists, this is a work to remind us that no picture of Mozart is complete without allowing that he, like everyone, had moments of eccentricity.

450 *in B flat*

This can fairly be said to be the first of the mature concertos. There is no advance in form, indeed Mozart falls back upon the simple Melodic pattern perhaps with some relief, and in comparison with 415 and 449 there is little counterpoint and no truly 'symphonic' writing. But within the familiar structure there are several notable advances. First, the wind band (oboes, bassoons and horns) is liberated from the strings and we hear for almost the first time three pairs of voices, strings and wind, piano and wind, and piano and strings. Secondly, the writing is full of little felicities which enrich the second appearance of many phrases by some witty adjustment. And finally the piano finds a style of relaxed assurance in each of its several moods. The piano introduction, for instance, is more magnificent, the skittish little passages are more elegantly turned, the brilliant passages have more bravura and the soloist assumes a larger and more authoritative *persona* throughout. Gone are the diligent contrapuntal passages of 415 and 449, the empty arpeggios of 413 and the simple Alberti basses of the earlier concertos, and for the performer the technical difficulty of the part puts it in a different class to the earlier works—it is indeed a concerto 'to make one sweat'.

The gentle first subject, although Melodic by nature, retains some vestiges of the Galant call and answer. The wind band announces the call, the strings reply and lead to the dominant chord. The second call slips forward by half a beat and the second answer arranges its ornaments differently, and thereby two of the indices of the concerto are established within the first eight bars—the fastidious detail in composition which shuns exact repetition, and the separate identity of the wind and strings as two partners in a duet. The First Subject ends with an operatic flurry (F+) from which a traditional but splendid Bridge passage springs out with huge leaps in the violin parts under chording in the wind. The Bridge ends on the customary dominant chord, not in the dominant key, and introduces the Second Subject, an elegant syncopated measure. This has an affinity to the first, not a filo relationship, but its likeness can be tested by inserting the First Subject's answer after the first phrase of the Second, and it will be found to construe perfectly. Mozart does not resolve the tension of the hesitant rhythm by the method of 414 where the same subject reappeared relaxed, and on the beat, as a Cadential. Instead he repeats the subject with a flowing counter-melody from the violins (bar 33) which smooths out its uncertainties. The First Cadential is a little Mannheim Crescendo leading to the Second, which is based on the second half of the Bridge, now forming an effective closing piece. This Cadential is repeated (bar 49) and at the head of this repeat there is another example of special attention to detail:

Example 39
bar 45

Example 40
bar 49

The third and last Cadential (bar 53) is one of Mozart's happy *envois*, and a distinct filo relative of the call. Again it is deployed in a duet between the wind and strings.

Now comes the piano introduction (with orchestral accompaniment), a majestic assertion of the key of B flat and fit to stand at the head of the grandest symphonic First Concerto. Instead, with carefully contrived bathos, the piano slips into the

First Subject which it carries through, in partnership with the wind, to an abrupt switch to G minor (bars 86/87) and the piano bridge. This begins with two transitional melodies in quick succession, scarcely substantial enough to be called episodes, and carries through in sequences through the double dominant to a point of entry marked by the customary gesture from the strings (bars 102/103). The piano second subject enters as a slender affair (again with some affinity to the outline of the First Subject) but gains in substance when the orchestra adds a sequential strain beneath the piano line, which now becomes pure decoration. Seven bars of close sequential writing bring the piano to the start of its climax (bar 119). This is constructed of a sophisticated little phrase still bearing the traces of the First Subject over a running accompaniment which develops by spontaneous combustion into a fiery virtuoso piece of fifteen bars. The closing ritornello is made up from the Bridge and the Second and Third Cadentials.

The piano snatches the last phrase of the last Cadential and works upon it with fury, insensibly changing its shape and meaning until it is free to run, in the most improvisatory style, up to the First Return (bar 182). Then, under a trill from the piano, the orchestra works up a second return, leading to a run of thirds on the piano and orchestra which hint broadly that the Reprise is at hand. This is the first time in the concertos that the First Subject is used as its own herald in the Return.

In the Reprise the call is taken by the orchestra and the answer by the piano. The first part of the original Bridge follows, stopping short to allow the piano's two transition tunes, considerably varied and now starting in C minor, to lead back to the remainder of the piano bridge, the piano second subject and its consequences. Here the original Second Subject, which was missing from the First Concerto, makes its entry (bar 248). After a first outing on the piano, the wind take over the second, as they did in the Statement. But this time the counter-melody is given to the piano, which embroiders it in double time with charming effect. The climax follows, heightened by an extra two bars before the trill. The First and Second Cadentials provide the cadenza platform.

The Cadenza opens with a light reference to one of the transition themes. Soon, however, it thickens and finds a driving rhythm from the bass figuration used at the start of the climax. The central section returns to the Second Subject for its melody and it finishes with a truly formidable set of runs both in free time and *in tempo*. It is a model of cadenza design for a Melodic movement, and, where no Mozart cadenza exists, would that all performers were content to follow its example. The final ritornello is made up of the Second Cadential (again) and the Third, the little *envoi*.

There is not one moment in this movement where invention flags, where repetition oversteps its welcome, nor is there anything, as there is in 449, that jars the ear or disturbs the senses. At the same time it moves in a larger world with more resources at its command and more reserves of power for the climactic moment. The material is particularly neatly balanced. A glance at the table of mentions (p.270) shows the Bridge passage to be more usefully employed than usual. The Second Subject (which is long) appears twice, the Second Cadential four times, but on its last two appearances it is not repeated (that is to say it is cut from eight bars to six to form the cadenza platform and after the cadenza only the repeat [four bars] is used).

This concerto is one which will distinguish the real musician from the good technician. It will also throw a light on his own character, for, like all truly great works, no two people will interpret it in the same way. It is by no means an easy movement.

The second movement is in the first class of Mozart's Andantes, a serene melody with exquisite variations and a short coda. The final rondo makes another leap forward; its scale is more spacious and its invention more bold than any before; it is deftly calculated to bring an audience to its feet. The use of the orchestra continues to be flexible, with some duetting between the piano and the wind in the second movement and an elegant dialogue with a solo oboe in the rondo. It was from movements such as these that the young Beethoven learned so much.

451 *in D major*

At first hearing this majestic movement reads as a straightforward symphonic piece, and the listener could be forgiven if he were to select it as the simplest example of Mozart's mature symphonic style. In fact the means used to create a sense of unity are more complex than in the later and bigger concertos. It relies upon a mixture of the methods of the filo and the motif. The opening subject has a set of characteristics some of which it passes to its successor. The new subject adds elements of its own, and some of these are adopted in turn by the next in line, until at the finish of this relay race the Statement ends with precisely the same notes as those with which it began.

Let us look at this process in some detail, eliminating for the time being the middle section of the Statement (from the end of the First Subject to the end of the Second) all of which lies outside this scheme.

The First Subject opens with a statement of the octave of D with an iambic beat on the bottom end of the octave, then with a series of trills on the notes of the common chord ascends the scale of D major to the extent of one octave and climbs more quickly and simply up to the second (F1). Here begins an imitative duet in thirds between the upper and lower strings which, for the sake of brevity, we can call a canon although the voices do not follow their parts precisely (F2: bar 10). The shape of the canon includes an octave at the start and a downward scale in the iambic rhythm. Now moving past the unrelated material to the First Cadential, we find a moving bass again going through a scale-like progression, but it slides downwards chromatically. The Second Cadential picks up the chromatic idea and reintroduces the pattern of the canon, a strong reminder of F2. The Third Cadential (no more than a short caesura) brings back the rhythm and trill of F1, and the Fourth, after some closing flourishes, ends with both the rhythm and the octave leap of F1.

To summarise:

	Octave	Iambic Rhythm	Trill	Scale	Canon	Chromatic Progression
F1	x	x	x	x		
F2	x	x		x	x	
C1				x		x
C2	x				x	x
C3		x	x			
C4	x	x				

The identity of the binding agent is too multifarious to be given any single label. The 'motif' has in effect some six separate elements, and in no single passage do they all appear at once.

But to revert to simple narrative, the First Subject's opening gesture amounts to a grand and static introduction, and the action begins only with the iambic scale which forms the second half of the First Subject. This runs on into a Transition section (bar 17), different in kind from the old-type Bridge, which moves momentarily into A major but soon makes it clear that it is merely on the dominant chord. This is followed by a link passage (bar 26) anticipating the Second Subject with a whispered rustle of expectation thrown from the flutes to the strings and the oboes, all over a dominant pedal and ending in a scale in contrary motion to raise the curtain. The Second Subject, when at last it comes (bar 31) is something of a disappointment, a simple hunting-call from the horns and oboes answered by a simpering little phrase from the violins and flutes.

With the First Cadential, however, we are back in true symphonic country: there is an air of mystery; a walking bass moves stealthily and chromatically beneath a syncopated pattern in the upper strings (bar 43). Its similarity to the iambic scale becomes clearer in the Second Cadential which picks a part of the chromatic progression from the First and presents it in a loud canon, starting with the leap of an octave (bar 52). The Statement ends with the caesura plus a quiet answer, the whole played twice (the Third Cadential) and the Fourth Cadential, which takes us back to the beginning again, with a hustle.

The piano opens the First Concerto with its own filled-in version of the introductory octave and scale. The iambic canon enters quietly beneath it whilst it continues to work on with scales and arpeggios. And now strange things occur. In place of the usual piano bridge there is a short legato passage from the piano over the dominant pedal with a suggestion of the chromatic progression with it (bar 92). This is rudely interrupted by a call in the rhythm and style of the caesura (the Third Cadential) which switches the piano abruptly into B minor—the tonic parallel (bar 98). And here, where the piano second subject should be, there is instead a harmonic progression with a piano figure not unlike a passage from the Transition. Sequences follow accompanied by variations of the last tag of the call from the Third Cadential, and the tonality moves from the double dominant into the dominant and (this time unmistakably) into the end of the original Transition passage and then the Second Subject (bar 128), this time with the piano taking part in the preliminary whisper.

The Second Subject, although rescored and opened up to allow the piano in, comes off no better than before. It fades out into A minor and there is a temporary lacuna, filled by fragmentary figures and broken chords from the piano. But suddenly the impetus is restored (bar 143) by the walking bass (the First Cadential) now given new vigour by a bubbling piano accompaniment, followed by an octave canon (the Second Cadential). Here the piano adds scales, at first of two octaves to the bar, but becoming a free chromatic sweep. The two cadentials leave the piano in command and form what is, in effect, the first part of the piano climax. Next comes the conclusion of the climax, free passages for the piano (bar 158), including two bars in contrary motion (162 and 163) and ending with a sweeping scale in thirds. The canon on the octave leap and scale (the second part of the First Subject) begins the ritornello and acquires a new tail, which is interrupted (bar 181) by the caesura (the Third Cadential). The first answer comes sweetly enough from the strings but after the second caesura call, instead of a second answer, the piano replies with another call, moving it towards E minor, and the Development has begun.

After some play with the caesura phrase, the piano runs on freely, soon supported by another walking bass with the same beat but without the chromatic slide of the original (bar 202). The dominant pedal booms out in bar 211 and is given four heavy beats before the piano makes a somewhat hurried return to the Reprise.

We first heard the opening of the First Subject played by the orchestra alone, then by the piano, now we have both and the richness of the piano's scales within the orchestral texture gives it a marvellous extension of depth and power. This is one of the happiest and most effective moments in the movement. The piano accompaniment to the iambic scale is then changed to fast triplet arpeggios and the foreshortened Transition passage returned to something nearer its original shape with the piano holding a leading part. In the rustling link passage which follows, the roles of the piano and the wind instruments are reversed. From the start of the Second Subject, however, all goes as in the First Concerto until the centre of the piano climax, where the caesura (the Third Cadential) intervenes yet again (bar 283). As at the end of the First Concerto the piano takes it up after the call (bar 289) but this time develops it into a quiet little cadenza-like passage. The beat is picked up again (bar 297) and the climax is completed with a new set of scales and runs. The iambic scale of the First Subject appears for the fifth time to form the cadenza ritornello, followed by a part of the Transition section.

The Cadenza begins by playing with the iambic scale, then follows up a chromatic idea at some length, jumps into the two bars of contrary motion from the first piano climax, then adopts the run of thirds and finally, before its departing sweep, it lingers a little on a figure like the chromatic phrase that it had just developed out of the caesura in the second piano climax. But although it touches on five separate retrospective thoughts it does not sound like a potpourri but a spontaneous extempore piece. The final ritornello is made up by the neglected Fourth Cadential.

With this movement the piano concerto has finally entered the world of the later symphonies. It is not easy today to remember the magnitude of this event: it was not achieved by Haydn nor by any other of Mozart's contemporaries. In Mozart's own calendar only the Linz symphony had by this time reached this Olympian level. It is therefore not unreasonable to classify 451 as his second mature symphonic work. 451 is assured where 415 was tentative: it fully justifies the ambition of the enormous opening: it is, above all, a modern work in the new and powerful idiom of the later eighteenth and early nineteenth century with liberated orchestra and a dynamic range equal to that of the young Beethoven. It is the first Mozart concerto that *can* be played with a modern concert grand and an orchestra of seventy, and still keep its true character.

The complex network of relationships gives the work a true symphonic unity: the material is wonderfully balanced in its use: what weakness there is lies in a thin Second Subject without a complementary piano subject to relieve the symphonic texture and to beguile the ear with a simple melody. Mozart, in his first attempt to write a symphonic concerto, realised that there was not room for two proper second subjects, adding up to five mentions in all (see pages 75-80). Thus in 415 he avoided a lyrical Second Subject altogether and substituted the pedal relief passages. In 451 he kept a full orchestral Second Subject and dropped the piano second subject. In its place we have the strange little passage starting in B minor (bars 98–105) which can only be regarded as an episode within the piano bridge. This is not unlike the episode at the same point in the First Concerto of 365, and like its predecessor the episode is dropped in the reprise. The only other weakness lies in the piano climaxes which do not rise to the orchestral challenge of the movement. As we have seen, the earlier part of the climaxes is formed by rapid piano accompaniments over symphonic material. When they are done, the piano's solo climax seems to lack a continuous drive towards the final trill.

The second movement is a pleasing andante burdened with a first strain which becomes wearisome on the third or fourth hearing. It is distinguished by some elegant writing for the wind instruments. The rondo is a simple high-spirited affair with the piano allotted a decorative role in *perpetuum mobile.* Neither of the two movements, however, is quite up to the scale of the first.

453 *in G major*

This movement is far removed from the grandeur and power of 451: it moves in the world of Jane Austen's Anne Elliott and Jane Bennet (the sensible young women, not the headstrong ones), and it is all tenderness, elegance and good feeling. Viewed from without, its architecture is in the mode of the earlier Melodic concertos, but within it is furnished more richly.

The sprightly First Subject runs a smooth course for eight bars and then, after a slight caesura and answer, there follows a particularly attractive Bridge in the old style, but growing out of the First Subject's last phrase. A link passage joins the Bridge to the Second Subject, a happy witticism uttered by the bassoons, flute and oboes, which is more introductory than conclusive (bar 30). As we shall see, it is to be given a favoured position in the work. The Second Subject is exquisite, and, once heard, lives in the memory forever. It is played first on the strings, who give it a pleading tone. When repeated in the wind section it acquires a more plaintive note. The First Cadential plunges darkly into E flat with an operatic arpeggio and a menacing trill (bar 49), the Second a smooth farewell adapted from the closing phrase of the First Subject (bar 58), the Third an even more moving farewell (bar 65), a filo relative of the opening melody, and the Fourth a final dynamic explosion.

The piano, with some early encouragement from the wind, deals with the First Subject in the accustomed manner. After six bars of the old Bridge, the piano bridge strikes out at a tangent, which runs a fluid and direct course to its second subject, another of the family of 365 and 415, but more playful and less strenuous.

More fluid sequences modulate up to a point on A major when the link passage (bar 133) again heralds the Second Subject which is played first on the piano with the lightest string accompaniment and then repeated on the woodwind with piano interpolation. Then a traditional Melodic climax, consisting of what Girdlestone would call 'passage work'—neat arpeggios and then scales. The closing ritornello is made up from the beginning of the original Bridge; this is followed by the Fourth Cadential.

After two bars of orchestral hinge the piano takes off into a free fantasy in three sections, first a stream of modulatory arpeggios, then after a short launching ritornello (bar 207) a poignant little episode in C minor (which has some distant relationship to the opening melody). This is an unusual event, for Melodic Fantasies usually keep up the impetus of the movement with some strenuous piano work. A first return begins in bar 224.

All goes according to plan in the Reprise. The whole of the old Bridge is played and out of the last phrase the piano picks up the bassoon part to make a link, not with the Second Subject but with its own subject, presented delicately in the high register (bar 261). After some modulatory sequences the little link crops up again (as in the First Concerto) and this time it does lead to the Second Subject (bar 290). There is a slight adjustment to the end of the piano climax. The First Cadential makes up the Cadenza ritornello.

The first Cadenza opens with a reference to the First Subject and between its free passages lingers a little with the Second Subject and throws in the slightest reminder of the end of the piano second subject. The alternative cadenza starts with some play on the caesura from the end of the First Subject and passes, with some free working between, to the piano second subject and the link. Both are gentle cadenzas and lead out into the quiet and docile Second Cadential, followed by the Third and Fourth and then—the link passage as a diminutive coda, this time presented with a dying fall.

There is little more to say about this simple and beautitul

movement except to wonder at the fertility of invention and to admire the variations of pace which are interspersed to animate its unusually long and placid sections. It is effectively scored for the woodwind, but the horns do little more than add to the texture.

It presents the performer with a nice problem of steering between a soft and affectionate interpretation throughout, whereby the momentum will flag, and too drastic an accent and rhythm in those passages (such as the piano second subject) where a contrast can be made to invigorate the steady beat of the piano part.

The second movement has an opening strophe which is one of Mozart's perfect miniatures. It is followed by a long theme which is treated by the orchestra and piano in equal partnership and moves through a golden haze, interrupted by two contrasting *minore* sections from the piano. It is not a bar too long.

The final theme and variations on the 'starling' tune are the greatest success, and, where Mozart steps outside convention and adds a buffa operatic finale, it again comes off to a perfectly calculated conclusion. Like 450, the concerto has three movements each perfect of its kind, and each moving through the progression of a gentle allegro, a spacious andante and a big, theatrical and fast last movement.

456 *in B flat*

After the excellence of the last three concertos, this movement is something of a disappointment. It reverts to the early Galant form and only by the scoring could we recognise this as a concerto of 1784. What felicities it has are hidden in unlikely places.

The simple First Subject has a double call followed by the conventional Galant answer, the whole is repeated with the call given by the wind and an extended answer running into a thoroughly ordinary Bridge of the old type which ends in strange little turns and arpeggio jumps:

Example 41
bar 24

Then follows a mysterious link passage in the dominant (bar 28), a dying phrase in the wind fading out over shifting semibreves and minims in the strings. The relief-type of Second Subject has a call in thirds on the oboes answered by the flutes and bassoons and ending in a quirk (bar 43) which is related to those at the end of the bridge.

Example 42
bar 43

This is worked over again and again, first in the wind band, then in the strings, to form the First Cadential. Then comes the first moment of magic, a slow hymn-like strain (bar 54) in four parts played by the strings and ending still with the same quirkish closing figure. This is played twice and is followed by the second joy of the movement, the Third Cadential developed from the same figure but now in the form of a pert bugle call (bar 60).

Example 43
bar 60

The Fourth Cadential is a conventional closing flourish.

The piano plays the call (which is unusually gentle and soft) and the answer; the second time it adds ornaments to the orchestra's version and provides its usual closing flourishes. The old Bridge, rescored, runs for six bars and then the piano embarks on a somewhat banal 'passage' sequence, a functional but inelegant piano bridge. The switch to the dominant is sketchy but the dominant tonality is reinforced by the Fourth Cadential which unfurls its flourish in F major. The piano second subject is of the sonatina type, light and unmemorable, but it is followed by bolder and more pleasing sequences which give this section a moment of heightened interest which is extended by the link passage, now with an in-filling of rapid piano figures, and transformed into a grand and imposing introduction to the Second Subject. The piano runs straight on to the First Cadential, and to the Second which is repeated in the orchestra with the piano sweeping through the centre of the texture with good effect.

The next section is unusual. In the old Galant form of Christian Bach it was common enough for the piano to work on with the Cadential material from the Statement after the Second Subject, as in this concerto, but now we have a series of what can only be called 'piano cadentials' for each one has the cadential sense and the cadential close, and, laid out as they are one after the other, they cannot possibly be construed as a part of the piano climax. The first of these unusual specimens begins in bar 149, the second in bar 152, the first is then repeated, then the second, and finally a third cadential (bar 162) leads to the short piano climax. The closing ritornello is made up of the Bridge and the Third and Fourth Cadentials.

The piano opens the Fantasy with two elegiac and affecting strophes. Then the bugle-call Cadential (the Third) breaks in on the oboes and bassoons (bar 201). This is developed at some length to the accompaniment of rushing scales in the piano. The third section (bar 211) is another free piano passage leading to what is remarkably like an old-style cadenza, which is hinged to the Reprise by three bars in the wind section which suggest a return to the mystery of the link passage.

The Reprise goes much as expected: the old Bridge is note for note the same as in the Statement. The awkward piano bridge is dropped and with a simple scale the piano runs into its unimpressive second subject. The rest goes as before until the piano climax where an extra half-dozen bars are inserted and the final bars are scored under the bugle call (Third Cadential) in the orchestra. This greatly adds to its effectiveness. The Cadenza platform is made up from the Bridge, and all four Cadentials (the first two without their repeats) follow it. The cadenzas themselves are both less interesting than usual. The first refers mainly to the Second Cadential, and the second starts with the turn and jump from the end of the Bridge, touches on the First Subject, the Second Cadential, and the First.

This is the most puzzling movement in the concertos, but not because of its complexity. It is indeed of quite a peculiar kind. Its methods are so unlike those of the surrounding concertos that it is tempting to speculate that it was an unused work, written perhaps for another genre, pulled out of a drawer and adapted to meet the performance deadline of 17 March. Much of the music has a simplicity we have not encountered since 242 and 246, and the subjects follow each other like beads on a string. The only strong filo relationship links the awkward 'turn and jump' figure at the end of the Bridge, the last phrase of the Second Subject, the First Cadential, the last phrase of the Second, and the Third Cadential. But the filo does not run; these are similar phrases tacked on the end of several sections and they do not seem to arise from the main subjects in an organised way. This snatching at tags (in the way that the Fantasies often begin with the last phrase of the preceding cadential) continues throughout the movement, and when we come to the 'piano cadentials' it is hard to avoid a suspicion that Mozart (but with his usual felicity) is merely out to gain time.

The second movement is very long. It is the least unsuccessful of the three, although it does not quite live up to the style of noble resignation which it strikes at the outset. The interest lies more in the orchestral writing than in the piano part which, for such a context, is somewhat ordinary for Mozart. There is not much hope today of riveting the attention of an audience throughout the 240 or so bars (including repeats) of its often rather wearisome *Andante un poco sostenuto*.

The third movement has a first strain to the rondo which Mozart could (and perhaps did) write in the nursery. In the other two movements there are occasional felicities, but here there is little magic to be found, except perhaps in the one rather conventional *minore* episode.

459 *in F major*

In 451 Mozart used a multitude of scattered components to create symphonic unity. Here, in the next Symphonic concerto, he sets out to achieve the same result by using an almost opposite method. The movement is held together by one long melody which sometimes re-appears in its entirety, sometimes in part, sometimes in small fragments. In one way or another the use of this First Subject as a main unit occupies some 200 out of the 400 bars of the movement, excluding the cadenza. The several mentions and references to the main theme are not filo derivatives but directly recognisable as a part of the original, and thus, despite the gentle melodic nature of its opening, the movement is truly 'symphonic'.

The First Subject is a gentle eight-bar melody, given the first time softly and delicately on the first violins and the flutes; three sharp wind chords introduce the repeat, which is *forte* and scored for the whole orchestra. The following elements are worth noting:

The dotted rhythm and the interval:

Example 44

bar 1

The triplet:

Example 45

bar 2

The simple intervals of the last phrase:

Example 46

bar 7

If this stately ritornello were heard in isolation we should half expect an aria to unfold, sung perhaps by a lady resigned to the bitterness of frustrated love. In this context, however, we have three beats from the bass strings matching the chords that linked the two halves of the First Subject. Over the last of them the violins breathe a series of three-crotchet sighs. This is the first section of the Transition (bar 16): the sighs pass to the woodwind and lead to the second section, some rising string figures, more bridge-like in nature but with the flutes and oboes still clinging to the dotted rhythm of the First Subject. This ends with a slowly moving figure in the lower strings given in sharp dynamic bursts, which we can call the 'repeating bass' (bar 32):

Example 47

bar 32

This is the second and lesser root from which later material will grow. During the next three bars the repeating bass adopts the crotchet beat:

Example 48

bar 37

The woodwind adds whirling triplets above, and with three conclusive bars the transition is over. In the course of transit we have not, however, been moved one hairsbreadth away from the tonic nor towards a Second Subject. Instead the Transition leads to the First Cadential (bar 42), a caesura-like question asked by the bassoons and oboes and answered by the strings based on the 'intervals' of the last phrase of the First Subject. The Second Cadential is a downward scale with a concluding bustle (bar 54) and the Third a cheerful duet between the first violins and the bassoons (bar 62). There is no open reference to the symphonic main units in any one of the three cadentials.

The First Concerto opens with the piano giving the First Subject in a clear treble: the three-note link is given by the strings and the repeat by the woodwind with a delicious piano accompaniment in triplets. The piano adds a descant to the sighs of the Transition (bar 91), then it strikes out into its own bridge passage, a vigorous little episode which leads through the double dominant to the dominant of C major. Here, instead of the expected piano second subject, the flutes start off a miniature fughetto amongst the wind section on the first strain of the first subject (bar 106). The piano picks this up and in a beautifully fluid series of shifting sequences reaches a clear cadential close, still in the rhythm of the First Subject, still in C major (bar 130).

All of this has been a preamble to what is, in fact, a substantial Second Subject, again a filo relative of the closing bar of the first subject, and given out by the strings and wind in alternate strophes. In the repeat the piano takes over the whole subject, adds some consequences and then moves into the first part of the piano climax (bar 149). Now for the first time we encounter what was to become Mozart's most telling weapon in defeating the isolation of the piano from the orchestral material and the symphonic idea during its long climactic passages. Over the piano's triplets we hear a light but definite reminder of the First Subject's rhythm and interval in the woodwind. This partnership continues for fourteen bars, the piano follows its own ascending line until the flow of the climax is unexpectedly halted by a sudden intrusion of the repeating bass and triplets from the last section of the Transition (begins bar 163). The piano smooths away the interruption and continues a free run to the trill. The final ritornello is made up of the First Subject which soon changes its shape and reveals unsuspected harmonic possibilities to become something very like a coda and so confirm its new function as an end-piece instead of a beginning.

The last bars of the First Concerto, however, do not run to a close. There is a drift to A minor and the piano opens the Development with broken arpeggios of the sort that might well lead to a free fantasy (bar 211). Almost immediately, however, the woodwind checks the piano's course with some chording in the rhythm of the First Subject (bar 217), and soon both the rhythm and the interval (extended first to an octave and finally to a twelfth) are there to be developed in a dialogue between the two partners that runs up to the first Return (bar 235). This avoids the dominant pedal and moves instead towards the relative minor. The second Return passes from the piano to the orchestra which gives out a succession of calls again in the rhythm of the First Subject, modulating quickly to the dominant and the start of the Reprise (bar 247). This is a unique method of Return, devised perhaps because of the static tonic/dominant emphasis of the First Subject which is to follow.

Now the piano takes the first appearance of the First Subject just as in the First Concerto, the orchestra the second, scored just as in the Statement. But the sighs of the Transition have the same piano descant as in the First Concerto and this section is joined to the fughetto entry, losing the piano episode altogether. This is parallel to the procedure of 415 and 451. From here to the end of the first part of the piano climax (the ground bass), all goes much as before. But now there is a novelty. At bar 340 the piano gives out the caesura-questions of the First Cadential to which the strings reply. Then the piano gives out the question a third time, answers it itself, and drives on into the closing part of the climax. But again there is a change, for the woodwind comes in with the rhythm and interval of the First subject above the piano to form what is, in effect, an extension of some twelve bars (bars 360–71) made up from the First Subject in the form of the quasi-coda which ended the First Concerto. The piano leaves the tonic key with some unusually emphatic modulations just before the end of the climax, which is rounded off with a ritornello starting like the First Subject and working towards the cadenza platform by methods similar to those of the closing ritornello of the First Concerto.

The cadenza is short and valedictory, mentioning only the First and Second Subjects in altered form and mood and with display writing fore and aft of each. The Second and Third Cadentials make up the closing ritornello.

It is clear on first hearing that the construction of this movement is something new. The First Subject has ten substantial mentions and, as we have seen, either in whole or in fragments it dominates almost a half of the work. Apart from the repeating bass, a minor agent, the rest of the 'given' material appears only twice. This was as far as Mozart was to go with the use of a unified theme: perhaps he felt he had gone too far, for in the last three great Symphonic concertos he reverted to a balance between the methods of 451 and those of 459.

He resolved the second subject equation in this concerto by inserting only one piece of second group material shared between the orchestra and the piano, in the First Concerto. This made more room for the pervasive first subject, but even so one of the

Transition sections disappears after its first outing, as does the piano episode, and the last two Cadentials are played only at the end of the Statement and the end of the Reprise.

The problem in this form of symphonic essay was that the remnants of the old concerto form offered an embarrassing superfluity of unconnected material. When Mozart wrote a movement, half of which worked on or around a main theme, then the other half was not large enough to contain an orchestral transition, a piano episode, two second subjects, four cadentials and a piano climax. There were two ways out: to drop some of the parts, or to adjust the independent passages so that, while they still did the same job, they did it by adapting the motif to their purposes instead of introducing new material. In 459 Mozart adopted both solutions in part: there is only one second subject and only three Cadentials and a dispensable piano episode. The piano bridge became a second Transition with orchestra and piano sharing material from the First Subject. A bridge passage used to be identifiable as much by the shape of its melody and the style of its rhythm as by its position in the work and its function. From now on the function of the Transition may be the same as the bridge but it will often use the same melodic and rhythmic materials as the First Subject.

In 459 the greatest advance was therefore the appearance of the main theme in the area of the piano bridge and the piano climax. The weakness lay in the inability to make use of the central part of the Transition and to have three Cadentials, two of which were no more than appendices to the Statement and Reprise. It may well be, however, that 459 more than 467 gave Mozart the cue for his ultimate solution: a merging together of the parts of the Statement by the use of a main unit, a reduction in the number and size of the independent cadentials, and a more concise and pervasive use of the main unit in the piano solo sections. It may also have pointed to the need for a First Subject which was more flexible than a distinctive eight-bar melody.

There are two subsidiary points. First the balance of power between the piano and the orchestra is more equal than in the previous concertos. The piano has its times of silence in the First Concerto and when it does play it has three different roles: its traditional role as the soloist (as in the piano episode, in its version of the Second Subject, and in the piano climax proper); the accompanist (as in the extended treatment of the First Subject material from bar 120 onwards); and as the equal partner to the orchestra, as in the descant it supplies to the first section of the Transition. A quick comparison with 415 and 451 will demonstrate the great reduction in the extent of the solo part. Second, Mozart indulges his fondness for dramatic stops and starts within the piano climax more successfully here than in the previous Symphonic concerto, 451. There the use of cadential material was impeded near the climax section by a number of full stops. Here his use of the repeating bass, the First Subject material and (in the reprise) the First Cadential, all add to the drama without unduly arresting the pace.

Both of these points pose problems for the performer. To find the right balance with an orchestra is more difficult than to play a solo part with orchestral accompaniment, and the conductor and performer have a delicate task in adjusting things nicely between the two voices. The problem of building continuous tension towards finality in an interrupted piano climax is also difficult, and few pianists indeed pass the test. It is never, of course, a matter of rubato, but rather of the right degree of weight required to let the interruptions make their point without losing the sense of the larger strategy of the climax.

The second movement opens with an unpromising theme, but soon redeems itself past all doubt with the ingenuity of what follows, in particular the canon of four voices at bar 103, the elegant *minore* section and the clever little coda. It is marked Allegretto and is naturally quicker, lighter and shorter than usual, and it does not pretend to any lofty sentiments, being content to entertain with gentle wit and decorous modesty. The finale too is a complete success. It has two main subjects and some broad symphonic writing, as in the fugal ritornello beginning at bar 289. The cadenza is most effective.

9

The Three Concertos of 1785

466 in D minor; 467 in C; 482 in E flat

In 1785 it first became apparent that Mozart and his public were drifting apart. Except in opera, where his sense of audience never deserted him, he was beginning to write for himself rather more than for his audience. In the earlier years he had been able to combine the two, and without any apparent effort. Some works, like *Figaro,* were still to please both; others, like the Haydn string quartets, were to please only himself and a few connoisseurs and professionals. The piano concertos of 1785 probably stood somewhere between the two. In writing a concerto like 466 he surely did not bear in mind what was 'a happy medium between what was too easy and too difficult', what was 'natural' and what 'could not fail to please the less learned'.

We do not know how the financial results of his six Mehlgrube concertos in 1785 compared with similar series in the previous years. (Leopold being in Vienna at the time, we lack their usual correspondence.) We do know that the Society of Musicians' concert on 13 March, which had as the second part a long work adapted by Mozart from the C minor Mass, was poorly attended and that the repeat performance was a disaster.

The reasons for the decline in Mozart's popularity, apart from those reasons of fashion, luck and exposure which affect all artists in all ages, were several. First there was his greater range and enterprise in harmony. Ernst Ludwig Gerber, a musician of the court of Prince Schwarzburg-Sondershausen, who was a good and intelligent critic of other contemporary composers, wrote of Mozart in 1790:

> This great master, because of his early acquaintance with harmony, has come to know it so deeply and inwardly that the unpractised ear has difficulty in following him in his works. Even practised ones must hear his pieces several times.

'Amateurs' and 'connoisseurs' alike were puzzled by the Haydn quartets: one customer is said to have sent the parts back to the publisher Artaria 'because they were full of engraver's errors'. Another story tells how a noble amateur tore the score in pieces when he ascertained that the discords he had heard were actually in print.

The second specific charge laid against some of the operas (and probably the concertos too) is that of 'too many notes'. The criticism, made in the Emperor Joseph's famous remark about *Il Seraglio* (to which Mozart replied 'not one more than is necessary'), probably reflected, as most royal criticisms must do, not so much a personal opinion as the general view of the musical establishment surrounding the court. It is likely to have been applied not only to the thickness of the texture, but to the fact that the soloists, instead of being provided with a respectful *sotto voce* accompaniment, had to contend with an emancipated orchestra which often played a part equal to their own. Dittersdorf, writing of Mozart's operas in 1786, said 'He has only one fault in his pieces for the stage, and his singers have very often complained of it—he deafens them with his full accompaniment'.

The third identifiable complaint against Mozart concerned the sheer profusion of musical ideas. His invention was too rich for the listeners' comprehension. Dittersdorf again wrote:

> I have never yet met with any composer who had such an amazing wealth of ideas. I could almost wish he were not so lavish in using them. He leaves his hearer out of breath, for hardly has he grasped one beautiful thought than another of greater fascination dispels the first, and this goes on throughout, so that in the end it is impossible to retain any one of these beautiful melodies.

(Both of these Dittersdorf passages are from his book *Lebensbeschreibung*, Leipzig, 1801, quoted by Hyatt King in his book *Mozart in Retrospect*, Oxford, 1955.)

One suspects, however, that all these criticisms were a rationalisation of something that critics never care to mention. Mozart's music disturbed them, because it assaulted their emotions in a manner to which they were not accustomed. Their well-regulated susceptibilities were not ready to accept the first beginnings of the *Sturm und Drang* of the Romantic age.

There is little value in speculating about the motives which compel a great talent to forsake a popular and profitable career in order to explore a private line of development. Today it might be called artistic integrity; this was not, however, an eighteenth-century concept. In those days the few lonely spirits in the arts were perhaps subject to the same sort of compulsion that drove the scientists and the natural philosophers to dedicate their lives to the advancement of knowledge. It is possible too that the influence of religion, or at least the Masonic code, had some bearing on Mozart's quite definite change in purpose as a composer. At any rate, during his early life and until his closer acquaintance with Bach's works, his entry into the Masonic lodge and his friendship with Joseph Haydn, there had been little evidence of any composition being undertaken except to serve an occasion, to please an audience and to enlarge his reputation. But now, in 1785, we find him composing music which no longer conformed to these criteria. There can be little doubt that a piano concerto on the lines of 175 would have been warmly welcomed by the audience at his concerts at the Mehlgrube. It is unlikly that the great concerto in D minor, which confronted the audience with unfamiliar harmonies and with a strange mood of heroism and tragedy, was nearly so well received.

Despite the few great successes that were to come, Mozart's chances of securing the highest position in Vienna's musical life grew less each year. The list of subscriptions to his concerts on the 17th, 24th and 31st of March 1784 probably represented the richest sponsorship he was ever to command. The concerts of

1785 were probably financially successful too, but from now on (except in the opera house and in foreign cities) we hear less of tumultuous applause, less of concertos that 'went magnifique' and more of the financial problems that culminated in the last series of desperate letters to Michael Puchberg.

The D minor concerto was composed in a few weeks for the first of six Friday concerts at the Mehlgrube. Mozart performed it himself, and in the audience was Leopold, who wrote to Nannerl:

> The concert was magnificent and the orchestra played splendidly,... we had a new and very fine concerto by Wolfgang, which the copyist was still copying when we arrived, and the rondo of which your brother did not even have time to play through, as he had to supervise the copying.

Mozart played the concerto a second time as an item in a concert in the Bergtheater on 15 February.

467 was composed presumably just after this and first performed at another concert at the Bergtheater on 10 March, this time organised by Mozart for his own benefit. There is mention in the billing for this concert of the 'large forte piano pedale' or pedal-board. In this bill it is said that it will be 'used by him in improvising'. Whether or not he ever used it to give himself a pedal bass in the performance of a concerto, we do not know. Its range was of two octaves, downwards from middle C.

There is no doubt that these months of February and March marked the high tide of Mozart's activity in Vienna. Leopold wrote, again to Nannerl, on 12 March:

> We never go to bed before one o'clock and I never get up before nine ... Every day there are concerts; and the whole time is given up to teaching, music, composing and so forth. I feel rather out of it all. If only the concerts were over! It is impossible for me to describe the rush and bustle. Since my arrival your brother's forte-piano has been taken at least a dozen times to the theatre or to some other house.

There was, however, no call for a new piano concerto until December. Leopold wrote to Nannerl on 13 January 1786 saying he had had a letter from Mozart dated 28 December 'in which he said he had given without much preparation three subscription concerts to 120 subscribers, that he composed for this purpose a new piano concerto in E flat (482) in which [a rather unusual occurrence] he had to repeat the Andante.'

466 *in D minor*

In this work, the first in a minor key and perhaps one of the best-known of all classical piano concertos, the concerto form reached its destination. Other composers were to do great and different things with it: no one was to take it further. In writing 466 Mozart brought to bear all the skill of a long apprenticeship. Although his life was short, by the time he was in his later twenties Mozart had more practical experience of composition, that is to say he had written a greater number of considerable works, than any composer who lived before or since. For eighteen years he had had a special interest in the piano concerto, writing and performing them as a matter of necessity. Now, to the in-grained memory of the old concerto form, to the experience gained from his several experiments and to the skill of a veteran performer, he added the final touch of genius and minted a new and perfect symphonic form. 466 can no longer be assessed in terms of partial success or failure: it has the authority of a masterpiece, and all we can do is to marvel at the means he employed to bring it off.

The symphonic method he used lies somewhere between that of 451 and 459. There are a number of small binding units or motifs, but they all lie within the first two long opening sentences, which we can now only call the First Group/Transition. The concerto opens softly and mysteriously with a series of upward triplet scoops in the bass under an uneasy and syncopated melodic line in the upper strings. The opening eight bars keep a tonic-dominant harmony, but then there is an upward movement in a series of suspended chords which move chromatically and return to close the tonic. The whole orchestra comes in *forte* on the chord of D minor (bar 16) and the triplet figure runs up to successive octaves of D and then strikes out an affirmative variation of the first uneasy phrase, ending this part of the First Group/ Transition with a series of insistent semitones rolling in unison around A, the foundation of the dominant chord. The thematic units in the First Group/Transition can be described as follows:

FIRST GROUP

The 'triplet in the bass':

Example 49

bar 1

The 'uneasy' figure 1:

Example 50

bar 3

with 'upward movement' 2:

Example 51

bar 9

The 'affirmative version':

Example 52

bar 18

The 'rolling semitones':

Example 53

bar 21

The transition continues quietly with an adapted version of the uneasy figure from the opening, and leads on to a loud assertion of the rolling semitones in the bass, now extended and moving more widely to form a two-bar pattern. Again these end on the dominant chord, and the Second Subject follows (bar 33). This is of the Relief type and begins in F major as a dialogue between the oboes and bassoons beneath and the flutes above (six bars) and has a five-bar tail provided by the two oboes reverting slowly back to D minor and with a string accompaniment (of which more will be heard). The opening of the Second Subject has picked up the semitone interval from the passage before (but which was also present in the opening sentence) and plays with it in the simplest possible manner. The whole passage gains its effect from its contrast in tone and form with the massive bustle of the closing bars before it. It is little more than a pause in the majestic progression of the Statement, and as soon as it is over the full orchestra continues with the Transition where it left off with the semitone roll extended in a new and third pattern rising in semitones and leading to the 'affirmative version' this time designed to end in a cadential close. The last five bars are repeated (bar 53). And then there is yet another and last pattern for the rolling semitones followed by a shortened and varied version of the cadential tail. This ends in a caesura (bar 67) and leads to the First and only true Cadential, a filo relative of the 'uneasy' figure, retaining its tied rhythms and intervals, and written in four-part harmony for the strings of a particularly rich texture. The second violin part is based upon the sequences which accompanied the tail of the Second Subject, and now they flower into an elegiac counter-melody to the first violin line.

The only sensible way to read the structure of this Statement is to divide it into a First Group, a Middle Section incorporating a Second Subject within it, and a single Cadential. For the Statement is one organic piece of music built from the motifs in the opening sentences and changing its nature to perform the several jobs of providing an opening, a forceful 'statement', a moment of relief, a lengthy continuation of the statement moving towards finality, and then a Cadential. For the purposes of comparing and indexing the concertos, however, it is still perfectly correct to describe the Statement in detail as follows:

First Group	Bars	1 – 22
Transition		23 – 32
Second Subject		33 – 43
Transition/Cadential		44 – 70
Cadential		71 – 77

As in 459 the Statement has made only the slightest move away from the home key which it has reinforced again and again in the true ritornello fashion.

The piano opens the First Concerto with a lucid assertion, all the more effective for being spoken quietly in its upper register. The phrases have relationship both with the opening 'uneasy' figures and the flutes' reply to the first phrase of the Second Subject. In the twelfth bar it breaks rhythm and, supported by the wind band, breaks into a broad but rapid introductory flourish which leads back to the First Group, opening in the orchestra alone (bar 91). In the fifth bar the piano enters the orchestral texture, supplying its own version of the 'tentative' figures and reinforcing the triplet runs in the bass. Gradually it gains ascendancy and usurps first place, running along brilliantly until it reaches the rolling semitones, where the orchestra joins it to round off the first part of the Transition section. Then follows the Second Subject, again in the tonic parallel, with the piano taking over the part of the flute and converting the tail into a concise piano bridge leading through C major to C the dominant of F (bar 127).

The piano second subject consists of a dramatic phrase in F major, again related to the opening 'uneasy' figure. The answer is accompanied by the strings; a second piano phrase follows, this time in G minor, but the answer returning to F major. The whole subject is then repeated in the woodwind with the piano supplying scales beneath the answer. A final scale in the reverse direction leads the piano straight into the piano climax. The first section of this (ten bars, 143–152) is a free climactic passage ending in a trill which, in another context, might itself have made up the whole of the climax. But the piano climbs out of the trill with a second spurt and this time its material is based on one of the later versions of the rolling semitone figure. It reaches a second trill in bar 158, goes on yet again with a mighty piano statement of the third version of this figure to a tumultuous final burst of arpeggios and scales to reach the truly final trill in bar 173. This marvellously constructed climax of thirty bars is no more nor less than an extended piano version of the Transition/Cadential section of the Statement and it grows in size from the first bar to the last, each trill signalling a false close and each succeeding passage springing on to extend and raise the tension. The second part of the First Group, followed by the first part of the Transition and the Cadential, all now in F major, form the closing ritornello. The lift into the major key transforms the main subject into a buoyant affirmation, yet the cadential is even more pathetic and affecting in the major mode than it was in the minor.

The piano introduction, now in F major (still in the two distinct parts of the assertion and the flourish) opens the Development. Again the shift to the major has transformed it; the shape of the melody is altered too. The orchestra breaks in with the first sentence of the First Group, and the cycle starts again with the piano introduction, this time in G minor and again worked into a slightly new form. And so to a third cycle. This time its problems are worked out happily in E flat and it runs into a free development with the piano's arpeggios supported from time to time with the triplet run from the First Group in unison from the strings. At bar 242 the piano reaches the dominant pedal and the first Return; the second Return is a four-bar passage for the piano alone which leads directly back to the first sentence.

In the Reprise the first sentence of the First Group remains with the orchestra; the piano enters at the eighth bar but the music follows the course of the Statement, not the First Concerto, and the second and *forte* sentence of the First Group follows without the piano which only rejoins after the first part of the Transition has begun. The piano adds a different tail to the end of the Second Subject (still in F major) and delivers its own second subject in D minor.

This, in passing, is one of the key moments of the Reprise. Instead of the buoyant move to the tonic parallel at this point, the reinforcement of the minor mode has a devastating effect. The one ray of hope which lit up the First Concerto has been extinguished.

After the piano has done with its second subject, the first section of the piano climax is reworked; the second extended by two bars, and the third by three, the whole climax being lifted to a pitch even higher than in the First Concerto. The cadenza ritornello is made from a simple statement of the second sentence of the First Group. Alas, no cadenza of Mozart's remains; what he would have done can only be a matter for speculation. Certainly his cadenza would not have been so powerful as to detract from the great climax just achieved, and certainly it would have referred to one or more of the symphonic motifs with either the Second Subject or, more likely, the piano second subject in its major version, lying in its central pool of peace and melody. It must, of course, have confirmed the concerto's purpose by ending with a reinforcement of the minor mode.

The final ritornello consists of the last cadential section of the Transition, followed by the Cadential. There is a short coda of eight bars which returns for its material to the uneasy figure of the opening bar. But now it has reached a new and final shape; the mood is one of resignation and the phrase has lost its tentative nature; it resolves peacefully into its last cadence.

This movement finally achieves Mozart's symphonic ideal. It has the same supremacy amongst the concertos as *Don Giovanni* amongst the operas. The old cut-and-dried sections have disappeared from view, and this new liberty allows the music to flow through the same phases of the dramatic scheme which lay behind the concerto form with a continuous (and developing) use of the same basic materials. It also allowed an economy in the time taken to make each point. The Statement is wonderfully compact; the long stream of Cadentials has been replaced by a working out of the basic material which leads to its own finality: the single melancholy Cadential supplies all the additional closing balance that is needed. In the Concerto sections several problems have been smoothed away. The second subjects are both short and easily managed: the piano bridge is reduced to three or four bars: the piano episode has disappeared: there are no loose sequential passages. Only the piano climax is enlarged to give it room to match the power of the orchestral framework. Once the structure of the movement is described there is little to add, except perhaps to point out that this concerto demands exceptional stamina and power in the performer.

The second movement is a simple little Romanza, nicely calculated to flow peacefully in the valley between the massive peaks of the movements on either side of it, and saved from sluggishness by an agitated *minore* section in the middle. The Rondo has a strenuous and noble theme far distant from the Tyrolean style of some of the earlier concertos. The piano's entry after the massive opening ritornello (bar 64) is very close to its first entry in the first movement, and the little relief phrase (bar 93) is an inversion of the Second Subject of the first movement. As happens quite frequently, the filo of the opening movement carries through to have its influences on the last. Unlike the first movement, however, the rondo moves steadily towards the major key and ends in a cheerful section in D major, far from the mood anticipated by its opening bars.

467 in C major

This movement lacks the taut construction of 466; it is more discursive by nature and it generates a number of new ideas as it goes along. In particular the two concerto sections are more loosely built. Nevertheless, from its opening bar it has the stamp of a symphonic movement and the looser piano writing is brought back to the symphonic idea by each ritornello.

The First Subject opens with a whispered statement of a theme with a martial air. The second phrase ends on the tonic, and is answered by two phrases from the violins rounded off by a flourish from the wind. The whole answer is then repeated, with some ornaments. Then the *forte* statement begins with the military tune forming the bass and the upper strings giving a new descant above it. The First Group ends with a series of insistent semitones over the dominant pedal.

The units in the First Group can be described as follows:

1 The 'martial air':

Example 54

bar 1

2 The 'answer':

Example 55

bar 5

2 Ditto, ornamented:

Example 56

bar 8

3 The 'closing flourish':

Example 57

bar 7

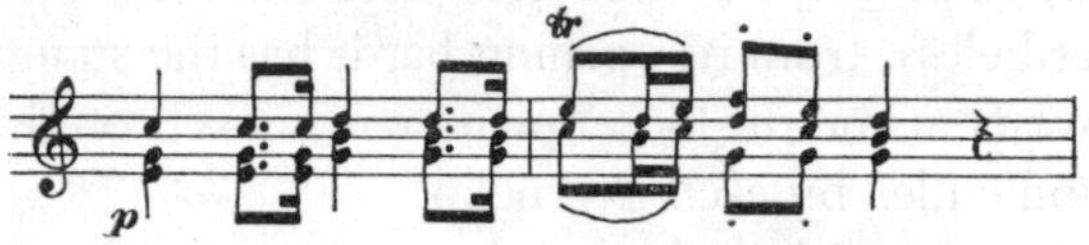

4 The 'descant':

Example 58

bar 12

5 The 'insistent semitones':

Example 59

bar 24

The First Group and the Transition have again been collapsed into a single unit. After the first two sentences the *forte* statement begins to wander towards a dominant tonality and, if the First Group were chopped off arbitrarily in the middle of a phrase, bars 16–27 could be called the first part of the Transition. A comparison with 466 will show the parallels and divergences in this part of the two Statements. For consistency, however, the whole opening section of 467 up to bar 28 is called the First Group.

But to resume, the dominant seventh resolves back to C major in a staccato falling scale, and the Second Subject sounds out in the horns and trumpets (bar 28). This is a light affair of some eight bars in length (as in 466), and consists of two sonorous chords with a frilly answer from the woodwind, the first part related to the ornamental phrase in the First Subject.

Then the middle section, or Transition towards the Cadentials, begins with soft fugal entries of the martial tune (bar 36), again leading to the semitones, this time carrying the sense of dramatic question mark and escaping from them into a series of cadential phrases. The first true cadential is a chromatic slide upwards from the flute, answered by a sweet strain in the first violins (bar 52). This is related to the original string answer to the martial air, now adapted into a cadential shape. After a repeat of the chromatic slide, this strain is extended with wayward and rapturous leaps. The Second Cadential (bar 64) is a compact reminder of two elements of the First Group—the martial tune and the closing flourish.

The First Concerto has an introduction from the oboes and bassoons giving out a linking phrase, again related to the original string answer. The piano takes its bow, and makes a leisurely ascent up the dominant chord to pause before the orchestra enters with the military tune while the piano provides a sustained trill. The piano takes over and decorates the answers and appropriates to itself the first military flourish. Then, as in 459, it embarks on an episode (bar 91) which widens out to provide a bridge to the dominant and ends with two bars in which the orchestra establishes the scale of G major. At this point, we have, instead of the piano second subject, a second episode in G minor (bar 109) of the kind we have already encountered in 451. This moves into a gallop and ends with a pedal on the dominant of G. Now at last comes the piano second subject, one of the full-scale melodious kind, played first by the piano and then by the woodwind. After this striking melody, the piano starts off towards its climax by giving the cue for a fughetto on the military tune, which is taken up by the strings. But after its third entry the tune is overlaid by two-handed arpeggios from the piano, the strings' staccato accompaniment dies out, and a new rhythmic figure appears in the orchestra (bar 154). This figure gives a new spring to the piano's tread. But its course is arrested by a short stop in the subdominant and a cadenza-like passage (bar 163) ending with a half-hearted trill. But now the piano moves into its second and true climax, at first playing with the new rhythmic figure itself and then exhorted by its presence in the orchestral accompaniment. So to the final stream of arpeggios and the final trill. The closing ritornello is made up from the *forte* version of the military tune with its descant. This has a new ending to link on to the First Cadential. All goes as expected until the violins reach their rapturous leaps, and then quite suddenly the Cadential broadens, modulates and extends for an additional eight bars (215–222), thereby leading into the Fantasy.

The piano gives out a figure which is a filo relation of the episode and has within it the triplet of the opening march. This phrase has the air of a subject for a cyclic treatment, but the piano drifts into a passage of growing power, developing a bass figure related to elements of the First Subject with a reminder of the Second Subject in the woodwind above it. These disappear as insensibly as they arrived and after some free writing the Return is reached with a theatrical gesture in bar 264. This is smoothly done, with the piano filling in between slow chording in the wind, and with an expectant pulse over the dominant pedal in the strings.

The piano is silent throughout the opening of the Reprise, which repeats the first part of the First Group. This, however, is cut short and followed at once by the fugal beginning to the second part of the Transition. But the piano joins in and soon diverts the 'reprise' into the same series of fluid chromatic runs which in the First Concerto led to the piano second subject (bar 313). This goes much as before and passes on to the fugal entry and the first section of the piano climax. Where before we had the quasi-cadenza, this section leads instead, with an extended run, to an elaborated version of the closing bars of the First Group, the semitones and the scale. Then comes the Second Subject (bar 351), played first by the orchestra and then the piano. The last section of the piano climax is lengthened and heightened by three extra bars. The cadenza ritornello is based on the *forte* section of the First Group, and after the cadenza there is the cadential ending to the Transition followed by the first part of the First Cadential and then the Second. This is rounded off by a short coda of four bars, still based on the opening military tune with which the movement began.

Even in this comparatively loose-limbed member of the Symphonic family it is clear that the Main Theme system of Emmanuel Bach has returned to the piano concerto. Although the forms are different some of the ideas are similar. The First Ritornello has a thematic identity and it is once again more a thing of related sequences than a succession of contrasted subjects. The light relief type of subject is used because it is easier to handle than the long lyrical Second Subjects of the kind used in 271. The Second, Third and Fourth Ritornellos all start with the Main Theme, or a part of it, at their head. It is true that the side-ritornellos have gone, or been absorbed into a texture which has both piano and orchestra playing together, but in the concerted sections reminders of the Main Theme once again crop up from time to time.

This movement adopts the easy solution of dropping the two piano episodes (and the cadenza-like interpolation in the piano climax) to make room for a full reprise of all the main subjects. Whether this was a deliberate choice, or due to the nature of the work, or because of pressure of time during composition, we can only guess. It is nevertheless a fine movement and, because of its less rigid structure, it leaves many options in the interpretation of the First Concerto. It is probably better for the performer to err on the side of a fairly summary treatment of the several interruptions to the progress of the movement than to try too hard to bring out the contrasting flavour of each one. It is easy to see that the First Concerto demands some placid piano tone to balance the speed and spontaneity of its own second subject. It is less easy, however, to see why Mozart did not use the Second Subject both in the First Concerto and in the Reprise, as in 466, instead of introducing two piano episodes and a quasi-cadenza, all of which are lost in the Reprise. It may be that he felt the Second Subject to be so static as to hinder the flow of the first piano section.

The second movement is one of those Andantes which inspired the Victorian soubriquet 'divine'. It moves with serenity through a golden haze, the strings supplying a continuous rustling pulse beneath the simple melodic line, and the horns and the bass register of the piano occasionally booming out with a deep and mellow serenity. The finale is gay, gallant and full of fresh invention. It is one of the last of its kind; open and straightforward in nature without the serious aspirations of the finale of 466 or the operatic excitement of 453.

482 *in E flat*

This concerto reverts to the stock Galant form for its construction and to more traditional methods of composition in its content. It is easy to believe that Mozart composed it very quickly.

The Galant tonic-dominant call is given out by the whole orchestra, the very agreeable answer played the first time by the horns with the bassoons working in counterpoint, the second time by the clarinets and violins. It is followed by an important pendant figure (F2) passing through the woodwind and answered by the horns. Within the accompanying violin line there is a phrase in bar 17 which will lead to many things. The pendant figure is repeated and the answer given twice, the second time by the whole orchestra. A magnificent Bridge of the old Galant type follows; it uses the violin phrase mentioned above as a powerful bass figure. The Bridge ends with a hustle on the dominant and is followed by a somewhat theatrical woodwind link to the Second Subject (bar 46). This consists of a lyrical sweep in the violins (a filo relative of the same violin phrase from bar 17). The First Cadential has a long figure in the strings over a strong two-bar bass figure, the Second (bar 64) a conventional series of phrases on the violins which relapse into scales, and the Third a wistful little *envoi*.

The piano introduction is of the sonatina type, which we

have not encountered since 415. Then comes the call in the orchestra with piano arpeggios filling in the reply, which is otherwise scored in the same way. In place of the pendant the piano moves straight into its own bridge, a filo relative of the *envoi*, but nevertheless a perfunctory and somewhat disappointing passage. The dominant key is confirmed by a conventional scale, with twirls, from the orchestra. Next there is a slow piano episode in B flat minor (bar 128), thickly chorded in the bass and of the kind with which we have become familiar in 365, 451, 466 and 467. The sequences from the episode lead, again in a somewhat offhand manner, to the piano second subject (bar 152), which, like many similar and peaceful melodies, has the cloud of the sub-dominant chord hanging over it. It is sixteen bars long with the repeat. The ensuing sequences run into the piano climax, considerable in length but weak in texture. The three cadentials provide the closing ritornello.

The Fantasy opens with some dialogue between the piano and orchestra on the theme of the last three chords of the Third Cadential; the piano then moves into a free fantasy. This passage is uneventful both in its outline and in its harmony until it surprisingly pauses to toy for a moment with a variant of the piano second subject (bar 248). The dominant pedal is reached in bar 254 and with a moment of magic in the return we are back to the comparative riches of the First Subject.

The first call and answer are given to the orchestra alone, the second time the piano gives its decoration in unison and then plays a leading part in the pendant section. The first part of the Bridge follows, rescored for piano and orchestra, followed by the second part of the Bridge (orchestra alone), and with the operatic link given by the piano. So to the Second Subject, also played by the piano the first time. There is a short new link to the piano second subject, which develops some new sequences and runs into an entirely new piano climax, shorter but no more original nor effective than the first. The First Cadential makes up the cadenza ritornello and the Second and Third end the movement.

This is one of Mozart's few first movements which deteriorate after the Statement. Perhaps Mozart's confession that the concerts for which this concerto was written were put on 'without much preparation' explains a good deal. The piano sections do not have the same degree of craftsmanship or of spontaneity as the original orchestral writing. Faced by a movement of this nature, the best the performer can do is play with precision and pace, and in particular to give the piano climaxes as much solid force and momentum as he can. Many good pianists make the mistake of allowing sections of the Melodic and Galant climaxes to drop in volume, perhaps encouraged by an often spurious *piano* marked in the orchestral part. No doubt such directions crept in as a signal to the orchestral players to 'let the soloist through'. The piano part should, of course, be clear and firm at the start and proceed in a controlled crescendo to reach its maximum volume by the trill.

The second movement is on a higher plane (we know that it was given an encore on its first performance). The opening theme has a truly Mozartean second strain and there are some pleasant variations, especially the serenade-like sections given to the wind band. Here at last the presence of the clarinets in the score is fully justified, perhaps because they were no longer overpowered by the horns on their home ground in E flat. The coda, once heard, haunts the ear forever. The finale is the last of the simple rustic rondos with a mild contrasting Andantino section in 3/4 time.

All in all, there are indications that Mozart may have composed the Andante and the Statement of the first movement with his usual care and affection, and then been forced to complete the rest of the work as best he could in the time available, which, knowing how fast and how well he could work, cannot have been much.

10

1786—The Year of *Figaro*

488 in A; 491 in C minor; 503 in C

On 1 May 1786 Mozart's opera *Figaro* had its first performance. The composition of *Figaro* had been begun in October 1785 and according to da Ponte had been completed in six weeks, Mozart writing the score as he received each part of the libretto. This is likely to be broadly true, but for once there was a gap of months between 'setting the music on paper' and the performance, and it is possible that *Figaro*'s polished and elaborate score was revised and reworked in the interval. We know that the overture at least was not written until the week leading up to the first night.

1786 was the year of Mozart operas. *The Impresario,* a small thing, was performed at the Imperial Court in February; there was a revival of *Idomeneo* in March at Prince Auersperg's palace; *Figaro* had nine performances during the year at the Burgtheater; in November *The Seraglio* was revived also at the Burgtheater; and in December *Figaro* opened in Prague.

The reception given to *Figaro* in Vienna, although by no means hostile, must have been a crushing disappointment to Mozart. He must have known that he had composed an opera incomparably better than its predecessors, that the libretto was brilliant and the cast strong. He must have hoped that by redeeming the *buffa* convention and by transforming it into a style of true human comedy he would still please the Vienna public and score a great popular success. The 'connoisseurs' and the 'amateurs' were indeed delighted, but the rank and file of the audience were less than enchanted. Perhaps two entries in the diary of a high court official, Count Zinzendorf, are indicative:

> At seven o'clock to the opera *Le Nozze di Figaro* . . . Louise in our box, the opera bored me . . . (1 May)
> At the opera *Le Nozze di Figaro*. Mozart's music is singular, hands without head . . . (4 July)

It was after the summer of *Figaro* that Mozart thought of emigrating to England or France, and no wonder. The great success of the opera in Prague, although it may have refreshed his spirits, did nothing to advance his career in the musical capital where he was now beginning to be out of favour. No high appointment seemed likely any longer; his band of supporters was thinning out; his talents were appreciated only by the few professionals, such as Haydn and 'amateurs' like Baron van Swieten, who had no cause for jealousy and were sufficiently flexible in their musical tastes to follow Mozart's astonishing progress.

Two of the greatest of Mozart's piano concertos were written between the composition of *Figaro* and its performance. 488 is marked 2 March, and 491, 24 March. Both were written for the usual season of Lent concerts on days when dramatic performances were forbidden. 491 probably had its first performance at Mozart's Grand Musical Concert at the Burgtheater on 7 April.

Between the production of *Figaro* and the end of the year he wrote music for the piano, chamber works and the last horn concerto (495). During the autumn of doubts there were no major works, but in December came the Prague symphony and the great piano concerto in C major.

This concerto, 503, may have been played at one of four Advent concerts at the Trattner casino on 5 December. There is documentary evidence that these concerts were planned, but none that they actually took place. 503 may have been performed, but not by Mozart, on 7 March 1787 at a concert at the Karntnertor Theatre in which one Marianne Willmann and her brother and sister performed. The first fully authenticated performance by Mozart himself was in Leipzig on 12 May 1789.

These were the three last of the subscription concert concertos. They had begun with 449, and although some of them were written for a first performance by pupils or visitors, it is likely that all were played by Mozart himself at one or other of the concerts. All the symphonic concertos he wrote for his own first performance, and there is no record that they were subsequently played by others in his lifetime, with a very few exceptions, which are in themselves interesting.

Leopold reports on a performance of 503 by one of his own pupils named Marchand which sounds as if it had been something of a scramble: 'Marchand took it rather quickly . . . We had to practise the rondo three times before the orchestra could manage it.' There is something infinitely touching about this family scene at Salzburg, Leopold presiding, his pupil playing the clavier, Michael Haydn turning the pages, and all of them marvelling at 'the art with which it is composed, how delightfully the parts are interwoven, and what a difficult concerto it is'. Although technically it may have been 'difficult', in its emotional range it must surely have been even more formidable.

Apart from this Salzburg occasion and the possibility mentioned above of a performance by Marianne Willmann, there is one other recorded instance of a performance of 503 by Mozart's pupil Hummel on 10 March 1789 in Dresden. This was an amazing work to choose for a child prodigy (he was nine years old). Apparently, however, he carried it off very well.

488 *in A major*

With this concerto we return to the exquisite and gentle pleasures of 450 and 453. This is one of the most gracious and most popular of the Melodic concertos, and, but for one surprising deviation, it runs true to the Melodic form. And also, until that deviation occurs, it is nearer to sonata form than any concerto since 271.

The First Subject opens with a phrase which might almost read: 'As I was saying before I was so rudely interrupted by those noisy symphonic concertos'. It is a mellow eight-bar tune with a first part played over a Melodic pedal by the string quartet; they provide the answer and then the first phrase is repeated in the wind, which give a different and slightly extended answer. The old-type Bridge opens with a phrase that is related to the first phrase of the answer (bar 5), and is to run on a strong filo throughout the movement. The Bridge runs a conventional course to a close on the dominant. The Second Subject is one of the pleading feminine kind—similar to that of 453—eight bars in length and played first by the first violins, doubled by the flutes and bassoons in the repeat. The Second Subject closes, and runs into a caesura, which is the start of the First Cadential, and since it is the most sophisticated Cadential we have yet encountered and will play a large part in the work, it is perhaps worth some investigation.

The shape of the caesura (violins, bars 46 and 47) is derived from the Second Subject (itself descended from the Bridge phrase) and, after stopping the flow by appearing twice in two different shapes, it pulls out in the next three bars (49–51) with a reference in the strings to the second bar of the First Subject. Now the caesura reappears in yet another shape, this time on the first beat of the bar and in the woodwind, and stops all progress with three insistent repetitions. An extra bar is inserted to slide up to the pulling-out point, which goes as before, but then too it fails to close and repeats itself (bar 55), creating in the process yet another caesura.

The Second Cadential is a brief and wistful farewell from the woodwind, and a reminder that many musical ideas lived on in Mozart's mind from one concerto to another, in this case from 467.

Before leaving the Statement let us trace the filo which spins out so smoothly from the fifth bar:

Example 60

bar 5

Then on to the Bridge:

Example 61
bar 18

So to the Second Subject, with a change in rhythm:

Example 62
bar 30

And the several varieties in the First Cadential:

Example 63
bar 46

Example 64
bar 47

Example 65
bar 52

The piano opens the First Concerto, and is given a light string accompaniment when it reaches the second phrase, which it varies according to custom. The orchestra alone starts on the Bridge but the piano enters after five bars and runs above the original harmonic ground for a short way until it is given a twist by a D sharp in the bass line (bar 90) and then completes a concise and elegant piano bridge of its own. Here we have the Second Subject played first by the piano, followed by the complex First Cadential, translated by the piano in its own terms, a very short piano climax (little more than an extension to prevent the First Cadential from closing at all) and a version of the Bridge to form the closing ritornello.

If the listener were to feel that this was the shortest First Concerto (some 60 bars) and the nearest to sonata form he had heard since the very early days, he would be right. But this concerto has something special in store. The Bridge soon departs from its old shape and runs down some scales to end in an abrupt octave cue. Then a new and serene melody sails in (bar 143). It is given by the strings in four-part harmony, and with some imitation between the voices. It ends as precisely as it began; the piano immediately begins to work on its melodic outline in a vigorous canon, and the Development has begun.

There are several ways of construing this unusual event. The Statement was exceptionally rich. The First Concerto was short and scarcely escaped from the pervasive filo of the Statement. There was no piano second subject. It is not of prime importance to decide on the label for this new subject so long as its purpose is understood. Mozart has, in effect, delayed the provision of second subject material for the piano. For although it is unlike the general run of piano second subjects and is first played by the orchestra, this, as we shall see, is undoubtedly the function of the new theme. It can best, perhaps, be called Second Subject (2).

But to return to the Development, after a brief but fiery little canon from the piano the woodwind gives out a minor version of the new theme which is answered by strong arpeggios from the piano. This dialogue goes on until the piano itself takes over an inverted version of the theme (bar 166) and then runs into a swinging development which is accompanied by overlapping sequences from the theme in the orchestra right through the First Return (bar 178, still related to the new theme) and up to the Second (bar 186). There is a short cadenza-like link which runs from the last dominant pedal of the Return right into the first bar of the Reprise.

The First Subject is rescored and rearranged, the orchestra taking the first entry and the piano the repeat. The Bridge is treated as in the First Concerto, the piano link being adapted to the minor mode and shortened to bring in the Second Subject in the tonic. From here all goes much as before until the end of the seemingly un-endable First Cadential where with the same abrupt octave cue the Second Subject (2) arrives (bar 261), this time coming from the piano, and with an air of inevitability, as if it had actually been in from the start. The woodwinds repeat it with an elegant accompaniment from the piano which insensibly gathers force and turns into the piano climax, a new one, larger and far more powerful than the first. The same version of the Bridge material as in the First Concerto starts the cadenza ritornello; then there is a brief reference to the new Second Subject, which falters and stops to provide the cadenza platform. The cadenza, although a good one, contains no reference to the main subjects of the movement we have heard and might almost have been written for another work but for a central reference to a passage in the Development and to the filo (bars 11–15). The final ritornello starts in the middle of the First Cadential which is followed by the second, and the movement ends with a short, lightly scored coda, a cheerful and mildly affectionate farewell.

This is a great Melodic movement, softer and more gentle than 453, and more reflective than 450. From the first bar to the last it moves without faltering and without flaw. It also fulfils one of the criteria of any great work: once heard it seems to have existed always and to be an immutable and inevitable part of the world we live in. It moves graciously within the Melodic form and the one irregular happening does not in any way disturb its peaceful balance. This is because Mozart had so artfully contrived affairs that the plot actually gains in effectiveness by the introduction of a leading character so late as in the third act. There is no question here of an afterthought or of a spontaneous stroke of inspiration occurring when he reached this point in the work. His plan was to repeat the Statement in the First Concerto, for they are almost exactly the same length, and the only change in the succession of the main materials is that the last cadential (6 bars) is replaced by the piano climax (8 bars). The mildness of this climax is in itself a part of the scheme: it is pitched so low that the listener is scarcely aware that it has happened and is thus beguiled into a state of placid calm until the closing ritornello gives its sudden cue, and the new theme makes its stately entry. By these simple means Mozart achieves complete surprise. Now the Reprise can have a new second half after the Statement material is done (23 bars where only 8 stood before), and the whole movement gains a new and magnificent final act to counterbalance the milder dramatic interest of the material itself and the uneventfulness of the drama in the earlier stages. To gain the best effect from this plot the performer should enter into Mozart's conspiracy and play down the first climax and bring in the canon at the head of the Development with the proper intensity. The last climax should, of course, be given with full power. For the rest, so long as the pianist avoids a too feminine approach, this concerto can be played well by anyone who has mastered the style of 450 and 453.

The Adagio is another of Mozart's penetrating slow movements which only need the right touch and tempo to raise them to what, in less inhibited days, was called 'the sublime'. The Finale has a strength and size that places it too in the highest class.

491 *in C minor*

466 has a first movement full of strenuous activity: 491, although its power is no less when it is unleashed, does not strive so hard. Its mood is one of resignation—but it is the resignation of wisdom, not defeat. Where 466 seemed to supply the final solution for the Symphonic concerto, 491 moves yet further onwards and outwards, using new methods. It is geometrically less exact than the perfect symmetry of 466 but none the less convincing for that.

The Statement opens with a mysterious passage played *sotto voce* by strings and bassoon. We need only look in detail at the second phrase to find the genesis of a great part of the movement, and even this fragment can be divided into smaller generating units:

1 The whole rhythmic figure ('the main unit'):

Example 66

2 The 'iambic beat':

Example 67

3 The 'three crotchet strokes':

Example 68

4 The 'final leap':

Example 69

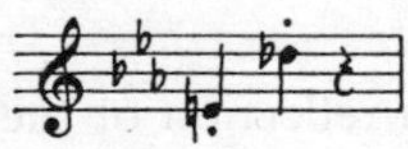

The first sentence ends at bar 12 and the *forte* statement follows at once and, as is usual at this point, leads towards the dominant in bar 27. It is always an arbitrary matter to lay a finger on a point of junction between the First Subject and the Transition in a symphonic Statement, but here we may reasonably say that the first part of the Transition begins with the assertion of the dominant chord over the main unit in the bass in bar 28. The second part of the Transition is a gentle link with the Second Subject made up from the main unit and played by the flutes, oboes and bassoons. The Second Subject itself is of the Relief kind, some light scales in the woodwind followed by two pendants, both echoing fragments of the main unit and lightly scored for the woodwind. The Transition continues with a *forte* statement of the whole First Subject in the bass which has a cadential close and runs into the First Cadential proper (bar 74). The theme of this is related to the central four notes of the main unit with a phrase from the Second Subject in counterpoint above and, but for its position and for the fact that this affecting passage disappears from the rest of the movement until the coda, it might well have served as the Second Subject. In the second half of the Cadential the woodwind quietly slide upward over a tonic-dominant bass. The Second and final Cadential is a gathering together of power to signal the close of the Statement, emphasising the iambic beat and the inverted leap of the main unit.

The short piano introduction is a first cousin of that of 466. It is, however, all of one piece, designed to show off the piano's high clear tone in contrast to the thick texture of the last Cadential. It too, however, clings to the triple crotchet beat of the main unit. The first phrase of the First Subject comes in *forte* on the strings, the second is played softly by the woodwind, and then the piano takes over, but not as one would expect, to complete the sentence. Instead it uses the main unit to modulate quickly to the dominant of E flat which it reaches in twelve bars and then confirms in a series of runs for another twelve (135–146).

Next comes the piano second subject, a calm reflection of the main unit followed by the affecting little phrase in the First Cadential, resting on the pedal of E flat. The woodwind takes the repeat, and then the piano moves into its first climax (bar 165). After a dozen bars of free movement the piano runs into a dogged caesura, first on the dominant of B flat, then of E flat and A flat, and finally runs out in ascending sequences over a jerky bass figure with the iambic beat and the leap (inverted) of the main unit. The climax runs to a trill which could well lead to the closing ritornello (bar 199). If the First Concerto were to end here it would, indeed, be almost exactly the same length as that of 466. Instead a new theme in E flat enters on the oboes and is passed down the woodwind. Again its nature is simple, almost rustic, but when the piano repeats it the Tyrolean rhythms are broken up into triplets and runs. This theme, the second Second Subject, departs as promptly as it arrived, and the piano plunges darkly into E flat minor with menacing arpeggios under the line of the first theme, played by the flute (bar 220). This dies away as the piano gathers force and moves into the final stages of its second and massive climax. The closing ritornello is adapted from the main unit, now in the major mode and with an octave leap downwards at the tail. This draws to a peaceful close in E flat.

The Development opens with dialogue between the piano and the woodwind on the subject of the early part of the piano introduction. In bar 302 the main unit enters in F minor; it soon changes its shape and is given a cadential turn by the bassoons, ending in an octave leap upwards. For the next sixteen bars the orchestra tosses this tag around the piano's arpeggios. Then after a short solo passage (bar 325) there is a romantic progression, again related to the main unit (bar 330), from the dominant chord of C to that of F, B flat and E flat, in which the orchestra provides the home base from which the arpeggios can depart and return. After eight more bars the dominant of C minor is reached, and the Return. This is carried out by the woodwind punctuating a piano run with a part of the main unit and both returning to C minor as if by the law of gravity.

The Reprise opens like the First Concerto until, after some new modulations, the piano gives its version of the end of the first part of the Transition, which is taken over and completed by the orchestra. The piano then provides a new link to the second Second Subject (bar 387), which is now in the tonic minor and much altered in character by the change of mode. (When repeated by the piano it moves even more sadly to the sub-dominant.) This is followed immediately by the piano second subject, which begins on the same E flat, but is now in the minor and with a different interval in the main line of the melody. In its new position this reads as a sad little pendant to a Second Group. Now, after a few bars which seem to be the beginning of the piano climax, the linking Transition theme appears in the woodwind over an insistent piano accompaniment (bar 435) and heralds the return of the original Second Subject. The piano moves into the lead and picks up the pendant theme (shorn of its triplet ornament) and then allows the woodwind to play the final passage alone. And now, at last, there are eight bars of quasi-climax (marked *legato*) and the final trill (bar 471). The first theme comes in with its full force to form the cadenza ritornello. The movement ends with three new bars from the orchestra marked *forte*, the Second part of the First Cadential, the Second Cadential and a coda. This is a sad and peaceful parting gesture: the piano runs quietly up and down arpeggios over a pedal with the wind and the violins throwing in farewell gestures, all of them still reminiscent of the main unit.

This movement has an Olympian spaciousness and, although it is made by unconventional methods, from the first bar to the last it moves as if its course were predestined. There are two main elements in making its character what it is, the drop from the major mode in the First Concerto to the minor in the Reprise, and the abundance of lyrical and elegiac material to contrast with the gravity and power of the Main Theme. Not only is there a second subject (with a slow introduction) and an affecting cadential passage in the Statement, but there is a new Second Subject and a piano second subject in the First Concerto. All four reappear in the Reprise, all in the minor, and together they take up over sixty bars out of just over a hundred. It is interesting to reflect that Mozart, who had so clearly striven to reduce the balance of second subject material in so many concertos, evidently felt that in this one he had created a vehicle which would carry an abundance, and consequently dispensed with the usual big climax in the reprise.

The second piano climax of the First Concerto, the quasi-climax in the Reprise and the cadenza set the performer an important question of interpretation. The movement has a dying fall, and the last quasi-climax can be no more than a short final assertion of the piano's role. If, however, the marking 'legato' is authentic it can be read (almost in the same spirit as the coda) as the piano's solo farewell. The cadenza, too, could take either of two courses. An heroic cadenza would alter the balance of the movement decisively, and perhaps rightly, for the noisy two or three bars of ritornello after the trill would seem to give the cue for a big cadenza. Conversely a wistful, elegiac cadenza might overload the atmosphere with grief and sadness, which is there in considerable force already. Finally, to job backwards to the last climax of the First Concerto, it would seem that to make the most of the contrast between the end of this act and the last, this climax should be given a bracing and vigorous treatment, in particular bars 241–253 should not be allowed to fall away to a gentle tinkle.

The second and third movements are both well known and both supreme of their kind. The finale of the concerto is without doubt one of the finest sets of variations in the wide range of works that Mozart wrote in this form.

503 *in C major*

This movement achieves its majestic proportions through the addition of two new orchestral sections. The first is a spacious introduction of some twenty bars which occurs three times, before each of the main sections. It is quite detached from the rest of the work, and is not to be confused with an introductory First Subject. This addition is a difference in kind. The second is a difference in degree. The movement proper begins with a combined First Group/Transition section which is 'new' because of its massive proportions. It is half as long again as the similar passages in 466 and 491. Its greater size and power also come from the abundance of ideas within it and from the extraordinary strength of the fabric of which it is built.

This movement is similar to the first movement of 491 in that it is built on one single symphonic unit. The unit is short, but it is malleable and there are many filo derivatives to add to its symphonic uses. On its first appearance it has three quaver beats leading to two crotchets moving up in semitones on the first and second beat of the next bar. It is overlapped by its second entry, where the movement is downward and a different beat:

Example 70
bar 18

Very soon there is an interval between the first two quavers:

Example 71
bar 23

and later between the two crotchets:

Example 72
bar 41

then it loses its second crotchet (and now it becomes a filo derivative because it is no longer the same thing):

Example 73

and gains another four:

Example 74

and so on.

To start at the beginning, the introduction opens with a full and stately rendering of the chord of C major. A little figure in thirds trails on after the close and leads to an equally formal treatment of the dominant chord. This time the figures trailed by the oboes and bassoons are clouded by suggestions of the minor mode. Before the last pendant is finished the motif or main unit enters softly in the strings and with close imitative working moves up the scale of C minor to G and then begins to withdraw downward again. As it reaches the home note the violins spring into a sequence of rapid scales in C major over a bass which climbs up at the speed of the motif. As both move towards the dominant the roles are reversed and the central climax of the section hammers at the motif over a double dominant pedal (bar 36). Then the downward descent begins (bar 41) but now with an interval between the last two notes of the unit. This mighty section ends with a last scale and a close in G major, which is repeated.

A pedant would have some trouble in deciding what labels he should use to describe this movement so far. The first eighteen bars are not the First Subject but a preparation for it. When the main subject does enter it is in C minor. As soon as it resolves into C major it moves towards the dominant and becomes a transition theme. The simplest description, however, is to call the opening section the Introduction, and to regard the following section (bars 18–49) as a combined First Group/Transition section (the 'opening section') in which the characteristics of the two are completely merged.

At the close of the opening section the whole orchestra hammers out the octave of G in unison twice. This short punctuation mark is worth noting, because it changes the pervasive rhythm and will crop up again. Although so short, it deserves to be accorded its own title—Transition 2.

The Second Subject picks up the rhythm of the punctuation mark, and enters in the form of a deceptively simple march in C minor played by the violins. In response to a touching appeal from the woodwind it swings to E flat major, but returns to close in C minor. The second time, however, it is played by the woodwind in C major throughout. The flute joyfully endorses the shift to the home key with a lyrical descant. A whole world of changing emotions has been encompassed in 16 bars. After this relief from the mighty opening, the punctuation mark reappears, now with a brass fanfare before it and hanging upon a half-close (Transition 3: what Tovey calls the 'Hallelujah' passage).

The First Cadential follows (bar 70), a little romantic and a little rhapsodic, and breaking the emphatic rhythm of all that has gone before (although still related to the main unit). The last phrase picks up the rhythm of the tympany in the introduction. The Second and last Cadential (bar 82) is a final and farewell version of the main unit in which the first violins have the melodic line (a version of the main unit), and the woodwind echo each phrase like a commentator who is slightly behind the action.

The strings invite the piano to enter with a broad gesture. Three times the orchestra extends its welcome, and twice the piano hesitates. The third time it runs on with a number of tentative phrases in its high register. It begins to gain some confidence, is rejoined by the orchestra and with a slender and fastidious run leads into the Introduction. The piano joins after the main chords and fills in the trailing figures. On the ensuing dominant version, however, it puts in its own chords quietly and off the beat in the spaces left vacant by the orchestra's rests. Again it fills in the trailing chords and punctually, as in the Statement, the main unit makes its surreptitious entry. Now the first part of the opening section begins with the piano running with increasing strength above. In bar 136 it smothers the accompaniment and in accelerated runs it settles into a more static figure over the pedal of G minor. The orchestra then gives out the punctuation mark with an embellishment from the first violins. The piano snatches the violins' last two notes, moves swiftly to E flat and embarks on a bridge subject (bar 148) which starts as if it might be the piano second subject but soon shows its transitory character by modulating towards some sweeping runs which place the tonality firmly on the double dominant. Now all is ready for the piano second subject, which is gentle and melodious and not unlike its antecedents in 365, 415, 453 and 467. It too, like the First and Second Subjects, has some ambiguity between the major and minor modes. This beguiling eight-bar melody is repeated by the woodwind, and then the piano moves into its climax (bar 187) with a series of scales reminiscent of those in the opening section, above a groundwork of the main unit moving up on the strings, again much as they did in the first section, but now in the major. Again the piano smothers its accompaniment and speeds on in a big climax obstructed twice by interruptions from the woodwind (bars 195–198 and bars 202–204).

The closing ritornello is made up from a part of the opening section, the last eight bars being note for note the same as in the Statement, but this time the passage is truly in G major, not in G, the dominant of C.

The First Concerto ends with the punctuation mark given out on the orchestra as the octave of G as before. The Development starts by the piano answering with octaves of the major third in the same rhythm, which the strings convert to the dominant of E minor. The piano then gives a full statement of the Second Subject (the march) in that key (bar 230). The punctuation mark comes in again in the woodwind, and this leads to another full statement by the woodwind of the Second Subject in A minor (bar 240). The punctuation mark then hangs fire for four bars whilst the tonality moves towards F major, and now the second section of the development begins (bar 252). The piano plays only four bars of the tune and then starts again in G minor and yet again in A minor. This is the cue for an elaborate treatment of the curtailed subject, which is described by Tovey as follows:

> Though the sequences are simple in their steps, they are infinitely varied in colouring, and they rapidly increase in complexity until, to the surprise of any one who still believes that Mozart is a childishly simple composer, they move in eight real parts. These eight parts are in triple, or, if we count added thirds, quadruple canon, two in the strings, four in the wind with the added thirds, and two of light antiphonal scales in the pianoforte. No such polyphony has occurred since in any concerto, except one passage in the middle of the finale of Brahms' D minor.

This marvellous passage ends on a long dominant pedal (bar 282) over which the piano makes leisurely preparation for the Return, which begins in bar 286 and ends in a single bar of scales from the piano and woodwind moving in contrary motion (the 'curtain-raising' effect).

The first strophe of the Introduction opens the Reprise on the orchestra alone; the piano joins in the second as it did in the First Concerto, but this time the piano takes the first beat in the bar, the woodwind the third. In the next section the piano part is the same as in the First Concerto but the orchestral texture is thickened by the addition of the woodwind. From the punctuation figure all goes as before until the latter part of the piano's bridging theme changes direction to move the tonality back to the tonic for the entry of the piano second subject (bar 354). The closing bars of the woodwind's version of this happy tune reach a sticking point, then continue with imitative calls between the flutes and the oboes and bassoons popping out clearly over the continuing rapid piano accompaniment. This leads, with no preparation, into the Second Subject now firmly in the major and played with force by the whole orchestra, but only once (bar 364). The piano climax follows, extended by three bars and with the wind interruptions slightly diminished and altered. For the closing ritornello the orchestra provides the *forte* passage of the opening section with full vigour for the last time, with its ending adjusted to form the cadenza platform.

The cadenza trill returns to the Hallelujah passage and the two cadentials. There is no need for a coda because Mozart had already provided one for the Statement in the form of the last Cadential.

The construction of this movement has the classical simplicity and economy of 466, but it is larger in scale and quite its opposite in mood. The balance between the main sections is maintained by a large-scale orchestral development to offset the weight of the Introduction. The two concerto sections are, within a bar or two, equal in length, yet, in spite of the insertion of the Second Subject into the Reprise and the slight extension to the piano climax, nothing of any thematic importance is left out from the First Concerto. The other equation generally applied to the concertos, namely that the length of the Statement and the Fantasy/Development together should be just greater than the length of the concerted sections, is also observed, the relative figures being, to the nearest few bars, $90 + 60 = 150$, and 140.

503 has a mood of great buoyancy. This is achieved partly by the Jupiter-like quality of the symphonic material, but also by reversing the major/minor emphasis which was used in 466 and 491 to darken the later scenes. In the first few bars the sunny assurance of C major is clouded over and the main section opens in the minor key. The Second Subject too is ambivalent, now minor, now major. The First Concerto moves in sunnier country. The piano's melodic passages are in the major (except for the slight shadow in its second subject); the entry of the main unit at the start of the piano climax is in the major, and the closing ritornello selects a part of the opening section which is also in the major. The Development works through many keys and, although the minor mode is used a great deal, this carries the

impression that it will soon pass, as it does in all middle sections. But in the Concerto Reprise all the shifts towards the major employed in the First Concerto are reinforced by the triumphant entry of the Second Subject, now clearly and forcefully presented only in C major. This blows away, once and for all, the cloud that has been hanging over the tonality since the seventeenth bar.

For the performer no concerto asks for a more careful graduation of tone and power than this one. The nature of the introduction asks that the piano should speak in its smallest voice. Its runs within the texture of the Introduction are only a whispered accompaniment to the oboes and bassoons. Its chords within the second strophe (which is marked *piano*) should also be quiet. (It is worth noting that Mozart may have intended the introduction when first played before the Statement to be *piano* first and *forte* second—for the *forte* marks against the first strophe are not necessarily authentic—and these markings are reversed in the First Concerto and in the Reprise.) The piano's voice must be heard more powerfully in the section after the introduction so that it can seem to obliterate the orchestra's insistent use of the main unit. But then it can drop again throughout the bridging passages and its own second subject until the start of the climax, which can be played with a graduated crescendo and offers the piano its only opportunity to match the size of the orchestral writing. The movement seems to demand a cadenza of greater bravura and power than usual so that the piano can consolidate its position. In many of the concertos the piano can very easily win its supremacy: in this one it must always be 'a damned close-run thing'.

The second movement does not reach the heights of those of 466 and 491. It has no obvious deficiency except that the touch of magic is missing and there does not seem to be quite enough invention to fill the time available. This, however, is not great, for it is, happily, short. With the finale we go back, too, not to the simple jollity of 482, but to a good straightforward rondo that has little affinity with the noble finales of the two symphonic concertos in the minor key.

11

The Two Valedictory Concertos

537 in D; 595 in B flat

By the end of 1786 Mozart had completed the cycle of his great piano concertos with 503, the Jupiter of the set. The two lone outriders that were still to come lie outside the main stream. 537, the Coronation concerto, is an occasional piece of the second rank with all the traces of hurried composition. 595, on the other hand, is an individual work whose beauty lies mainly in the melancholy intensity of the orchestral writing. It could almost as well have been written for a viola or a clarinet (it bears some resemblances to the clarinet concerto 622 written in the same year) and it lacks any one of the several characteristic styles of piano writing that Mozart had developed in the long line of piano concertos. At any time throughout his life he had one central stream of composition in which his main effort was applied. The emphasis shifted from the piano concerto, to opera, to the symphony. There was, of course, some overlapping. The shifts were caused more by external events than by choice, but he appeared to be able to direct his talent to meet the needs of the market without favouring one form above another. Only in the field of opera do we know that he constantly hankered for an opportunity. It is interesting to chart the major works of reconnaissance and the major masterpieces in these three fields to show how the full application of his talent switched from one to the other. The selection of the works under this definition must, of course, be arbitrary and personal. Nevertheless the list in Table 24 may help

TABLE 24

Dates of Mozart's principal masterpieces

Date	Operas	Symphonies	Piano Concertos	Other works
1773		183 G minor	175	
1774		201 A major		
1775				Violin concertos
1776			271	
1778		297 Paris		
1779			365	364 Sinfonia Concertante
1780				361 Serenade for 13 wind instruments
1781	*Idomeneo*			388 Serenade for wind instruments
1782	*Seraglio*	385 Haffner	413, 414, 415	
1783		425 Linz		427 C minor Mass Haydn quartets
1784			449 450 451 453 456 459	,, ,,
1785			466 467	Haydn quartets
1786	*Figaro*	504 Prague	488 491 503	
1787	*Giovanni*			525 Eine Kleine Nachtmusik
1788		543 E flat 550 G minor 551 Jupiter	(537)	
1789				581 Clarinet quintet King of Prussia Quartets
1790	*Cosi*			,, ,, ,,
1791	*Magic Flute*		(595)	622 Clarinet concerto Requiem

to explain the isolation of the last two piano concertos.

Whereas in the years from 1784 to 1786 the piano concertos had been in the mainstream of his effort, sharing it in the winter and spring 1785/86 with *Figaro*, by 1788 the emphasis had switched to the last three symphonies. The one piano concerto, 537, is dwarfed by the power and size of these masterpieces. Similarly in the last year, 1791, *The Magic Flute*, the Clarinet Concerto and the Requiem are all mainstream works, in comparison to which the gentle 595 is no more than a footnote on the record.

It is perhaps a tenable theory that Mozart, who could always write good music quickly, could only write great music, or make important new experiments in music, at a much more deliberate pace. Perhaps it took all of the nine months after the great effort of creating *Don Giovanni* to restore his energy for the next Olympian effort with the last three symphonies. And perhaps, although they were 'written' in six weeks, the period of gestation had been much longer. It may well be that by the early summer of 1788 he was carrying the greater part of them in his head.

The major musical events of 1787 and 1788 can be seen from Table 24. Mozart's private life presents a less magnificent tale. Leopold died in May. Although this came as no surprise, it was the end of a relationship stronger than any other in Mozart's life. The grip that Leopold exerted in his first fifteen years never completely relaxed. Up to the last he was the one who worried, who urged industrious habits, who condemned dissipation of time and money. When one end of an axis, strongly polarised as this one was, is removed, it liberates the other from psychological pressures, and this release may lead to marked changes in behaviour. It may be that had Leopold lived on (he was seventy-eight when he died) Mozart would still have been sucked down to the level of penury and importunity that made such a misery of the last three years of his life. On the other hand, it could well be true that the threat of a visit from the great touring manager of his youth, or indeed the mere knowledge that he was standing at his listening post in Salzburg and sooner or later would catch all the news from Vienna, would have had its effect upon the way he conducted his affairs. Leopold had always been frugal, humble and diligent in court diplomacy, and realistic in financial affairs. Mozart was extravagant, maladroit in place-seeking, and would turn his back on financial advantage if vanity called him another way. He was blindly optimistic in drawing his forward budgets. He felt the world owed him a living: perhaps two of the most revealing lines he wrote were scribbled on a receipt for the payment of his fee for the dance music which he was contracted to supply for the court of Joseph II:

> TOO MUCH FOR WHAT I DO
> TOO LITTLE FOR WHAT I COULD DO

537 was written for Mozart's last series of Lent concerts. It bears the date 24 February 1788. There is no record of its first performance. He played it on his northern European tour on 14 April 1789 at Dresden and also at the festivities surrounding the coronation of Leopold II at Frankfurt on 14 October 1790, for which occasion the trumpets and drums may have been added to the score. This concert (from which the inappropriate soubriquet 'Coronation' was gained) took place strictly on the fringe of the festival. It had no place on the official calendar.

By the beginning of 1791 Mozart could no longer raise a body of subscribers to support a series of Lent concerts. 595, the last piano concerto (it is dated 5 January 1791) was first played at a concert given by Josef Bahr, a clarinettist in the Imperial service, on 4 March in 'Herr Jahn's Hall', a city restaurant. This was Mozart's last known appearance at the keyboard at a public concert. It may have been performed again in April at a public concert in Prague by a young pianist, Johann Wittassek.

537 *in D major*

This concerto does not step off the mark with quite so springy a tread as the more favoured Melodic concertos 450, 453 and 488, nor does it have their self-confident poise and balance. Nevertheless it has good things to say even if it does take a considerable time in saying them.

The First Subject is eight bars in length and not immediately attractive. The violins play the melody in a single line over the tonic pedal; there is a slight thickening of the texture, however, in the next four bars which add an alternative answer to the four. The Bridge is a good one in the old style with a pleasing sonority due to the added presence of the trumpets and drums. It is in two parts, a typical violin bridge tune played twice, and with a four-bar conclusion to lead on to the dominant chord, and then a striking new semi-quaver figure in the violins over a pedal for a further six bars. There is a slender violin linking passage (scarcely important enough to be given a title of its own) and then the Second Subject. This lively tune is the most memorable item in the movement and in shape and character it is surprisingly like a piano second subject. The strings play it through the first time and start it over again, but when they reach the third bar (44) they diverge into a new ending in neat imitative four-part harmony. The First Cadential is an explosive little figure in the strings (which has a blood brother in the E flat symphony). It is joined by the woodwind in a loud cadential close, the whole repeated and given three bars of reinforcement at the end. Then after some hesitation the first violins bring in the Second Cadential (bar 59), a sweet four-bar strain with no apparent relationship to what has gone before, and repeat it with ornaments and a short rhapsodic extension. The Third Cadential is from stock, and it makes full use of the trumpets and drums to give the Statement a sturdy close.

The piano extends the last phrase of the First Subject in the traditional manner. This is sealed off by the First Cadential without its noisy tail, a practice we have not encountered since the early days. A long and loose piano bridge follows, running in pleasing but again old-fashioned sequences of scales for twenty-four bars before introducing the piano second subject. This turns out to be an important but wayward passage that soon leaves A major to pass through the dominant of A minor to D minor and then to dissolve into sequences which are fiercely broken off by a stirring series of triplets (bar 145) rising and falling again to the dominant of A minor. These are followed by a more flowing passage which reaches a trill in bar 163. The whole of this section from the end of the piano second subject to the trill is unsettled in its tonality and has the characteristics of a transition. The latter part is not unlike the structure of some of the looser piano climaxes in the earlier concertos, and the trill, as in 491, could be taken as the cue for the closing ritornello. Instead it ushers in the Second Subject played by the piano as if it were its very own. The orchestra takes the melody in the repeat and, at the point at which the diversion took place in the Statement, the piano resumes command and in one of the best passages in the concerto it works with parts of the subject in close counterpoint for some twelve bars (178–189). It then gives a run, as if to free itself from intellectual preoccupations, and moves into the true piano climax, a long one of twenty-three bars. The Bridge makes up the start of the ritornello: it steals the last two bars of the Second Cadential to run into the Third which ends the section.

As often happened in the Galant Fantasies, the piano picks up the last tag of the Cadential and starts to develop it in a dialogue with the orchestra. But instead of forgetting the tag and moving into a free fantasy, this fragment is developed in a symphonic manner for another twelve bars. Here the piano does run free until the Return (bar 281) which again is extensive, with three changes of pulse in the scales that the piano throws out over the dominant beats of the orchestra.

The first eight bars of the Reprise are given by the orchestra alone, the piano joining in to provide a new variant for the end of the fist subject. There is no ritornello and a much shorter piano bridge to the piano second subject which is in itself cut down in length; but from there to the start of the Second Subject all goes much as before. This time the piano's contrapuntal passage flows out of the tune on its first appearance, not on the repeat. The piano climax follows the same course for some twelve bars and then suddenly falters. Now the unexpected happens, the orchestra enters with the melodious Second Cadential (bar 384) which we have not heard since the Statement. The piano joins in its repeat and echoes the violins in the gentlest and most urbane manner. But when its twelve bars are up the piano plunges back into yet another, and entirely new, piano climax of fourteen bars. The end of the first part of the Bridge makes up the Cadenza ritornello and the Third Cadential on its own completes the movement.

This concerto is uneven in workmanship and might seem somewhat ramshackle in construction. There is a world of difference in the quality of writing between, say, the first piano bridge and the contrapuntal passage which the piano develops out of the Second Subject. The orchestration generally has slipped back to the pre-449 style with scarcely any individual writing for the woodwind, and the string accompaniment to the piano is quickly sketched in without the felicities that we have come to expect. Above all there is no evidence of a filo, and none, except in the Development, of symphonic writing. The movement therefore consists very much of one thing after another, and by the time it comes to the reprise there are a lot of things.

It is interesting to speculate why Mozart threw the melodious Cadential into the Reprise and followed it by a new and additional climax. The most charitable is that he was attempting a *grand coup*: a first mild climax leading to the Second Subject, a second larger climax leading to the Cadential, a third and massive climax leading to the final trill. This, at any rate, is certainly the best that can be made of it in performance. The least charitable is that when writing the concerto he was even more pressed for time than usual, and, liking the little tune, packed it in where best he could. In support of this theory there is also the omission of the excellent latter part of the Bridge which he would surely have used again if he had given the matter full consideration. Two comparable eccentricities, the suddent insertion of the First Subject at the end of 365 and the surprising appearance of the new theme in 488, both carry the conviction that they are part of a grand design. This intrusion of the Cadential does not. But the movement has undoubted strengths as well as failings, and many a worse work has been saved by a tune less vivid than the Second Subject of 537. Whatever the style of cadenza adopted for this movement, it should be short.

The second movement has the virtue of simplicity, but without much charm, and it fails to break through the barrier that divides Mozart the proficient from Mozart the genius. The finale, too, fails to do more than remind us of some of the earlier and jollier rondos, although it too has some rare moments of beauty.

595 *in B flat*

This melancholy and beautiful work stands in isolation at the end of the long line of piano concertos. It does not belong to their tradition, for it is not a typical Melodic concerto, nor does it sound like a work for the concert hall. It does not aim to excite or to impress an audience as the others have done. It has instead the air of a chamber work, of a private meditation to be played perhaps in front of a few friends. Mozart's interest in the concerto form has passed away; instead he writes in his late melancholy vein a number of exquisite passages which are joined together by links drawn from his vast repertoire of musical joinery.

The First Subject is given quietly by the violins over a pedal bass and smooth accompaniment from the second violins and violas. Beneath the simple outline of the first phrase there is a feeling of peaceful resignation more often found in the Andantes. At the fifth bar the woodwind and horns interject a gentle call; the second strain flows out; there is a second call, then the third strain which ends in a complementary call given by the strings in their own idiom, joined by the wind in imitation and brought down gently to the tonic B flat (bar 16). Next comes a transition theme of great beauty (B) which appears at first to be a second part of the First Subject. Soon, however, it modulates to F and leads to two bars of the type that conveniently close a bridge passage. But within the close are a series of semitones which are to influence the rest of the Statement. From these a link (B/S) spins out to reach across to the Second Subject. This is yet another haunting melody, played by the first violins, a long downward scale which has a filo connection with the First Subject. The first time it is in B flat, but the second time in B flat minor. It has a dying fall, and lingers in the memory. It is followed alas, by a stock Mannheim type of tonic/dominant cadential figure, directly descended from the semitones, repeated twenty-four times before its final close. The Second Cadential is a pair of Caesuras (bar 47) and their answers, the Third is another dark and plaintive theme played by the first violins, again linked to the same filo. Its closing phrase is picked up by the whole orchestra and serves as a *forte* cadential close. The Fourth and last Cadential is a sad *envoi,* spoken by the violins and echoed by the woodwind.

The First Concerto opens with a solo version of the first subject, only the calls remaining with the orchestra. The melody does not transfer well, at least to our modern keyboard: it is given in a single line over an Alberti bass and its deep and melancholy overtones are lost. In place of the Transition theme the piano provides a bridge which is pleasing enough, but out of character in such a movement. This ends with the second part of the Transition, without ever touching the double dominant. The orchestra merely asserts the key of F major. The piano then runs into its second subject (bar 100), a fragile series of phrases modulating from F minor and with something of the same opening shape as the Second Subject. Over the last four bars the flute adds a poignant descant. The next dozen bars are occupied by sketchy figures in the piano doubled by *pizzicato* strings, all on or near the dominant of F. Then the piano runs into the strong melody from the Transition (bar 123), which leads through the same closing figures to the link passage (still in the piano) and then to the full sweep of the Second Subject, played first in the strings and then by the piano (bar 136). The tedious First Cadential follows, at full length, and then we have a pause. This is filled by one of those translucent Mozartean pendants, played by the woodwind in slowly resolving chords (bar 157). The piano then advances into four bars of mild quasi-climax. A new and undistinguished ritornello follows the trill and the Second Cadential ends the section.

Or not quite. For the second of the two caesuras is repeated first by the wind and then the strings, and modulates to the dominant of B minor. Here the piano starts a plain statement of the First Subject. This B minor passage in a B flat major work has an unnerving quality which becomes more mysterious as the tonality shifts again through C major to E minor. The calls at the end of the First Subject are passed between the strings, the wind and the piano, and the oboes lead into the first phrase, shortly to be imitated by the piano, followed in turn by the bassoons. So, as entry follows entry, the development moves out of the shadows into a golden haze. The texture thickens and soon the call joins in (bar 210), and this leads, whilst the piano continues on an independent course, to a strict canon at a fifth between the first and second violins. A Return sounds at bar 224, but it is a false dominant—that of the relative minor and not of the major key of B flat. In an intricately worked passage of ten bars, however, the shadows lift again and we return to the tonic major for the Reprise.

The First Subject is played by the orchestra as at the outset, and thereby regains its true character. The piano joins to repeat the last call, and then the Reprise runs the same course as the First Concerto right up to the final trill. Here instead of a ritornello there are the two caesura bars of the Second Cadential, and then the piano enters again to give the answer. Once started it continues with the melodious Third Cadential and only fades away when the orchestra takes over the noisy closing bars, from which they project the cadenza platform. The cadenza is a good one, starting with the First Cadential and mentioning the calls from the First Subject and the main Transition theme. It ends with a reference to the melody of the First Subject. The New Tutti from the end of the First Concerto and the Fourth Cadential end the movement.

This concerto is written by two people, both of them Mozart. One is the Mozart of the last years seriously engaged on an elegiac style of composition (which finds perhaps its best expression in some parts of the clarinet quintet). The other is the Mozart of the Court dance music, hastily putting musical patterns together from the huge stock that has accumulated in his memory over the years. The two are as distinct as oil and vinegar, and can be identified:

(*a*)	(*b*)
First Subject	Second Transition Subject
First Transition Subject	First Cadential
Second Subject	Second Cadential
Third Cadential (beginning)	Third Cadential (end)
Fourth Cadential	
piano second subject	piano bridge
The Development	piano link (bars 112–122)
	piano climax
	New Tutti

Mozart's powers were still supreme, but his interest in the construction of a concerto movement had fallen away. Except for the masterly Development, this movement consists of a string of quiet reflective passages lying within the dead letter of concerto form. To interpret this work in such a way as to reveal its considerable beauties, its weaknesses must be concealed. The orchestral *fortes* should be *mezzo forte*, the long and empty First Cadential should be played as lightly and as unobtrusively as can be, and the devastatingly weak link between the piano second subject and the Transition theme should be a conspiratorial whisper—a mysterious pause—with the piano part scarcely audible above the *pizzicato* strings. The piano climax is best treated, perhaps, as a placid cadential close. This is a movement for the pianist who can play the deepest works of Brahms, and who can also skate so lightly over the weaker piano passages of Schumann that their virtues and their charms are all that is left in the listener's memory.

The second movement, too, despite some beauties in the middle section and a happy conclusion, needs all the help that the performer can give it. The finale shows some spirit, but there are several hollow passages and the movement as a whole is on a lower level of invention than in the great Melodic finales of 450, 453 and 488.

Although an uneven work, the first movement of 595 is both unique and touching. The gaiety and wit of the Melodic concertos have gone, the bustle and drive of the Galant style has become mechanical. The work does not aspire to the heroic plane of the great Symphonic concertos. Nevertheless the first movement of 595 is an appropriate epitaph for the long and glorious stream of piano concertos. Where it calls up ghosts of the past they do no more than remind us of what was once a living form; when it penetrates into its own new and peculiar world of resigned melancholy it reminds us that even in the desperate private and personal circumstances of his final year Mozart's musical genius was still supreme.

Musical References and Construction Tables

175—Construction

STATEMENT	F1F2F3 B1B2 S C1C2C3
FIRST CONCERTO	f1 f2 f3 F1 pb ps B2 s++ B1 px F2 C1C2C3
FANTASY	F1 developed. Free. Full Close
CONCERTO REPRISE	F1 f1 f2 f3 F1 pb ps B2 s++ B1 px B1 | cd | F2 C1C2C3

175—Mentions

F1	F2	F3	B1	B2	S	C1	C2	C3	ps	s+	s++
12	5	5	7	3	3	3	3	3	2	2	2

First Subject

.1 bar 1

2. bar 4

3. bar 7

Bridge

1. bar 10

2. bar 14

Second Subject

bar 16

First Cadential

bar 21

Second Cadential

bar 24

Third Cadential

bar 29

Piano second subject

bar 59

Extension to second subject

bar 76

238—Construction

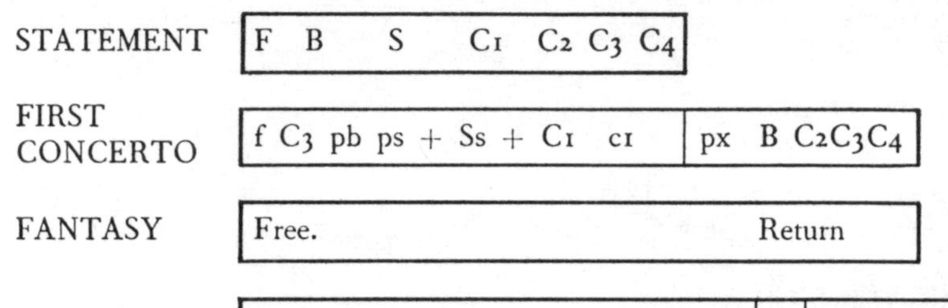

REPRISE | Ff C3 pb ps + Ss + C1 c1 px C3 | cd | B C2C3C4

238—Mentions

F	B	S	C1	C2	C3	C4	ps
3	3	3	5	3	6	3	2

First Subject
bar 1

Bridge
1. bar 12

2. bar 15

Second Subject
bar 17

First Cadential
bar 21

Second Cadential
bar 25

Third Cadential
bar 29

Fourth Cadential
bar 32

Piano Second Subject
bar 55

242—Construction

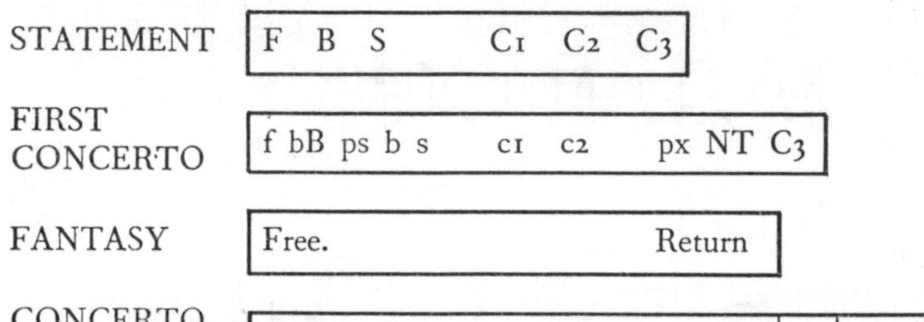

242—Mentions

F	B	S	C1	C2	C3	ps	NT
4	6	3	3	3	3	3	2

First Subject

1. bar 1

2. bar 4

Bridge

1. bar 15

2. bar 17

Second Subject
bar 27

p

First Cadential
bar 34

Second Cadential
bar 38

fp *fp* *p*

Third Cadential
bar 44

f *tr*

Fourth Cadential
bar 47

f

Piano Second Subject
bar 74

p *tr*

New Tutti
bar 122

f

246—Construction

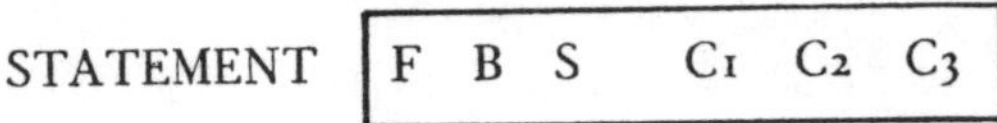

FIRST CONCERTO | f Bb ps + b s + px C1

FANTASY | NT Free Return

CONCERTO REPRISE | Ff Bb ps + b s + px C3 C2 | cd | C1 C3

246—Mentions

F	B	S	C1	C2	C3	ps
3	5	3	3	2	3	2

First Subject

1. bar 1

2. bar 5

Bridge

1. bar 12

2. bar 16
Second Subject
bar 19
First Cadential
bar 23
Second Cadential
bar 29
Third Cadential
bar 33
Piano Second Subject
bar 57

271—Construction

STATEMENT	Ff1 F2 B B/S S C1 C2 C3 C4
FIRST CONCERTO	Ff1 pb(f1) b/s sS+ px C1 c2 C3
DEVELOP-MENT	F2 Ff1 developed Bb b/s
CONCERTO REPRISE	Ff1 pb(f1) b/s Ss + px Ff2 px C1 c2 Ff1 | cd | C3C4CODA

271—Mentions

(General note: In the early concertos (175, 238, 242, 246) if a subject is repeated at any entry after the first this is counted as two 'mentions'. In the later concertos such precision is not always appropiiate and if a subject is repeated at a greater length it is normally counted only as one mention.)

F1	F2	S	C1	C2	C3	C4
10*	3	3	3	3	3	3

* With many variations and developments.

First Subject

1. bar 1

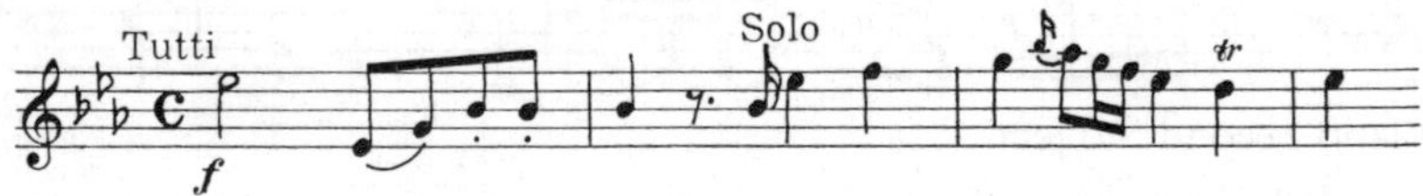

2. bar 7

Bridge
bar 14
f
Bridge/Second Subject
bar 22
p
f
p
Second Subject
bar 26
p
First Cadential
bar 41
f
tr
Second Cadential
bar 45
ff
p
Third Cadential
bar 50
f
tr
Fourth Cadential
bar 54
p

365—Construction

STATEMENT	F1 F2 B1 B2 S C1 C2
FIRST CONCERTO	f1 f2+ cC2 pb/e ps1+ ps2 px C1
FANTASY	b2 developed Free Return Ss Return
CONCERTO REPRISE	Ff1 f2+ ps1 · ps2 f2 px B2 | cd | C1 C2

365—Mentions

F1	F2	B1	B2	S	ps1	ps2
3+	4	1	1§	2†	2	2

+Plus a reference in each piano climax and in the coda.

§ The last few bars used in the Cadenza ritornello: one phrase used in the Fantasy.

† Plus a reference in the Cadenza.

First Subject

1. bar 1

2. bar 4

Bridge
1. bar 14
f
2. bar 18
p
tr
Second Subject
bar 30
p
First Cadential
bar 42
f
Second Cadential
bar 48
f
Episode
bar 84
tr
Piano Second Subject
1. bar 96
2. bar 104
3
p

413—Construction

STATEMENT	F B (B/S)S C1 C2 C3
FIRST CONCERTO	pi Ff pb(b) ps+ (B/S)S+ px C2
FANTASY	Cycle 1 (s) Cycle 2 (s) ps developed R1R2C3
CONCERTO REPRISE	pi Ff pb(b) ps+ (B/S)S + px + B | cd | C2C3

Mentions

F	B	B/S	S	C1	C2	C3	ps
3	2	3+	3	1	3	3	2§

6

+ also mentioned in the Cadenza § also mentioned in the Development

First Subject

bar 1

Bridge

1. bar 12

Bridge/Second Subject

bar 24

Second Subject
bar 26

First Cadential
bar 41

Second Cadential
bar 45

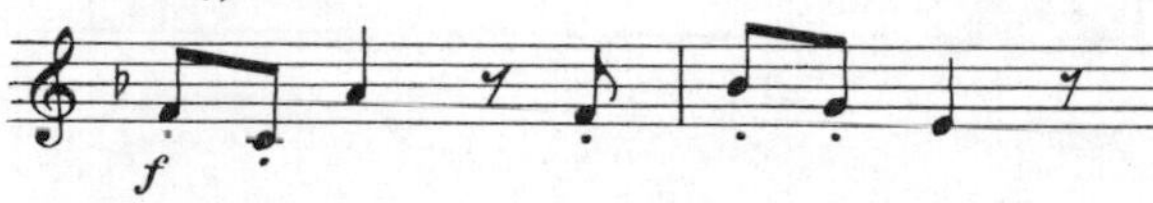

Third Cadential
bar 53

Piano Second Subject
bar 102

414—Construction

STATEMENT	F B S C1 C2 C3
FIRST CONCERTO	f c3C3 pb ps+ Ss + px C3
FANTASY	2 Cycles : Free passage No return
CONCERTO REPRISE	Ff c3C3 pb ps Ss+ C2c2 px C1 cd C3

Mentions

F	B	S	C1	C2	C3	ps
3	1	3	2	2	5	2

First Subject
bar 1

Bridge
bar 17

Bridge End
bar 29

Second Subject
bar 32
p
First Cadential
bar 40
p
Second Cadential
bar 50
p
Third Cadential
bar 58
f
Fourth Cadential
bar 62
f
Piano Second Subject
bar 98

415—Construction

STATEMENT	F	T	S	C1	C2	C3	C4		
	1		2	1		2			
FIRST CONCERTO	pi	Ff	pb	ps	px	(c3)	px	F	C4
		1			2	2		1	

FANTASY	Cycle 1	Cycle 2	F developed	Return 1	Return 2
			1		

CONCERTO REPRISE	pi	Ff	pb	ps	px	(c3)	px	T	cd	C2	C3	C4
		1			2	2			2		2	

1 The original 'canon' subject: the main unit
2 The 'upward runs' from the Second Subject

First Subject
bar 1

Transition beginning
bar 10

Transition end
bar 18

Second Subject beginning

bar 24

Second Subject the upward run

bar 32

First Cadential

bar 36

Second Cadential

bar 47

Third Cadential

bar 52

Piano Second Subject

bar 93

449—Construction

STATEMENT	F B B/S S C1 C2 C3 C4		
FIRST CONCERTO	f pb ps b/s s+ px C2 C3		
FANTASY	C3 developed in cycles R1 R2 R3		
CONCERTO REPRISE	Ff pb ps b/s s+ px + B	cd	C3 C4

Mentions

F	B	B/S	S	C1	C2	C3	C4	ps
3	2*	3	3	1	2†	3§	2	2

* Plus two fragments before the b/s in the two concerted sections
† Also mentioned in the coda
§ Developed extensively in the Fantasy

First Subject
bar 1

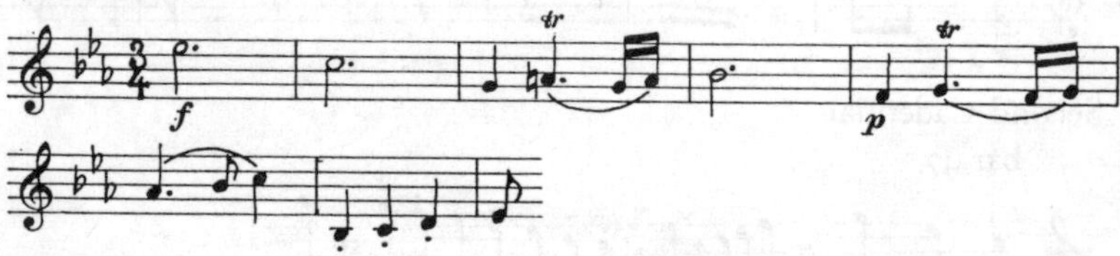

Bridge
bar 16

Bridge/Second Subject
bar 31

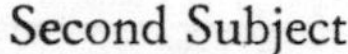

Second Subject

bar 37

First Cadential

bar 54

Second Cadential

bar 63

Third Cadential

bar 70

Piano Second Subject

bar 121

450—Construction

STATEMENT

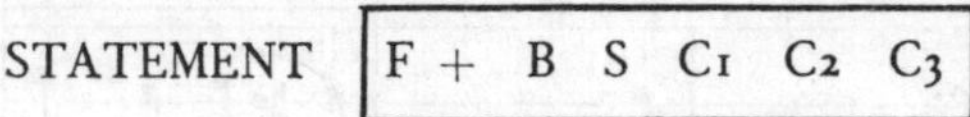

FIRST CONCERTO

pi	f	pb	ps + px	B	C2	C3

FANTASY

c3 developed. Free. Returns 1, 2 & 3

CONCERTO REPRISE

Ff	B	pb	ps+	Ss	px	C1 C2	cd	C2 C3

Mentions

F	B	S	C1	C2	C3	ps
3	3	2*	2	4	3	2

* Also mentioned in the cadenza

First Subject
bar 1

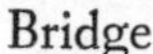

Bridge
bar 14

Second Subject
bar 25

First Cadential
bar 41

Second Cadential
bar 45

Third Cadential
bar 53

Piano Second Subject
bar 103

451—Construction

STATEMENT	F1	F2	T/S	S	C1	C2	C3	C4
	1234	1245			46	156	23	12

FIRST CONCERTO	f1	Ff2	pb	e	t/s	Ss+	px	(C1C2)	px	F2	C3	continues
	12345							46		1245	23	

FANTASY	Cc3	Free	Return 1	Return 2
	3			

CONCERTO REPRISE	Ff1	Ff2	Tt	t/s	Ss+	px	(C1	C2	C3)	px	F2T	cd	C4
	12345						46	156	23		1245		12

Units
1 The octave leap
2 The iambic rhythm
3 The trill
4 The scale
5 The canon
6 The chromatic progression

First Subject

1. bar 1

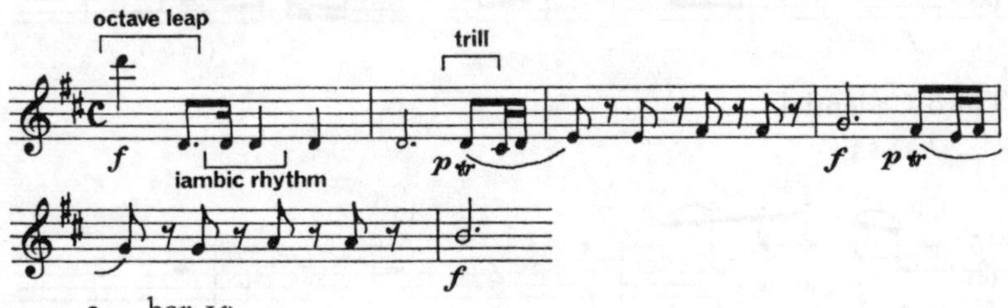

2. bar 10

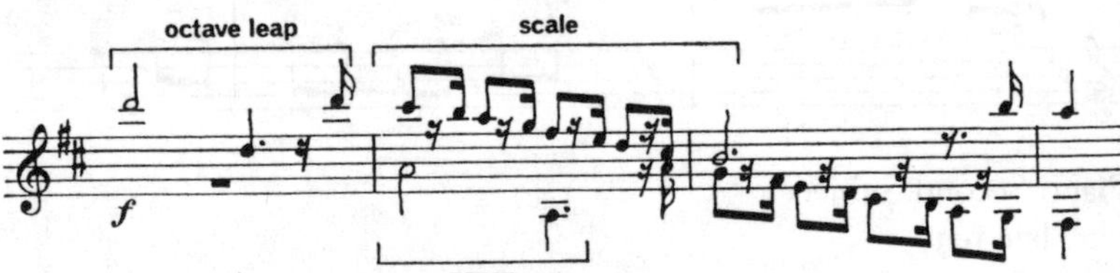

Transition

1. bar 14

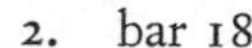
2. bar 18

Transition/Second Subject

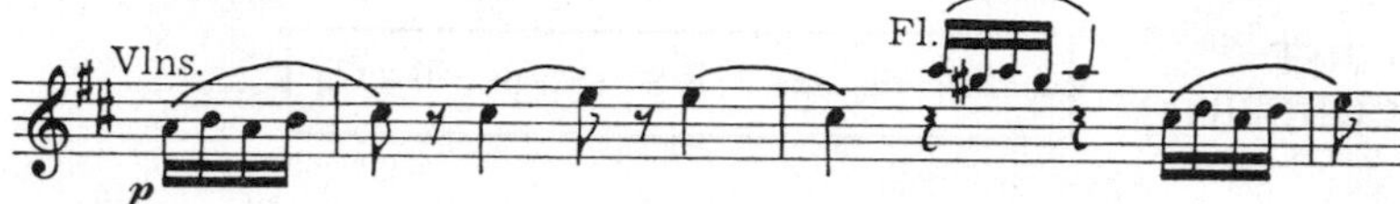

Second Subject
bar 39

First Cadential
bar 43

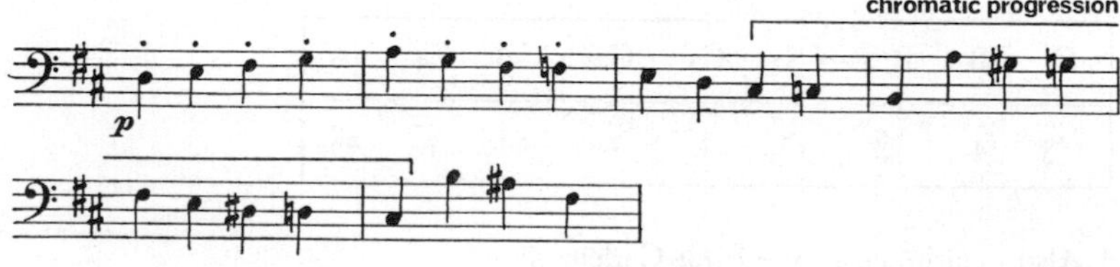

Second Cadential
bar 52

Third Cadential
bar 60

Fourth Cadential (end)
bar 73

453—Construction

STATEMENT	F + B B/S S C1 C2 C3 C4
FIRST CONCERTO	f Bb pb ps + B/S sS px B C4
FANTASY	Free Returns 1 & 2
CONCERTO REPRISE	Ff B b/s ps+ B/S sS px C1 | cd | C2 C3 C4 B/S

Mentions

F	B	B/S	S	C1	C2	C3	C4	ps
3*§	4	5§	3*	2	2	2	3	2§

* Also mentioned in the First Cadenza
§ Also mentioned in the Second Cadenza

First Subject
bar 1

Bridge
1. bar 16

Bridge/Second Subject
bar 31

Second Subject
bar 35

First Cadential
bar 49

Second Cadential
bar 58

Third Cadential
bar 65

Fourth Cadential
bar 69

Piano Second Subject
bar 110

456—Construction

STATEMENT	F B B/S S C1 C2 C3 C4
FIRST CONCERTO	fF B pb C4 ps + B/S Ss c1 c2 pc^s + px B C3 C4
FANTASY	Free C3 developed Free Return
CONCERTO REPRISE	Ff B ps + B/S Ss c1c2 pc^s px(C3) B | cd | C1C2C3C4

\+ 'piano cadentials'

Table of Mentions

F	B	B/S	S	C1	C2	C3	C4	ps
3†	5†	3	3	4†	4††	4*	4	2

† plus a mention in one cadenza
†† plus a mention in both cadenzas
* plus development in the Fantasy

First Subject
bar 1

Bridge
bar 18

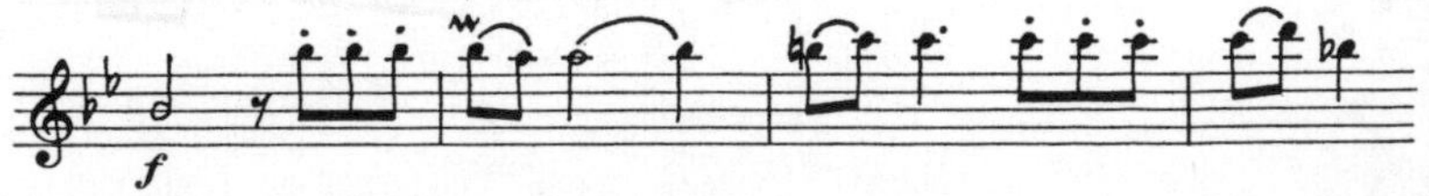

Bridge/Second Subject
bar 28

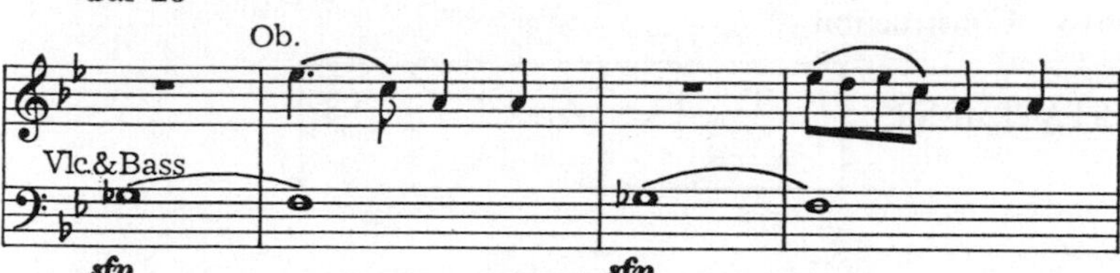

Second Subject
bar 39

First Cadential
bar 47

Second Cadential
bar 54

Third Cadential
bar 61

Fourth Cadential
bar 67

Piano Second Subject
bar 103

459—Construction

STATEMENT	F T1 T2 T/C C1 C2 C3 123 4

FIRST CONCERTO	fF t1 e pb Ss px (t/c) px F 123 12 (3) 123 4 123

FANTASY	Free Ff Return 1 Return 2 1 1

CONCERTO REPRISE	fF t1 pb Ss px (t/c c1) px F 123 12 (3) 123 4 123 12	cd	C2 C3

1 The dotted rhythm and the interval
2 The triplet
3 The intervals of the last phrase
4 The repeating bass (begins bar 32.See bar 37 below)

First Subject
bar 1

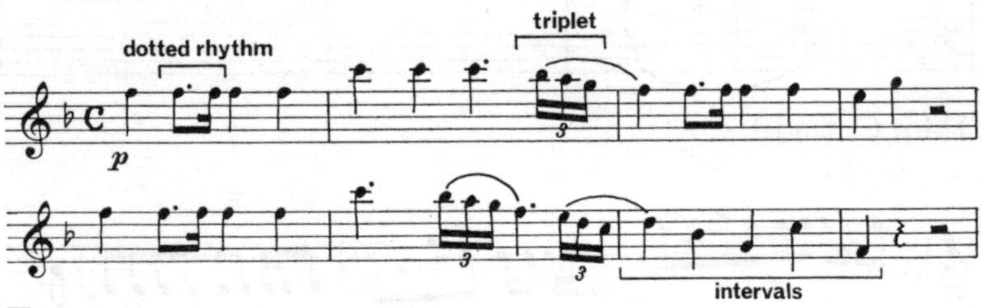

Transition
1. bar 16

2. bar 24
p
f
3. bar 37
p
3
First Cadential
bar 42
p
f
Second Cadential
bar 54
p
f
Third Cadential
bar 62
p
Second Subject
bar 139
Strings
Ob.
p

466—Construction

STATEMENT	F / T		S	T/C	C
	1234	24	(4)	34	(2)

FIRST CONCERTO	pi	Ff/Tt	Ss	pb	ps	px1	px2	px3	F/T1	C
		1234	(4)				4	4	1342	(2)

DEVELOPMENT	pi	F	in cycles	F developed	Return 1	Return 2
		12		1		

CONCERTO REPRISE	Ff/Tt	Ss	pb	ps	px1	px2	px3	F/T	cd	T/C	C	CODA
	1234 24	(4)				4	4	134	cd	4	(2)	12

1 The rising triplets
2 The uneasy figure
3 The affirmative version
4 The rolling semitones

First Subject
bar 1

Uneasy figure

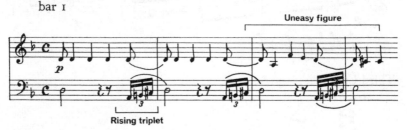

p

Rising triplet

The affirmative version
bar 17

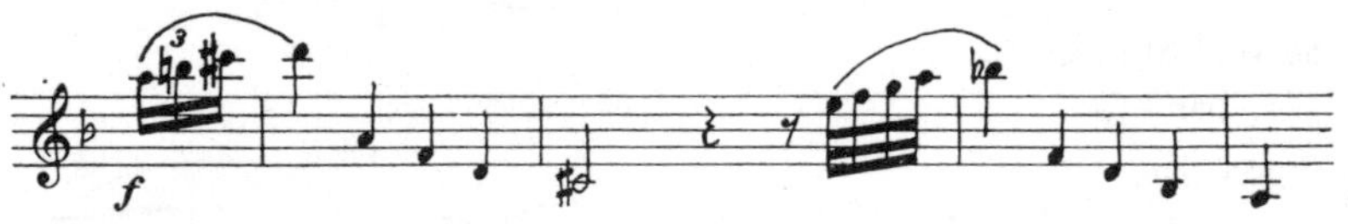

Rolling semitones
bar 21

Transition

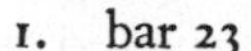

2. bar 28

Second Subject

bar 33

Transition/Cadential

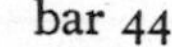

Cadential

bar 71

Piano Second Subject

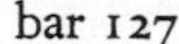

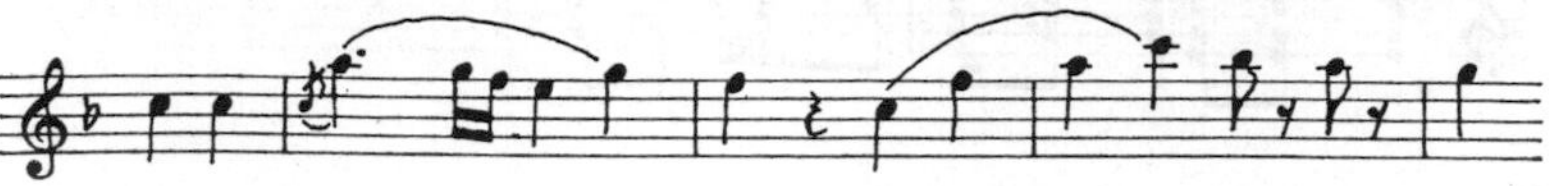

467—Construction

STATEMENT

F	S	T/C	C1	C2
12345	(2)	15	(2)	13

FIRST CONCERTO

pi	Ff	e1	e2	pb	ps	px1	px2	F		C1
	123					1(5)		14	2	

FANTASY

C1	Free	Return
(2)	(5)	

CONCERTO REPRISE

Ff	pb	ps	px1	Ss	px2	F	cd	T/C	C1	C2	CODA
12345	1		1(5)			14		5	(2)	13	1

1 The military air
2 The answer
3 The closing flourish
4 The descant
5 The semitones

First Subject

1. Military Air. bar 1

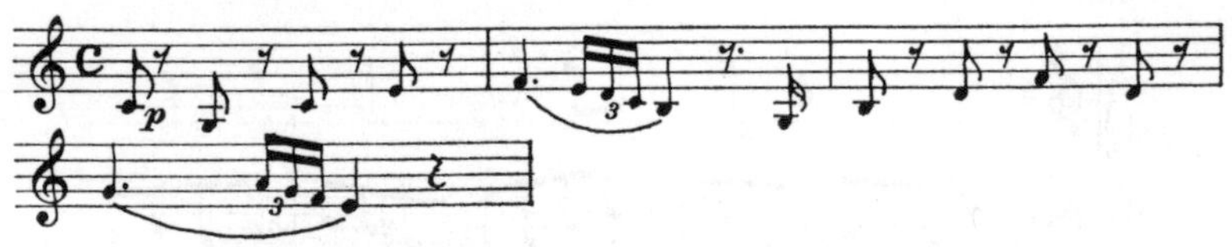

2. Answer bar 5

3. Closing flourish bar 7

4. Descant bar 12
f
5. Semitones bar 24
f
Second Subject
bar 28
Hn.
Fl.
p
Ob.
Transition
bar 44
f
First Cadential
bar 52
Fl.
Vln.
p
p
Second Cadential
bar 64
Hn.
f
f
Vln. I
Piano Second Subject
bar 128

482—Construction

STATEMENT	F1 F2 B B/S S C1 C2 C3
FIRST CONCERTO	pi Ff1 pb e+ ps+ px C1 C2 C3
FANTASY	C3c3 developed Free ps mentioned Free Return
CONCERTO REPRISE	Ff1 Ff2 Bb b/s sS+ ps px C1 | cd | C2 C3

Mentions

F1	F2	B	B/S	S	C1	C2	C3	ps
3	2	2	2	2	3	3	3+	2+

\+ Plus a mention in the development

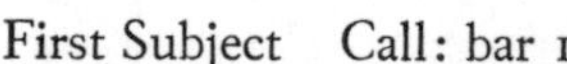
First Subject Call: bar 1

Answer: bar 9

First Subject
2. bar 13

Bridge
bar 31
f
bar 46
p
Second Subject
bar 51
p
First Cadential
bar 58
f
Second Cadential
bar 64
f
Third Cadential
bar 72
p
Piano Second Subject
bar 152

488—Construction

STATEMENT	F B S1 C1 C2
FIRST CONCERTO	f B pb sS1 c1 px B S2
DEVELOP MENT	s2 canon Ss2 dialogue S2 accompanied Returns 1 & 2
CONCERTO REPRISE	Ff B pb sS1 c1 sS2 px BS2 cd C1 C2 CODA

Mentions

F	B	S	C1	C2	S2
3	5†	3	4*	2	3§

always abbreviated after its first appearance
but on its last mention, only in part
and used throughout the development

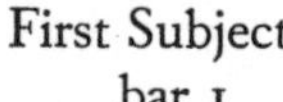

First Subject
bar 1

Bridge
bar 18

Second Subject 1.

bar 31

First Cadential

bar 46

Second Cadential

bar 62

Second Subject 2.

bar 143

491—Construction

STATEMENT	F/T1	T2	S1	T / C	C1	C2
	123 123	123	(2)	123	(2)	13

FIRST CONCERTO	pi	Ff	pb	ps	px1	Ss2	px2	F / T1
	(2)	123	123		13	(2)	123	123 13

DEVELOPMENT	pi dialogue	F developed	Free	Return 1	Return 2
	(2)	123			

CONCERTO REPRISE	Ff	pb	tT1	Ss2	ps	px1	Ss1	px2	F	cd	C1	C2	CODA
	123	123	123	(2)		123	(2)		123		(2)	13	123

1 The iambic beat
2 The three crochet strokes
3 The final leap

First Subject
bar 1

First Transition
bar 28

Second Transition
bar 35

Second Subject 1.
bar 44

First Cadential
bar 74

Second Cadential
bar 81

Piano Second Subject
bar 148

Second Subject 2.
bar 201

503—Construction

STATEMENT	I	F/T	T2	S	T3	C1	C2
		12	3	(3)	3		1

FIRST CONCERTO	pi	Ii	Ff/Tt	pb	e	ps	px	F/T
			12	13			1(2)	12

DEVELOPMENT	T2	S developed	Retrun 1	Return 2
	3	(3)		

CONCERTO REPRISE	Ii	Ff/Tt	pb	e	ps	S	px	F/T	cd	T3	C1	C2
		12	13			(3)	1(2)	12		3		1

1 The 'main unit'
2 The scales
3 The changed rhythm of T2 – the 'punctuation passage'

Introduction

bar 1

First Subject/Transition

1. Main Unit bar 18

2. Scales bar 26
Vln.
f
Vlc.
3. Changed rhythm bar 48 (Transition 2)
f
Second Subject
bar 50
p
Transition 3.
4. bar 66
Brass
f
Vln. I
f
f
First Cadential
bar 70
p
Second Cadential
bar 82
p
Piano Second Subject
bar 170

537—Construction

STATEMENT	F B S C1 C2 C3
FIRST CONCERTO	f+ C1 pb ps+ sS + px B C3
DEVELOPMENT	C3 developed Free Returns 1 2 3
CONCERTO REPRISE	Ff pb ps + s + px C2 c2 px B | cd | C3

Mentions

F	B	S	C1	C2	C3	ps
3	3	3*	2	2†	3 §	2

* The last mention has the repeat and sequences only
† Plus a mention of the last two bars in the closing ritornello of the First Concerto
§ Also used in the Development

First Subject
bar 1

Bridge
bar 17

Second Subject
bar 28

First Cadential
bar 50

Second Cadential
bar 59

Third Cadential
bar 74

Third Cadential
bar 78

Piano Second Subject
bar 128

595—Construction

STATEMENT	F B B/S S C1 C2 C3 C4
FIRST CONCERTO	fF pb ps + b b/s Ss c1 C1 + px NT C2
DEVELOPMENT	Ff developed Return
CONCERTO REPRISE	F pb ps+ b b/s Ss c1 C1+px C2c2 c3 | cd | NT C4

Mentions

F	B	S	C1	C2	C3	C4	ps
3*†	3†	3	3	3*	2	2	2

Used at the start of the Development
† Also mentioned in the cadenza

First Subject
bar 2

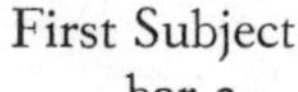

Bridge
bar 16

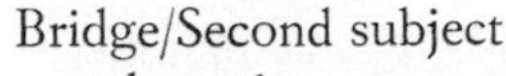

Bridge/Second subject
bar 26

Second Subject
bar 29

First Cadential
bar 39

Second Cadential
bar 47

Third Cadential
bar 55

Fourth Cadential
bar 69

Piano Second Subject
bar 100

General Index

See separate index on page 301 for references to the piano concertos

Index to the Piano Concertos

Note: *Bold type refers to main entries; italic type refers to musical examples and construction tables*

Symbols

Capital letters
mark passages played by the orchestra:
lower case, passages played by the piano